Fine WoodWorking *on* The Small Workshop

Fine WoodWorking *on* The Small Workshop

41 articles selected by
the editors of
Fine Woodworking
magazine

The Taunton Press

Cover photo by John Lively

First printing: January 1985
Second printing: August 1985
Third printing: June 1986
Fourth printing: March 1987
Fifth printing: August 1987
Sixth printing: May 1988
Seventh printing: June 1989
Eighth printing: December 1990
International Standard Book Number: 0-918804-27-2
Library of Congress Catalog Card Number: 84-52098
Printed in the United States of America

A FINE WOODWORKING Book

FINE WOODWORKING® is a trademark of The Taunton Press, Inc.,
registered in the U.S. Patent and Trademark Office.

The Taunton Press
63 South Main Street
Box 5506
Newtown, Connecticut 06470-5506

Contents

Introduction

I know a professional woodcarver who works outdoors all year long, his bench a stump. He has a perfectly good indoor workshop, but he only stores tools and wood there. I know a furniture artist who is always moving out of his shop, into a bigger and better place. No sooner does he re-equip one than he begins scheming about the next. And one of the finest artisans I've met, a maker of musical instruments, has no shop at all. Instead, his workbench stands in the living room, where he can have the best light from the biggest window.

For some people the workshop is only another tool, one of the things you need to get the job done. For others, the workshop itself is the project, with the work done in it serving mainly to justify the work done on it. In this book of 41 articles reprinted from the first nine years of *Fine Woodworking* magazine, diverse woodworkers compare notes about their shops. The workbench, naturally, is at the heart of the discussion. Thay also share a variety of answers to the problems of storing tools, clamping and holding the work, managing dust, and keeping safe so you can continue to enjoy woodworking.

John Kelsey, editor

Limited space need not mean an inefficient workshop. Open central area of Henry Jones' former shop gives ready access to bench and machinery, leaving ample room for assembly. Platform in alcove at right is piled with 8/4 mahogany, out of the way but easily reached.

Five Ways to Set Up a Small Shop
Expert woodworkers tell how they'd do it

How can you set up a serious woodworking shop on a slender shoestring? Many readers have asked us variations of this question, so we made up our own composite question and put it to five expert craftsmen:

"I am an amateur woodworker, and I wish to start building a proper shop. As my skills improve, I'd like to make at least part of my living from the craft. I can move into a single-car garage (about 10 ft. by 20 ft.) with an overhead door. I have some basic hand tools, but no machines yet. What machines should I buy first, and what should I add as my finances permit? How should I arrange them in the available space? What about lighting, ventilation, storage, finishing?" The answer men are as follows:

—Henry Jones of Vineyard Haven, Mass., an industrial designer turned professional woodworker. His article on how to produce square frames in batches of 100 appeared in the Sept. '79 issue of *Fine Woodworking*.

—Tage Frid, professor emeritus at the Rhode Island School of Design and contributing editor of *Fine Woodworking*.

—Franklin Gottshall, of Boyertown, Pa., cabinetmaker and author. Most of his fifteen books, including *How to Design and Construct Period Furniture*, are still in print.

—Andy Marlow, consulting editor of *Fine Woodworking*, a professional wood craftsman and author of several books on reproducing antiques. His most recent book, *Classic Furniture Projects*, contains plans and instructions for 13 different pieces of furniture, most of them with inlay.

—Frank Klausz, a cabinetmaker in Bedminster, N.J. His article on cutting mortise-and-tenon joints appeared in the Sept. '79 issue of *Fine Woodworking*.

Leave room in the middle

by Henry Jones

When I opened a commercial cabinet shop about six years ago, I had to decide whether to rent suitable space or attempt to work in my detached single-car garage. The convenience of having a shop only a few steps from my front door was incentive enough to favor the garage, but economic considerations decided the issue, and I set about transforming the tiny 10-ft. by 26-ft. building into a production shop.

To cram my entire operation into 260 sq. ft. meant that I would have to use every available square inch. My first step was to prepare a diagram that included every machine, fixture and cabinet and the clearance paths required for the use of each machine and for my bench as well. I had to make many changes once I actually started setting up, but the original plan helped me decide that the limited space could be made to work. From the plan I knew that if I managed the space properly, I wouldn't have to move my machines around much to make room for other operations and that I would still have storage for lumber, fixtures, supplies, patterns and miscellaneous tools. In the midst of all this I had to have room to set up and assemble work in progress, without having to shift furniture parts and tools all over the shop every time I needed to use a given machine.

Deciding from the outset to limit stock length to 12 ft. or less on all but rare occasions, I was able to compute the amount of space needed to operate each machine. A 12-in. planer requires an unobstructed path 26 ft. by 24 in. by 6 in. A radial arm saw or a shaper needs about the same. A 4-in. to 6-in. jointer needs a space about 16 ft. long and 8 in. wide. And my 8-ft. workbench has to have at least 10 ft. on either side of the vise. Having satisfied myself that I could fit all these into the existing space, I was confident that somehow I could squeeze in my band saw and my Shopsmith.

With only minor modifications and several simple, inexpensive additions to the basic structure, I managed to produce a meager but acceptable income in this shop for five years. But last year I tore away about half of the garage and built it anew, doubling the floor space and tripling the volume. However, the methods I worked out to cope with limited space and which I'll describe here were successful in enabling me to run a cabinet shop on a small budget until it was financially feasible for me to enlarge the space.

To make the old shop workable, but without disturbing the existing roof or major structural members, I added a narrow shed and a bay clear of the ground—a kind of elevated alcove—to provide areas for storing and working large plywood sheets. I also cut ports through the two walls at opposite ends of the planer so the machine could be operated across the short end of the shop. The ports were then fitted with lift-out covers that latch in place. Because the arrangement precluded the use of a table saw, obliging me to use my radial arm saw for ripping (which I find entirely satisfactory), I cut another port in the wall that stands about 10 ft. from the saw. This lets me rip boards as long as 14 ft. and provides almost unlimited crosscut capacity.

I located my shaper to the left of the radial arm saw's 6-ft. table, and the band saw to the right of it. To keep the work

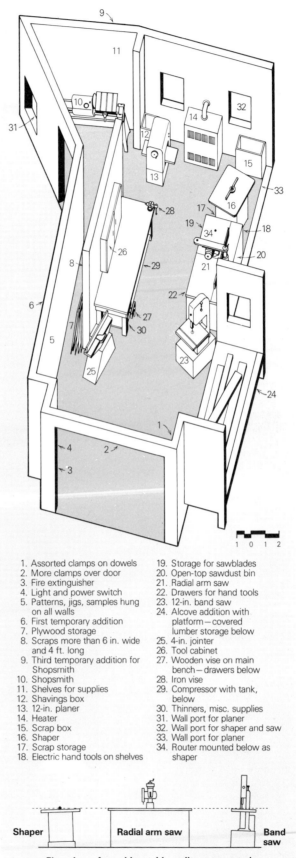

1. Assorted clamps on dowels
2. More clamps over door
3. Fire extinguisher
4. Light and power switch
5. Patterns, jigs, samples hung on all walls
6. First temporary addition
7. Plywood storage
8. Scraps more than 6 in. wide and 4 ft. long
9. Third temporary addition for Shopsmith
10. Shopsmith
11. Shelves for supplies
12. Shavings box
13. 12-in. planer
14. Heater
15. Scrap box
16. Shaper
17. Scrap storage
18. Electric hand tools on shelves
19. Storage for sawblades
20. Open-top sawdust bin
21. Radial arm saw
22. Drawers for hand tools
23. 12-in. band saw
24. Alcove addition with platform—covered lumber storage below
25. 4-in. jointer
26. Tool cabinet
27. Wooden vise on main bench—drawers below
28. Iron vise
29. Compressor with tank, below
30. Thinners, misc. supplies
31. Wall port for planer
32. Wall port for shaper and saw
33. Wall port for planer
34. Router mounted below as shaper

Elevation of machine tables, tilt exaggerated. Canted surfaces provide clearance for long stock.

Shaper · Radial arm saw · Band saw

on one machine from running into the table of another required precise angular as well as linear positioning. First I spaced the tables at least 1 ft. apart. Next I placed the shaper spindle and the band-saw blade about ½ in. behind the rearmost fence position of the radial arm saw, so boards being ripped pass in front of them. Then I turned the shaper and the band saw so that a long workpiece going through either machine clears the radial-arm-saw fence by running in front of it. Long pieces from the shaper run out the radial-saw port, while those from the band saw run into the alcove.

The trickiest problem to overcome with in-line machines is height. A board with a downward bow will run into the edge of the adjacent table on the outfeed side. Since I couldn't solve this problem by raising or lowering one table or the other, I simply tilted the shaper and the band saw slightly. This allowed me to lower these tables about ⅜ in. and still maintain good clearance as their workpieces passed over the radial-saw table, and vice-versa.

With its two extension wings, the underside of the radial-arm-saw table serves as a storage cabinet for two dozen sawblades, dado heads and buffing wheels. The base also contains shelves for twelve portable electric tools and finishing supplies as well as six heavy drawers for hand tools, hardware and fasteners. I've still got room under the saw for a trash box, a small scrap box and a sawdust bin. I keep the four most frequently used portable power tools plugged in on their shelves so they can be grabbed, used and as quickly put away again. The area beneath my bench is also used for storage. Here I keep my air compressor with tank, thinners, glues and seldom used tools. Two drawers hold sandpaper and sanding belts.

Handling and storing plywood had to be given special consideration because laying out a 4x8 sheet took up so much work space that I couldn't step around it. So I built an alcove, 3 ft. by 11 ft. with a floor 18 in. above the main floor; the alcove's platform is ideal for cutting sheets of plywood, better than sawhorses. The alcove is also useful for stacking wood I'm about to use and for assembling kitchen cabinets.

I like to stock 20 to 30 sheets of various plywoods, and such a stack just leaning against a wall is very difficult to manage. You can't extract one sheet while holding those in front of it against your stomach. So I built a narrow extension to the building, a kind of storage corridor only 16 in. out from the existing wall and still under the existing eaves. This has been so convenient that I've kept it in the new shop. Because they're supported on either side, I can shuffle through a large number of sheets like pages in a book, then slide out any one of them with ease.

The main hand-tool box hangs over the bench. Measuring 48 in. by 36 in. by 6 in. closed, with its two doors open it's 8 ft. long. I built this cabinet many years ago so that I could move into a new shop, hang it on the wall and be at work in a few minutes with over 100 tools in front of me.

I would not have had room for all the machines I needed if it weren't for the Shopsmith, which has its own space in the shop's third modest addition. It has served me faithfully since 1954 and I have gotten out a great deal of work with it, although I rarely use it as a saw. However, as a 12-in. disc sander it is unbeatable. As a drill press, horizontal boring machine, grinder and light-duty lathe, it is perfectly adequate. The shiftovers have been so well designed that I don't object to the setup time as a trade-off for space saved.

Scrap storage needs attention too, and I've found that any such pile has a critical size. You don't use what you can't see,

and obscured scraps might as well not be there. But I'm basically a squirrel, and I can't bear to toss out a nice, clean block of cherry or even pine. So there are about six scrap stacks scattered around wherever one fits in conveniently. Blocks smaller than about 8 in. long and 4 in wide go in a box under the radial arm saw. Most of these are cut-offs and go there directly from the saw. Long, skinny rippings go directly overhead. Sticks and boards less than 40 in. by 4 in. lean between the radial arm saw and the shaper, where I can see the end of each one. Those shorter than 20 in. go vertically in a box under the other side of the shaper. Squarish small panels are stacked like books under one end of the bench. Larger panels lean against another wall, with patterns hanging above them. Most lumber is up on the roof collar ties, and since there are three tiers of collar ties, few boards have so many others on top that one can't be hauled out. Every inch of every wall is covered with tools, supplies, patterns, jigs or clamps. I have nearly seventy clamps of at least eight different types which hang on ¾-in. dowels, as many as six per dowel. I hate to hang a tool on a nail, and I despise pegboard holders. A dowel with a nice, crowned end is much more respectful to the tool.

With all this, I still had space to assemble cabinets or produce small pieces in batches of 100. But a lot of time was wasted keeping things out of the way, stowing each item just so. It was like working aboard a boat. To turn a 14-ft. board end-for-end meant walking outside. The final straw came with a load of new lumber I couldn't store. My new shop, constructed phoenix-like from the old, eases everything. But there still is not enough space. There never is.

Start with a table saw

by Tage Frid

The most versatile machine is the circular saw. The choice comes down to the radial arm saw vs. the table saw, and my advice is to buy the table saw. The radial arm was designed for crosscutting lumber to length, but even there it is limited by the length of its arm. Though it can be made to do all the things a table saw can, it is more difficult to use and less accurate for fine joinery. Some joints would be impractical and even dangerous to make on a radial arm saw, sawing tenon cheeks or ripping small pieces of wood, for example.

When buying a table saw, get at least a 10-in. one; it doesn't cost much more than an 8-in. saw. The motor should be at least 1 HP; 2 HP is even better. Make sure the arbor tilts for angle cuts, not the table. I find a long extension rail on the side of the table helpful for ripping large pieces of wood. You will find the table saw the most used piece of equipment in the shop, so don't stint on quality. I don't have experience with all the brands on the market and can't give advice about which might be the best, but I can say that I have had a Rockwell saw for many years and we are old friends. If I had limited space, I would definitely look hard at the Inca 10-in. cabinetmaker's saw, although I have never worked with it, only seen it demonstrated. The disadvantage is its tilting table, very awkward for beveling long boards. But it has a mortising spindle that you can use like a horizontal boring machine, and this might offset the inconvenience of the tilting table. It is a lightweight machine, easy to move around, and that is an important consideration where space is limited.

After the table saw, I feel the jointer and thickness planer are the most important big machines. These two machines can be a big investment, but if you want to make a living out of woodworking, they will pay for themselves. A used jointer or thickness planer can sometimes be bought inexpensively and will usually do as well as a new machine. But don't buy a jointer with a square cutterhead; it is just too dangerous. The smallest jointer I would buy is a 6-in. model (an 8-in. is better) with at least a 1-HP motor. The smallest thickness planer I would buy is a 12-in. model with a 2-HP motor. If I had limited space I would give serious consideration to combination planer/jointers. Both Inca and Makita have them, and so does Parks, and there are a number of other imported machines available on the American market. The disadvantage of combination machines is that the infeed and outfeed tables might be too short for handling long boards. So it pays to find people who already have the machine you are interested in, to see how they like it.

After these big machines, it all depends on what kind of work you are going to be doing. The possibilities include a mortiser, band saw, shaper, drill press and lathe.

For the mortiser, the cheapest would be to buy the hollow chisel attachment for a drill press. I find these attachments fine for soft wood, but the chisel tends to stick in hard wood, and I would rather have a long-hole boring machine, or slot mortiser; with the right bit, it is one of the fastest ways to cut a mortise. Like a high-speed drill lying on its side, it has a table for the workpiece in front of the bit. The table can be moved up, down, in, out and sideways.

If you will be cutting many curves, or if you will be resawing boards for laminating or bookmatching, you will need a band saw. The 14-in. saw might be large enough if you are making musical instruments, but for cabinetmaking I would buy a 20-in. saw with a 2-HP motor. A lathe, I have found, is a very useful machine and does not take up much space. The shaper is important if you plan to do production work.

Sometimes I see advertisements for combination machines that do everything. A machine like this might be fine if your space is tight, if you do woodworking as a hobby, or if you have a small production shop making little things like boxes or toys. If you plan the work so the change from one operation to another is minimal, that type of machine might do. But if you have the space and want to have a more flexible shop, I suggest you buy separate machines.

Actually, after I had some good hand tools—saws, planes and chisels—one of the first things I would buy, before any stationary machinery, would be an electric router. It can make joints, including half-blind and sliding dovetails, and it can cut small moldings. It has many other uses as well. Get a good router that can take ¼-in. and ½-in. bits, with at least a 1-HP motor. Make sure the mechanism that moves the router up and down in its base is easy to work and accurate, and make sure the switch is easy to turn on and off while routing.

If I were setting up to work in a single-car garage with an overhead door, I would put my bench right in front of the door. It is not too hard to move out of the way when big things have to go in and out, and this would be the best place to work in the summer with the door open. The table saw is the most used machine, so I would put it right in the middle

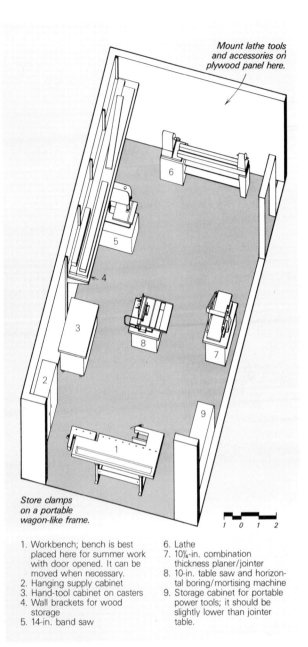

Mount lathe tools and accessories on plywood panel here.

Store clamps on a portable wagon-like frame.

1 0 1 2

1. Workbench; bench is best placed here for summer work with door opened. It can be moved when necessary.
2. Hanging supply cabinet
3. Hand-tool cabinet on casters
4. Wall brackets for wood storage
5. 14-in. band saw

6. Lathe
7. 10¼-in. combination thickness planer/jointer
8. 10-in. table saw and horizontal boring/mortising machine
9. Storage cabinet for portable power tools; it should be slightly lower than jointer table.

of the room, where I could get at it from all sides with all sized pieces of wood. The jointer and thicknesser should be nearby because while preparing stock you have to move the wood back and forth between these machines and the table saw. There shouldn't be anything else along the wall with the jointer/planer that will be in the way of long boards. The exception would be a low cabinet near the bench for portable electric tools, low enough for boards to pass over the top. I would keep my hand tools in a cabinet on casters, and I would make a portable frame for storing clamps. Lumber could be stored along the walls overhead, on wall brackets or on racks hanging from the ceiling.

In designing a small shop, don't underestimate the space you need to leave open for assembling work, and for storing parts of jobs in progress. In a one-man shop, I would not have any specific finishing area—it takes up too much space. Instead I would plan my work so the finishing could be done late in the day and cleared away in the morning.

High ceiling, wood floor, good light

by Franklin H. Gottshall

A good shop should have a high ceiling. A minimum height of 7 ft. will do, but 8 ft. or 9 ft. is much better. My shop, a part of which is shown in the photograph, has a 9-ft. ceiling. I do not like a cement floor in a shop, and unfortunately most garage and basement shops have one. A wooden floor is much easier on the feet and the work, and if either a garage or a basement is to be made into a workshop I strongly advise superimposing a wooden floor over the cement, though this will mean lowering the ceiling. Walls and ceiling should be adequately insulated to keep the shop warm and dry.

Proper lighting is extremely important, and is often inadequate both in home workshops and in buildings used for commercial purposes. You need natural daylight as well as enough artificial lighting. Walls and ceiling should be white to make full use of all the light you can bring into the shop. Good eyesight is precious.

The drawing shows what I think is an ideal natural lighting situation, with the workbench situated to get lighting from the north. This eliminates a lot of glare and shadows you might get having to work facing in another direction. You need enough overhead lighting at your machines and workbench to eliminate shadows and eyestrain, and in my shop it is possible to move some lights as necessary.

As to equipment and machinery, first priority should be given to a good workbench, equipped with a good vise or two. I recommend a bench with a flat, hardwood top, 2 in. or more thick, and a substantial base. It should not be fastened to the floor, because you may need to move it.

Machinery should be the best quality obtainable. I recommend buying single-purpose machines and avoiding multi-purpose machines that combine saw, jointer, lathe, and what-have-you. They are inefficient because too much time must be spent on the adjustments and changes needed to carry out sequential operations. All of my machines have sturdy cast-iron bases, and each has its own electric motor.

If I were to purchase machinery for a shop, one item at a time, I'd buy a good table saw first. You should be able to tilt either the saw or the saw table, and it should be equipped with a 10-in. combination crosscut and ripping blade and with a dado head. A radial arm saw could be substituted here but would require more room. My table saw has a ¾-HP motor, which meets all my cutting requirements.

Next, I would buy a 6-in. jointer, equipped with a ⅓-HP or ½-HP motor. A 14-in. or 16-in. band saw should be your third machine, and for this a ⅓-HP motor is adequate. A floor-type drill press (⅓ HP will do) should be next, and it would pay you to equip it for hollow-chisel mortising.

Fifth, get a woodturning lathe with one or more faceplates, as well as a good set of woodturning chisels. If possible buy a lathe equipped with an index head and a bed long enough so you can turn spindles 38 in. or more. A ⅓-HP motor will be adequate for this machine. A 12-in. surface planer is a good machine if you can afford one, but it might crowd you for space in a small shop. You need floor space for assembling large projects and for safety—don't sacrifice it for equipment you can get along without.

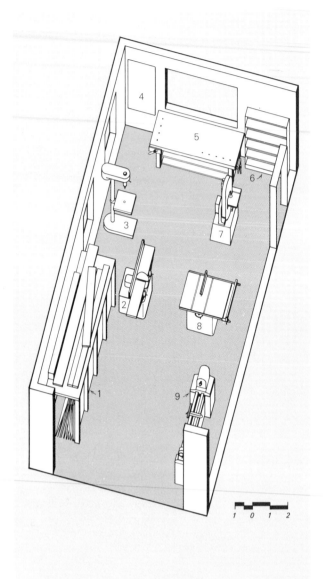

1. Lumber storage
2. Jointer
3. Drill press
4. Tool and clamp rack
5. Workbench
6. Tool cabinet
7. Band saw
8. Table saw
9. Lathe

Gottshall in his own shop, somewhat larger than 200 sq. ft.

Get a big band saw and a jigsaw too

by Andy Marlow

For a home shop I would start with a 10-in. table saw. This is one machine that requires space in all four directions for work maneuverability, so it must be placed with the fence running parallel to the length of the building and equidistant from all four walls. Though the power cable should come up through the floor (this is not too difficult to arrange if the floor is wood), it may not be worth the trouble of chipping away cement to bury the conduit. So to keep from tripping over the conduit, simply border it with chamfered strips of wood on each side. Your jointer, for convenience of operation, should be placed next to your table saw and can be powered by the same cable.

The placement of other machines and equipment is optional and deserves careful consideration. I would place the lathe along a wall somewhere near the workbench because extra space at the ends of this machine is unnecessary, and operational space out into the general shop area can be held to a minimum. A band saw is an indispensable tool, so don't buy a small toy. I believe that a 16-in. throat is the minimum, not only because of its width capacity but also because on smaller size saws the blade will wander, distorting the shape on the bottom of the cut, especially if the stock is thick. The column of the band saw may be placed quite close to a wall, though there should be plenty of room on the other three sides to move your body and negotiate the workpiece.

Two more machines I consider necessary are a drill press and jigsaw. As you continue to use your shop equipment, you will begin to realize how many different operations can be done on a drill press. In addition to light shaper work, you can do dowel boring and mortising. True perpendicular boring is, in many cases, quite important. A jigsaw is indispensable for fine scroll work on thin stock, and no other machine can saw a complete inside cutout. If you look at the shop sketch, it will become apparent that space is running out. Fortunately a jigsaw can be mounted on a table with casters so that you can move it about the shop. Two more machines for later consideration are a bench shaper and a homemade 6-in. belt sander needed for larger work.

The idea is to get as much daylight as possible on the bench, so you might want to place it close to the entry door. You could get by with a bench top as small as 48 in. by 20 in. At least 95% of your work will be performed at the right end of the bench (if you're right-handed), where two 7-in. woodworking vises should be mounted. The vise on the end should have a dog, and on the bench, in line with this dog, should be a series of 7/8-in. diameter holes to receive a bench stop. You can make a suitable bench stop by starting with a block 1 1/4 in. square by 2 3/8 in. long. Put it in your lathe and turn a 7/8-in. by 2-in. dowel on the end of it. This stop can be inserted in any one of the holes in the bench to hold workpieces of various lengths.

The kind of lighting you use is optional, but your fixtures must be placed so that no shadows will be cast on your work. Only one other suggestion—don't use a fluorescent light over your lathe. Rapidly revolving objects appear to writhe and squirm under this kind of light.

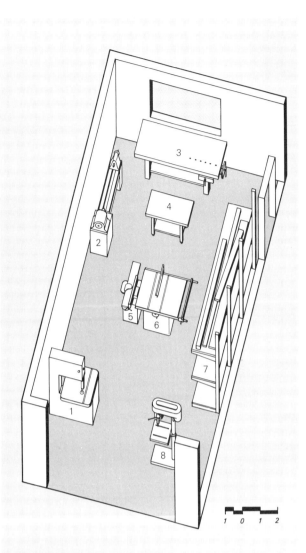

1. Band saw
2. Lathe
3. Workbench
4. Worktable—can be used as base for jigsaw
5. Jointer
6. Table saw
7. Lumber storage
8. Drill press

Though his shop is not much larger than a typical single-car garage, Marlow works quite comfortably and efficiently here reproducing period furniture. His work includes multiple productions and one-of-a-kind pieces.

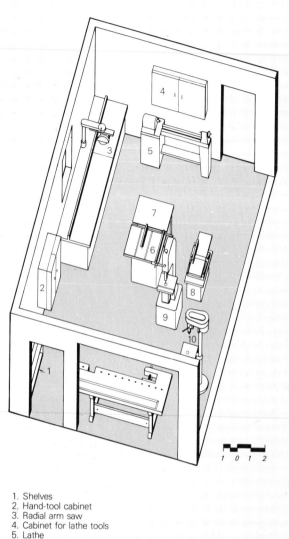

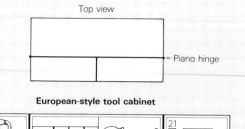

Top view

←— Piano hinge

European-style tool cabinet

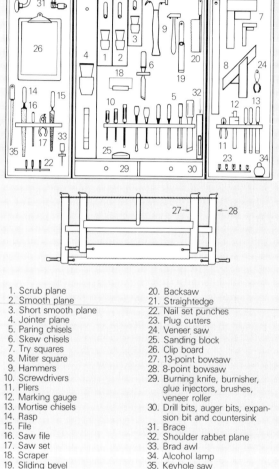

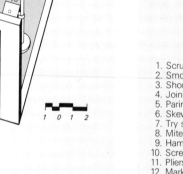

27 →   ← 28

1. Shelves
2. Hand-tool cabinet
3. Radial arm saw
4. Cabinet for lathe tools
5. Lathe
6. 10-in. table saw
7. Extension table
8. 12-in. combination jointer/thickness planer
9. Band saw
10. Drill press

1. Scrub plane
2. Smooth plane
3. Short smooth plane
4. Jointer plane
5. Paring chisels
6. Skew chisels
7. Try squares
8. Miter square
9. Hammers
10. Screwdrivers
11. Pliers
12. Marking gauge
13. Mortise chisels
14. Rasp
15. File
16. Saw file
17. Saw set
18. Scraper
19. Sliding bevel

20. Backsaw
21. Straightedge
22. Nail set punches
23. Plug cutters
24. Veneer saw
25. Sanding block
26. Clip board
27. 13-point bowsaw
28. 8-point bowsaw
29. Burning knife, burnisher,
    glue injectors, brushes,
    veneer roller
30. Drill bits, auger bits, expan-
    sion bit and countersink
31. Brace
32. Shoulder rabbet plane
33. Brad awl
34. Alcohol lamp
35. Keyhole saw

Build around bench and hand tools

by Frank Klausz

It is very difficult to plan a shop for a woodworker and to recommend specific tools without knowing the kind of work done in the shop. But for general furniture making, repairing and refinishing, I can make several suggestions for the woodworker with limited space. One of the most important items in the shop is the workbench. It should be at least 7 ft. long and equipped with a side vise, a tail vise and a good set of steel bench dogs. Of equal importance to the bench is a set of fine hand tools. Don't waste your money on cheap ones; buy the best and keep them well honed. Sharp tools are easier and

safer to use, and they do nicer work. If you have your bench and a good set of hand tools, you are ready to tackle almost any kind of furniture work. This is especially true if woodworking is your hobby and you don't care how long it takes you to make a piece.

If you want to make a living working wood or if time is at all important, you'll definitely want to buy some machinery. It would of course be preferable if you could buy your machines all at once, but few people can afford to part with that much money at one time. So if you're going to spread your investment out over a long period, I suggest that you buy your machines in the following order. The first one I would pick is a 14-in. or 16-in. band saw. The reason is that with this machine you can rip and crosscut as well as make contoured cuts, producing everything from a haunched tenon to a Queen Anne leg. If your budget is limited and you want a table saw too, you can make a temporary one by simply mounting a portable circular saw on a piece of ¾-in. plywood, inverting it and fixing the table to a base. Clamp on a straight-edge for a rip fence.

The second machine I would get is a radial arm saw, a very versatile machine that can be used for ripping, crosscutting, grooving and shaping. Actually, the machine is best suited for crosscutting, dadoing and mitering. A good 10-in. table saw would be my third choice, and you'll want to attach a sturdy extension table on the outfeed side of the saw. Next would come a jointer, the longer and wider its bed, the better. For a small shop, a combination jointer/planer would do very well. Finally I would get a drill press and a lathe, and be content with these machines until I could afford to move into a bigger shop.

With care, these six machines and a workbench can be arranged to fit into a small shop 12 ft. wide and 20 ft. long. I would group the table saw, the jointer and the band saw in the center of the shop. There are several reasons for this. One is that you can easily run the electricity to this central area, and you can run all three machines from a single breaker box or fuse box, minimizing the amount of cable necessary to power them. Second, you don't have to carry your workpieces all over the shop to perform various operations on them. Third, lighting can be concentrated on this central area; and finally, you have more space in your shop for storage, assembly and walking around.

If your shop is in a free-standing building, you have the option of feeding some machines across the width of the shop by cutting ports in the walls where needed. In Hungary my father has a cabinet shop, and all the machines are in a room that is only 12 ft. by 16 ft. His only machines are a 30-in. band saw and a combination table saw/jointer/planer/mortiser/shaper. There we used to cut our own lumber from 20-ft. logs that came in one window on a steel roller, were fed through the band saw and exited through the opposite window on a roller at the sill. Once the log was put in position, it wasn't that hard a job to cut it up, needing only two men working in close harmony.

In a small shop it's especially important to keep your machinery clean and your work areas orderly; you need to organize storage space so that tools and supplies can be put away as soon as they are used. A carefully planned, wall-mounted tool cabinet is essential. Lighting is another aspect of shop planning. The aim is to achieve shadow-free lighting wherever possible, certainly over your bench and machines. In addition to getting as much sunlight as you can in your shop, you need to install as many long fluorescent tubes as it will take to give you shadow-free illumination. Stand a dowel on your bench and on each machine; if it casts no shadow your lighting is good.

Finishing in a one-room shop is always a problem because there is going to be a lot of dust in the air, even long after you've stopped working and swept up. So it's best to use finishing products that don't require a dust-free environment. Shellac, linseed oil, Watco oil, and polymerized tung oil are best for finishing furniture in a small shop because they harden in the wood rather than on its surface like varnishes and lacquers, which become rough to the touch and unsightly when they dry in a a dusty shop. Sprayed finishes don't belong in the small shop. They are health and safety hazards and will never look right. □

Tool Carousel in Alcove

by Richard Starr

To save shop space and to organize a variety of jigs and tools, Charles Fox of the Guitar Research and Design Center, South Strafford, Vt., made a revolving tool tray. About 8 ft. in diameter, the turntable pivots on a large lazy-susan bearing and is supported two-thirds of the way out by a series of cabinet casters. The entire unit is situated in an alcove, which protrudes over a lower room, adding storage without taking up floor space. □

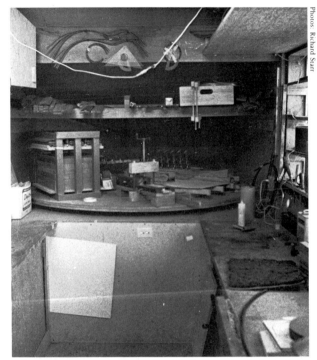

Photos: Richard Starr

Though used here to hold specialized luthier's tools, the basic design of this revolving tool tray can be adapted to suit the needs of almost any workshop in which floor space is at a premium.

Capacity of carousel tool tray is large enough to accommodate this veneer press, which operates on compressed air and is used for gluing tops to guitar bodies.

Woodworking in Seventy-Five Square Feet

It takes more time, and careful planning

by J. A. Hiltebeitel

Neither limited shop space nor a small tool budget need discourage an amateur woodworker from attempting serious projects. Respectable work can be done in less than 75 sq. ft. with a modest selection of hand and power tools. The tradeoff is time—time planning the work before the wood is cut, time to move and set up the tools, time to do what could be done faster with a more appropriate tool, and (in my particular case where the shop is a through-traffic room) time to clean up.

Identifying the particular limitations imposed by available space is a good place to start setting realistic limits on the size and type of work that you will undertake and will help avoid frustration. You shouldn't try to make a solid-top dining table or other large piece of similar proportions. To save on tools and the space they require, I decided to purchase them only when they were absolutely essential to the work planned. This has proven a valuable rule, and the only two hand tools purchased in violation of it I've since found unnecessary.

I began by using a sturdy 3-ft. by 6-ft. desk as my bench and a radial arm saw as my only power tool. The efficient use of space is the only basis on which this tool can be recommended, as it is very difficult to make it cut with the consistent precision necessary to good cabinetwork. However, acceptable accuracy can be achieved by truing up the whole tool

periodically and keeping it in tune. Make your most precise cuts (like slip joints) with the blade stationary, moving the work into or through the blade with appropriate guides, jigs and guards. In addition to the saw, I bought a few hand tools—a smoothing plane, a marking gauge, an offset dovetail saw, a ¼-in. chisel and a router. I discovered early that routing hardwood with a bit chucked in the radial saw gives unsatisfactory results and can be unsafe.

For my first project—a padauk jewelry box with a frame-and-panel lid—I devised a leg vise for cutting dovetails and for edge-planing small pieces. I found that a small-diameter dado blade is good for slotting the frame with only a small amount of squaring up and cleaning out necessary at the ends of the members. When attempting to rout inner edges of the frame, I learned my first lesson on the importance of planning operations in the proper order. A router bit's pilot bearing does not guide very well against an already-cut slot.

Planning for my next project—a wall cabinet with inset doors and a through-mortised shelf—suggested a few more tools—a rabbet and bullnose plane, a ½-in. mortise chisel, a jointer plane, and as an alternative to the offset dovetail saw, a *dozuki* saw. I found the latter easily controlled as you can stand well back from the work and improve the accuracy of that important initial cut. Because I had to rip a few long

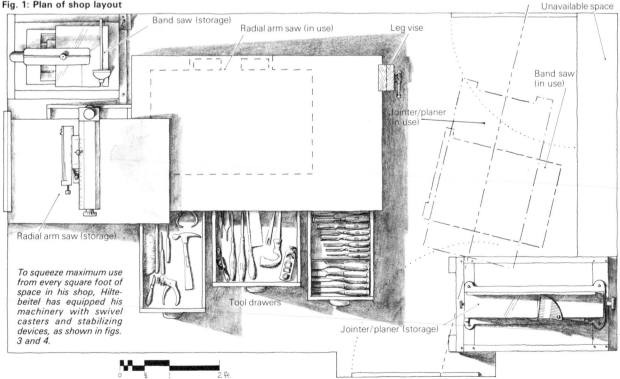

Fig. 1: Plan of shop layout

Band saw (storage)

Radial arm saw (in use)

Leg vise

Unavailable space

Band saw (in use)

Jointer/planer (in use)

Radial arm saw (storage)

To squeeze maximum use from every square foot of space in his shop, Hiltebeitel has equipped his machinery with swivel casters and stabilizing devices, as shown in figs. 3 and 4.

Tool drawers

Jointer/planer (storage)

0   ½   1   2 ft.

Illustrations: Christopher Clapp

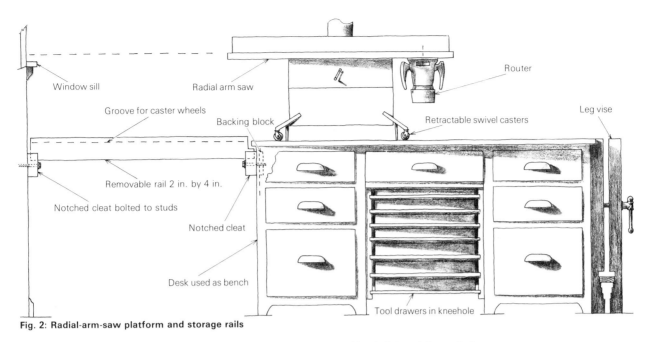

Window sill
Radial arm saw
Router
Leg vise
Groove for caster wheels
Backing block
Retractable swivel casters
Removable rail 2 in. by 4 in.
Notched cleat bolted to studs
Notched cleat
Desk used as bench
Tool drawers in kneehole

Fig. 2: Radial-arm-saw platform and storage rails

Fig. 4: Jointer/planer platform

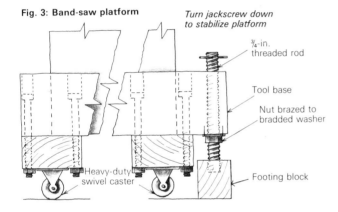

Fig. 3: Band-saw platform

Turn jackscrew down
to stabilize platform

¾-in.
threaded rod

Tool base

Nut brazed to
bradded washer

Heavy-duty
swivel caster

Footing block

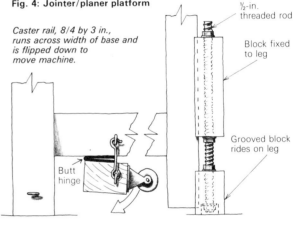

Caster rail, 8/4 by 3 in.,
runs across width of base and
is flipped down to
move machine.

½-in.
threaded rod

Block fixed
to leg

Butt
hinge

Grooved block
rides on leg

boards, I mounted the radial saw on a platform which allowed the boards to extend through an open window (figure 2). This put the saw table at elbow height and provided me a better view of the work. I added retractable casters to the platform along with removable, grooved rails between the bench and the wall, which allow the saw to be rolled off the bench when I need more work surface. The saw can be used in this stored position as well, though only for cutting relatively short pieces. I found an out-of-the-way place for tool drawers in the kneehole of the desk.

Later I got a band saw and made it mobile too using heavy-duty casters. I added threaded rods that passed through fixed nuts near two of the casters to jack one end of the platform off the floor and keep the machine from rolling. Wood blocks on the ends of the rods eliminate skidding. The result is a portable platform that is very stable on an uneven floor (figure 3).

Mounting the router under one wing of the radial-arm-saw table provided modest shaper capability without taking up any extra space. I use it in this position with either a pilot bit or a fence clamped to the table, and it is easily removed when necessary. Though not without its hazards, it does an acceptable job of slotting, rabbeting, molding and other guided shaping operations.

After hand-planing many resawn boards, I decided to buy a jointer/planer. I made it portable with a wheel and leg-stabilizer scheme. One end of the stand is lifted and a hinged rail with casters is flipped down (by foot) and then hooked in place; the stand may then be maneuvered wheelbarrow fashion. Once the jointer/planer is in operating position, I flip up the caster rail and then adjust the legs at the opposite end (figure 4).

In a situation where I'm forced to move, use and replace one machine prior to doing anything with another, an organized work schedule is essential. I have found the following quite dependable for preparing rough stock. Cut to approximate length; plane one face and joint one edge; resaw; rip; joint all edges; plane the opposite face; cut to precise length; scribe and proceed with joint details. A floor-plan layout with the various work and storage positions for each tool is shown in figure 1. Things are indeed cramped, but with realistic goals (I can't, for example, make several large pieces of case furniture at the same time) and thoughtful planning, you can do rewarding work.   □

J. A. Hiltebeitel, an electrical engineer and amateur woodworker, lives in South Burlington, Vt.

A Cabinetmaker's Tool Cabinet
Updating a traditional design

by David Powell

When I first started making furniture in Edward Barnsley's workshop, the tool chests used by the craftsmen there were of the traditional sort. They were simplified versions of a design that had developed over centuries, originating probably as medieval oak chests or coffers. All of them were rectangular boxes that sat directly on the floor. Their lids were hinged in the rear and locked in the front to discourage borrowing and pilfering. The underside of the lid was fitted to hold tools, and the inside of the chest contained one or two banks of drawers which faced each other and opened into a central well (see drawing below). Under the drawers there was usually a space to hold tools too large or awkward to fit into any of the drawers or to hang from the lid. These tools might fit into partitioned compartments or just be wrapped in cloth and placed into an undivided bin. At the bottom of some chests there would be a wide drawer that opened to the outside, so a person could get at its contents without having to rummage inside the main part of the chest.

By the late 18th century cabinetmaker's chests had evolved into refined pieces of furniture. Though outside they remained plain and unadorned, the interiors of these chests were often finely fitted, veneered, inlaid and otherwise decorated. Such refinements proclaimed the skill of the maker to a prospective customer or employer, and no doubt brought a sense of satisfaction to the cabinetmaker who had to live with the chest and work out of it.

When I decided to make my own tool case about 25 years ago, the chests I saw around me in Barnsley's shop were superbly straightforward and well made, but without any in-terior inlaying, decoration or veneering. Looking at these chests, it seemed to me that their big disadvantage was that too many of the tools they held were not easily accessible. A lot of the tools were stored below the drawer cases, which could mean having to move a whole bank of four to six drawers to get the shoulder plane you wanted. And then perhaps you'd have to go to the added trouble of unwrapping it. Retrieving a tool from the bottom of the chest was about like resurrecting a mummy.

Another disadvantage with these chests was that they were low to the ground. You had to do considerable bending and crouching to fetch and replace your tools. Finally, I felt that there was much wasted space in an already confined area inside these chests, because the well between the facing drawer units had to be left clear to allow the drawers to be opened.

I wanted to have my tools as readily accessible as possible, while still having a case that I could close and lock. I also wanted it to be reasonably transportable, and to fit into my workplace unobtrusively. An upright tool cabinet seemed to be the answer. Sitting on a squat base, such a cabinet when fitted with a bank of drawers would hold all my tools at a comfortable height and would minimize the amount of stooping I'd have to do, and I wouldn't have to remove some tools to get at others. Having a pair of doors would give me two large surfaces on which I could mount saws. And below the drawers, I decided to build pigeonholes for my planes.

Initially, I tried to measure every tool or set of tools I owned and to assign a place in the chest or a drawer for each. This, of course, proved impossibly complex, and couldn't take into account future acquisitions. So I designed the bank of drawers to general dimensions that seemed likely to accommodate my smaller tools, and in particular to keep together sets of related tools such as squares, chisels and gauges in a single drawer, or in a group of drawers. Then I estimated what further small tools I was likely to buy and added drawers for these. This estimate has fallen sadly short of the mark, and after 25 years the drawers are overflowing with tools.

Next, I got out all my planes and lined them up, measured them and assigned each a place in the bin below the drawer case. I also made allowance in this allotment of space for planes I knew I would buy later, and have found to my pleasure that all my planes still fit neatly where I planned for them to go. Then I fell into the trap of including an open well above the drawers. At the time I conceived the design, I reasoned that this space could contain tools that didn't fit conveniently anywhere else in the cabinet, and I could use the underside of the lid for hanging more tools. Over the years this well has collected a pile of tools and dust, and has become something of a junkheap from which it is difficult to disentangle a tool I want. This is exactly the feature in the traditional tool chests that I had wanted to avoid.

Now I'm redesigning the cabinet and will make a new one

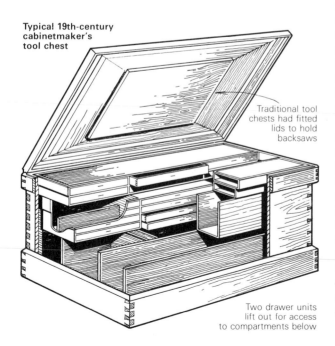

Typical 19th-century cabinetmaker's tool chest

Traditional tool chests had fitted lids to hold backsaws

Two drawer units lift out for access to compartments below

Drawing, this page: Lynn B. McVicker

without the well in the top. The area it would have occupied will be taken up by additional drawers. The drawers' basic dimensions won't change, and I will still provide fitted spaces for indispensible tools, but will create more in the way of flexible space for new tools.

Building a tool cabinet brings all of your joinery skills into play, and gives you the chance to make one large case and a lot of little drawers. Make the main case from 4/4 pine. If you want to omit the upper tool well and devote this space to drawers as I plan to do, then you can through-dovetail the four sides of the case together, cutting the pins on the top and bottom pieces. Groove the inner rear edges of the case to receive a ¼-in. plywood back panel. The main horizontal divider, which separates the drawer unit from the pigeonhole section below, is through-tenoned into the case sides, with three wedged tenons on each end. This divider stiffens the sides of the case and supports the drawer unit as well.

If you are tidy, you might find the upper well useful. To make it you must let two wide rails into the sides of the case with through wedged tenons on each side as shown in the drawing on the next page. The bottom inner edges of these rails must be grooved to house the bottom panel, which is best made from ½-in. plywood. Also, the bottom edge of the rear rail is grooved to accept the ¼-in. plywood back panel.

The drawer unit includes two vertical dividers which are housed at the bottom in dadoes cut across the horizontal divider and in dadoes in the top of the case (in notches in the two rails if you build in the top well). These dividers are made from ¾-in. thick stock, and have ¼-in. deep, ¾-in. wide rabbets cut along both of their front edges. These rabbets accommodate the ¾-in. thick drawer fronts, which overlap the drawer sides ¼ in. The side of the case must also be rabbeted in the same amount to make room for the overlapping drawer fronts at the extreme ends of the unit.

The drawers slide in ¼-in. deep, ½-in. wide dadoes cut into the two vertical dividers and in the case sides. The dadoes are hidden by the overlapping drawer fronts, which also obscure the drawer runners. These are ¼-in. thick, ½-in. wide strips that are screwed to the sides of the drawers. When fitting the runners in the grooves, you'll probably need to plane a shaving or two off their width to get an easy sliding fit.

The drawers themselves are joined in a straightforward way. The sides fit into vertical stopped sliding-dovetail housings in the drawer front, and the back is joined to the sides with through dovetails. The ¼-in. plywood bottom is glued and bradded in a rabbet cut into the drawer front. The back and sides are cut narrow to ride entirely over the bottom, and therefore don't need to be rabbeted.

The three drawers across the bottom are really not drawers at all, but French-fitted trays for holding drill bits and wrenches. It's frustrating to go rummaging through a pile of wrenches when you're looking for just one, but in a fitted

To hold his cabinetmaking tools in a convenient and organized way, author built this tool cabinet, making maximum use of its interior space. Its design evolved from those chests he saw while an apprentice in Edward Barnsley's shop, and is well adapted to studio woodworking.

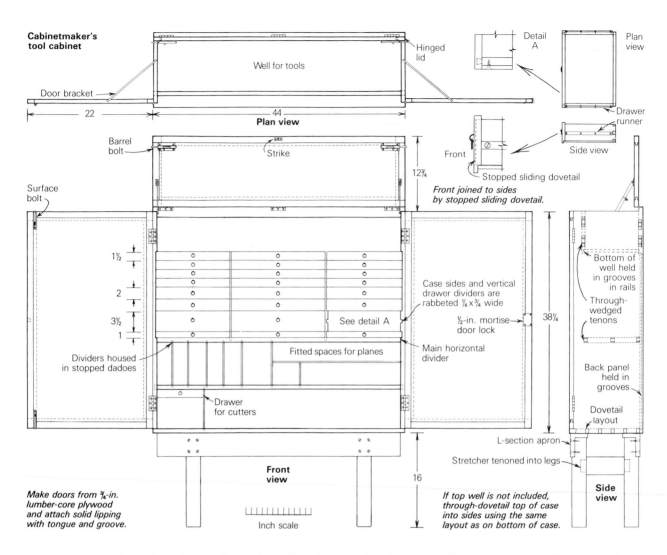

Cabinetmaker's tool cabinet

Door bracket

22 · 44 · **Plan view**

Well for tools

Hinged lid

Detail A

Plan view

Front

Drawer runner

Side view

Stopped sliding dovetail

Front joined to sides by stopped sliding dovetail.

Barrel bolt

Strike

12¾

Surface bolt

1½

2

3½

1

Dividers housed in stopped dadoes

See detail A

Fitted spaces for planes

Drawer for cutters

Case sides and vertical drawer dividers are rabbeted ¼ x ¾ wide

½-in. mortise-door lock

Main horizontal divider

Bottom of well held in grooves in rails

Through-wedged tenons

38¼

Back panel held in grooves

Dovetail layout

L-section apron

Stretcher tenoned into legs

Front view

16

Side view

Inch scale

Make doors from ¾-in. lumber-core plywood and attach solid lipping with tongue and groove.

If top well is not included, through-dovetail top of case into sides using the same layout as on bottom of case.

drawer, you can pick out the right wrench at a glance. I used ½-in. thick pine for the tray, and cut out the spaces for the wrenches and other items with a jigsaw. Then I applied the fitted tray over a ¼-in. plywood bottom, and edged both sides with solid lipping to which the runners are attached. The front edge of the tray fits into a groove in the drawer front.

The pigeonhole unit has two levels, and the top one is divided into nine bins that are dimensioned to hold planes of various sizes. The shelf that separates the upper and lower sections is housed in dadoes in the sides of the case, and the vertical dividers are secured in stopped dadoes in the shelf below and in the main horizontal divider above. The bottom half of this area is left unpartitioned, except for a single pigeonhole on the left and a little drawer I built to hold cutters for my router plane and electric router. Note that the drawer fronts and pigeonhole dividers are recessed 2 in. into the case to make room for the tools that will be mounted on the inside of the cabinet doors.

I made the two doors from lumber-core plywood and edged them on all four sides with solid wood. This lipping has a tongue milled onto one edge that fits into a corresponding groove cut in the edges of the plywood. The solid lipping wears better than the raw edge of the plywood and keeps the face veneer from snagging on a shirtsleeve and tearing up. Also, it's more attractive, and will hold screws better. The doors are hung to overlap the sides of the case and are secured

with butt hinges mortised into the edges of the case and the door. If you choose to make a top well, then edge its lid with solid lipping and attach it with inlet butt hinges.

To hold the doors open so they don't flop around when you remove and replace the tools mounted on them, you can fashion brackets by bending the ends of a 3/16 in. dia. metal rod to fit into sockets in the top edge of the case and the top edge of the door, as shown in the drawing above. These brackets can be put away when the cabinet is closed. The lid for the top well is secured by a pair of barrel bolts (one on each side), and the left-hand door locks top and bottom by means of two surface bolts (the strike for the top one is screwed on the underside of the lid). A half-mortise drawer lock installed on the right-hand door secures the entire cabinet.

The base I made from pine lumber also. The side stretchers are tenoned into the legs and the L-section aprons are held with screws and glue in notches cut into the tops of the legs. You could add a shelf to the base for holding tools and other items you don't mind having exposed to the outside. The cabinet sits unattached on the base; its weight is sufficient to keep it stable and in one place. This arrangement makes it easier for me (with some help) to move the cabinet whenever the need arises. □

David Powell is a designer and cabinetmaker, and the proprietor of Leeds Design Workshops, Easthampton, Mass.

Drawing, this page: David Powell

Bigfoot Tool Rack

by Ted Wick

A simple way to get your hand tools within easy reach of your workbench is to design and build a free-standing tool rack. I didn't have enough space in my shop for a wall-hung tool cabinet, which lacks the convenience of portability, so I made "Bigfoot," a tool rack with long feet for stability and an upper structure that can be adapted to changing needs as time goes by. To attach the crossmembers to the uprights, I adapted a Japanese joint called *sake-kama,* a modified through-dovetail joint held tight with a wedge, as shown in detail *A*. I used this assembly so I would be able to knock the rack apart easily and alter its brackets to accommodate changes and additions to my hand-tool collection. I used no glue or fasteners on Bigfoot so these future alterations would be easy to make. You can increase the capacity of the rack simply by using longer crossmembers or by adding more shelves and racks.

For the bottom rack, I made something that resembles a round-rung ladder lying flat. Between its rungs it holds mallets, squares and other tools with large heads and narrow shafts, and its design lets dust and shavings fall right through to the floor. I also keep all of my electric hand tools on this lower shelf, where they can remain plugged into the six-outlet fixture I've attached to the right-hand standard below shelf level. I like being able to use these tools right when I need them, without having to plug them in and then unplug them when the operation is finished. Their cords drop neatly behind the bench when they're not in use.

The middle rack, for my chisels and gouges, is a compound piece that works much better than a strip of wood with holes bored into it. My basic design is shown in detail *B*. I began with a board 1½ in. square and bored ¾-in. diameter holes on 3-in. centers all the way down its length. Then, setting my sawblade at an angle of about 75°, I ripped this board in two. These two halves, their slots staggered, were then joined with ⅜-in. dowels to a 1-in. by 2½-in. center strip so that there was a ⅜-in. gap remaining between the center strip and the two strips with the half-round slots in them. The gap, in conjunction with the angle, serves to accommodate the tapered sockets and handles of the chisels, holding them always perpendicular to the rack and keeping them from flopping around in their holes and damaging their edges by scraping against each other.

The top crossmember is a shelf for planes, spokeshaves and the like. The edges of the shelf are lipped, with the crossmember down the center. The back shelf is located high on the crossmember, while the front shelf is located at a low position on its front. The shelf is angled slightly toward the front; this elevates the tools on the rear half of the shelf and makes getting at them easier. ☐

Ted Wick, an amateur woodworker, is campus chaplain at Pacific Union College, Angwin, Calif.

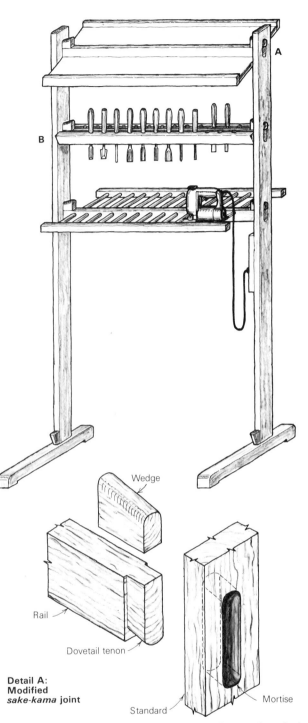

Detail A:
Modified
***sake-kama* joint**

Top of mortise is angled to accommodate wedge; bottom of mortise is angled in the same direction to house dovetail on tenon.

Detail B

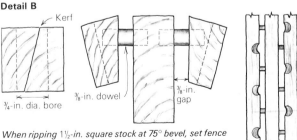

When ripping 1½-in. square stock at 75° bevel, set fence so kerf passes through the center point of section, producing two equal trapezoidal pieces. These are then connected to center strip with ⅜-in. dowels.

A Joiner's Tool Case
Wooden box holds all the essentials

by Tony Taylor

A few years ago I worked alongside a joiner who impressed on me the advantages of carrying your tools in a wooden case. His own case was a masterpiece of inventiveness and caught the eye of every visitor to our work site. The number of items he kept in this case amazed me. In addition to a full range of hand tools, he could produce on request just about anything the rest of us didn't carry—spare knife blades, chalk and line, scissors, tweezers, knife, fork and spoon, and, in case he worked overtime, toothbrush and paste, razor and aftershave and a corkscrew. Not everyone may feel the need to be so readily equipped for the contingencies of the working day, but those who regularly work away from the shop are familiar with the need to carry an organized tool kit.

My finished tool case weighs 16 lb. unloaded and up to 55 lb. when full, so don't count on walking to work if you make one of similar size. Strength of construction is vital; your tool case may have to withstand rough handling. So unless you can guarantee its safety, I would advise against making anything too fancy. A simple, well-made case will give years of service and will protect your tools. Because each tool has its own place, it's easy to find, and you'll notice if any are

missing at the end of the day. Furthermore, an attractive, well-made case will always get the attention of prospective clients and employers, and it will serve as a good example of your work.

Whether you plan to build a fine showpiece or a simple plywood box, careful planning is essential. List on paper all the tools you want to carry and sort them into categories according to size and usefulness. The saws can fit into the lid, where they lie flat and are easy to reach; a square can fit in here as well. Small tools fit easily into removable drawers or trays. Divide the drawers into separate compartments for chisels, files, brace bits and screwdrivers. Allow extra drawer space for mortise gauges, marking tools, measuring tape, drill bits and punches. My spirit level hangs on blocks glued to the back panel underneath the lowest drawer. This leaves the larger, heavier tools—oilstone, planes, hand drill, brace, pump screwdriver, coping saw and hammer—to lie in the bottom of the case.

The carcase is made of ⅝-in. thick pine boards dovetailed together. Front and back panels are of ¼-in. plywood. The depth of the lid must be determined before you lay out the

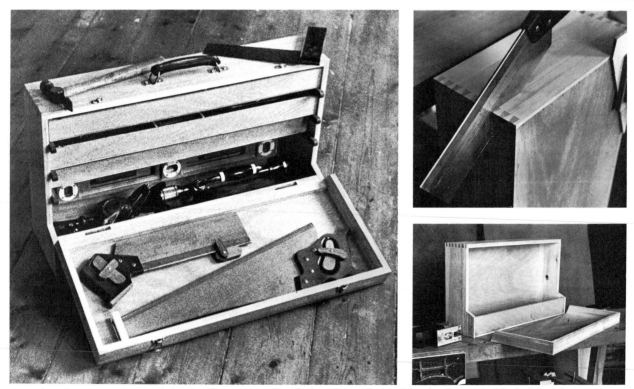

A sturdy tool case puts everything in its place for on-site work, with three drawers for small hand tools, saws inside the lid, and a storage compartment below for large, heavy tools. Top right, a tenon saw starts the cuts in the two upper corners and makes the beveled cut through the face of the front panel to form the lid. Note that the kerf neatly divides a dovetail pin. Once the corners and the panel have been cut, a portable jigsaw finishes the cuts along the sides and top. The lid will fall away as shown, lower right.

Photos: Tony Taylor

Wooden tool case

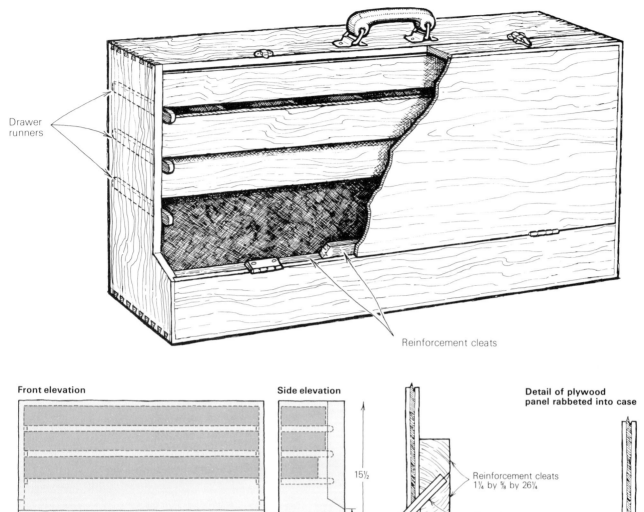

Drawer
runners

Reinforcement cleats

Front elevation

Side elevation

15½

3½

Measurements given in inches

28

7½

2

Bottom drawer is not as wide as two top drawers. This provides easy access to large tools stored in compartment below.

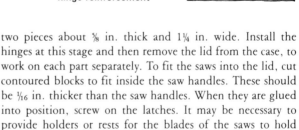

**Detail of plywood
panel rabbeted into case**

Reinforcement cleats
1¼ by ⅝ by 26¼

2½-in. brass butt hinge

**Detail of
hinge reinforcement**

dovetails so the sawcut that will separate the lid from the case will pass through the middle of one of the pins. It's best to glue the plywood panels into rabbets cut in the carcase rather than to fit them into grooves. The latter way may seem stronger, but will rob space from the inside of the case. Remember to allow for the rabbet when laying out the dovetails.

With the carcase glued up and the panels glued in place, the box is now completely enclosed. So the next step is to saw off the lid. Mark the depth of the lid with a gauge, and then make the first cut along the front plywood panel using a tenon saw. Cut from the outside edges of the panel towards the center, gradually lowering the angle of the saw as the cut proceeds. Complete the cut down the beveled line on the carcase sides. Next, saw in from the top corners so the kerfs will pass through a dovetail pin and will end at the beveled line on the carcase side and at the center of the top of the case. At this point the lid will fall free. Some cleaning up of the sawn edges will be necessary, but it should be kept to a minimum or else the gap between case and lid will be too wide.

Before fitting the hinges, the sawn edges of the front plywood panel must be reinforced and made thicker by gluing in

two pieces about ⅝ in. thick and 1¼ in. wide. Install the hinges at this stage and then remove the lid from the case, to work on each part separately. To fit the saws into the lid, cut contoured blocks to fit inside the saw handles. These should be ¹⁄₁₆ in. thicker than the saw handles. When they are glued into position, screw on the latches. It may be necessary to provide holders or rests for the blades of the saws to hold them in position.

Using butt joints throughout, I made the drawers from ¼-in. plywood with ⅛-in. plywood bottoms. You may prefer using solid wood with delicate dovetails. To permit easy access to the bottom compartment of the case, I made the lowest drawer 1 in. narrower than the upper two. The drawers slide on hardwood runners screwed to the sides of the carcase. The runners extend beyond the drawer fronts to allow the drawer to be pulled out farther than would otherwise be possible. When fitting the insides of the drawers for partitions, cut more dadoes than required; this will let you arrange things differently should the need arise in the future. □

Tony Taylor is a cabinetmaker and writer in London.

A Cabinetmaker's Showpiece

Removable trays are heart of tool cabinet

by Tage Frid

Why bother making a tool cabinet when a crate with shelves nailed in would hold the tools? I believe if a person wants to make a living as a woodworker and furniture designer, a well-designed and executed tool cabinet is very important. It's a pleasure to have a beautiful tool cabinet, where the tools are properly arranged and easy to find. And when a potential customer comes into the shop and sees a nice cabinet, half of the selling job is done right there.

For a cabinetmaker, a cabinet for tools is more practical than a tool chest like carpenters use. Usually a cabinetmaker does most of his work in the shop, while a carpenter has to move his tools from job to job and many times must use the tool chest as a workbench. Also, there is less wasted space in a cabinet, and because you can make it open from the front it is easy to arrange and get at the tools you need.

Most of my graduate students design and make a tool cabinet as their first project. They find it a difficult piece to design because every inch has to be used, but at the same time it has to be flexible, handy and easy to rearrange as you add new tools or replace old ones. The photos shown here are all of cabinets made by my students.

The drawing below is not a working drawing and the joints are left up to you—it is just an idea of how I would make a tool cabinet if I needed a new one. I prefer trays that slide out instead of drawers or shelves because I can take the one that holds chisels out of the cabinet, work with them at the bench, then put them back in the tray and return it to the cabinet. The same goes for screwdrivers and all my other small tools—each kind of tool has its own removable tray.

I wouldn't make the height of the cabinet any less than 40 in. if I wanted to have a bowsaw hanging inside the door, and in that case I wouldn't make any grooves in the door.

Personally, I would have the bowsaw hanging on the outside and use small shelves in the door grooves for storage of small tools. If you aren't going to hang saws inside the door, the height isn't that critical.

Through the years, I've found that 15 in. is the best depth for the cabinet, not counting the door, which should be another 4 in. This is deep enough for nearly everything, including heavy tools. The width, 30 in., is necessary so the jointer plane, slicks and other large tools can fit in the upper part, which can be an open shelf or a drawer.

I make the sides of the trays out of hardwood—use whatever joint you like at the corners—with a bottom of ¼-in. plywood. The grooves in the sides of the cabinet of course are ¼ in. by ¼ in., so the plywood can easily slide in and out. The space between the grooves is 1½ in., which makes the cabinet very flexible—the trays can be 1½ in. apart, or 3 in., or 4½ in. and so on, depending on whether they are used for chisels, planes or whatever. The center divider should be in the exact center of the cabinet, so both sides are the same width, in this case 13½ in., and all the trays and shelves are interchangeable. Remember that the plywood bottom of the tray slides into the groove and add ½ in., making the bottoms 14 in. wide. Inside the sides of the trays it is a good idea to make some vertical ¼-in. grooves for removable partitions. Part of the front of each tray is cut down for a handle, and to make it easy to see what's inside. If the cabinet is made out of solid wood, make the trays ⅜ in. shorter than the cabinet is deep, in case the wood shrinks.

Tage Frid is a professor of woodworking and furniture design at Rhode Island School of Design.

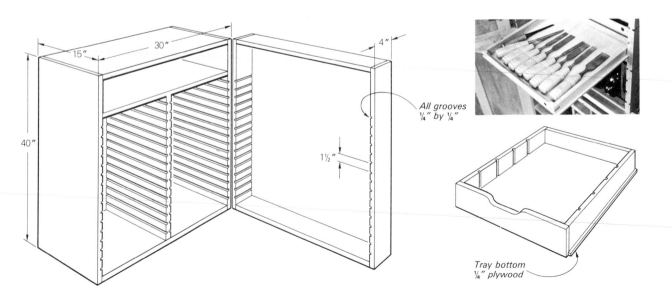

All grooves ¼" by ¼"

Tray bottom ¼" plywood

John Dunnigan's tool cabinet (41 in. by 34 in. by 19 in.; base is 24 in. high) is solid mahogany, with ply-wood door panels veneered in fiddleback mahogany. The inside of the door is 3¼ in. deep. One door holds saws; the other has adjustable shelves with holes and slots for screwdrivers and carving tools. The shelves are 14 in. deep and adjustable in height.

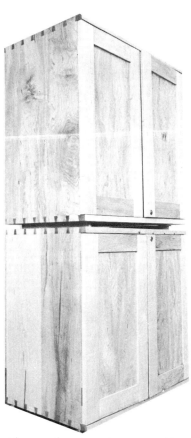

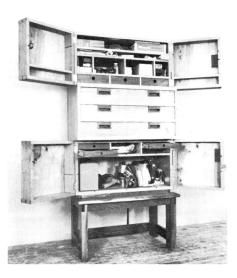

Above and center, these two cabinets (each 32 in. by 32 in. by 19 in.) by Douglas Hale can either stack on top of each other, or sit or hang individually. The doors are a flat frame-and-panel, and hold a few flat tools such as squares or small saws. The detail photo, opposite page, shows how the trays work.

Above and left, solid-oak cabinet by Richard Gallo is 48 in. by 32 in. by 19 in., with 18-in. high base. Stretcher at back makes space underneath usable for storage. Doors, 3 in. deep, have adjustable shelves; three large central drawers hold planes and saws. Lower cabinet was designed for electrical tools.

Workbench
Here's the European original

by Tage Frid

There are many workbenches available on the market to-day. Besides saving money, why should a woodworker build my bench? I can persuade my students and myself easily enough, but to convince you I should explain the benefits of this design and how I arrived at these specifics.

When I came to this country in 1948, I was given a tour of the school where I was to teach. I was guided to a large room and introduced to the teacher with whom I would work. We talked for a while, or rather he did the talking because my vocabulary didn't go much beyond yes and no. By waving arms and legs I finally conveyed to him that I wanted to see the woodshop. When I was told I was standing in it I just about passed out. In the room was a huge thickness planer I think Columbus' father must have brought over, and a few small power tools. I was really flabbergasted when I saw the student "workbenches." These were large tables for two persons with a vise on each end. Most of the time the students were holding down their work with one hand and working with the other. Some had taken much time to make special contraptions to hold their work so they could use both hands, which I'm sure was the Lord's intention when he de-signed us with two. (The Japanese sit on the floor and use their feet to secure the work, leaving both hands free.)

After being in school for a few months I realized that the bench I wanted did not exist in this country. So I designed my first workbench, which was quite similar to the one I was taught on in Denmark. Later we made one for each student. Since then we have been making workbenches every two or three years, so that the students each have their own when they graduate. I find it a good exercise in which they learn how to set up the machines for batch production and work

together as a production team. It takes us three days from rough lumber to have all the parts ready to fit and assemble, and to have the bench top glued up.

Over the years, having made the bench so many times and having had numerous people using and criticizing it, I have arrived at this design and these dimensions as best suited for a cabinetmaker. With its two vises and accessory side clamps there are five possibilities for holding the work—two in the right vise, one in the left vise, one between the bench dogs and one between the side clamps. Both vises are the European type with only one screw and no guide pins to interfere with the work. A piece can be clamped all the way to the floor if necessary. The left vise can hold irregularly shaped objects. With only seven bolts, the bench is easy to assemble and disassemble, and takes minimum storage space. The only glued parts are the bench top, the right vise and the leg sec-tions. Everything else bolts together so that any damaged pieces are easy to replace.

The bench is almost six feet long, but if you wish to lengthen it you can easily do so by extending the bench top at the center and the two leg stretchers (#18 on the plan) the same amount. You can shorten it in the same way. I would advise keeping all length changes in five-inch increments so that the distance between the bench dogs remains the same. The bench is designed right-handed, but could be converted to left-handedness by reversing the plans. You could make the bench top wider by doing without the tool tray. Americans who grew up with those school-shop work tables often prefer the larger work surface, but without the tray they must knock a lot of tools onto the floor, too. I suggest attaching a piece of plywood between the leg stretchers and inserting two

A With two steel dogs, the bench can trap just about anything.

B Auxiliary support will prop up the loose end of a long board.

end pieces to form a large storage compartment. If you wish you can add a piece behind the bench to hold gouges, chisels, screwdrivers, etc. But I find it more a bother than a help: if you are working on pieces larger than the bench top surface you have to remove the tools so they don't interfere.

If you are working on long boards or panels, you can make a simple device to support the weight of the board. Take a good heavy piece of wood (a 2x4 or 4x4 will do), and drill holes at least ½ in. in diameter and about 1 in. apart in a straight line down the length of the piece. By clamping this into the right vise and moving a dowel to the hole just under the work you can easily prop up a long piece. The side clamps can grab the edges of large pieces of plywood. They are wooden blocks with pairs of steel plates, which attach to the right-hand vise and bench edge through the dog holes.

Before beginning, get your hardware. That way, if you wish to make a substitution or if something isn't readily available, you can make all your dimensional changes before any wood is cut. We could not find a 14-in. bolt so we made our own by brazing a nut to the end of some ⅜-in. threaded rod that we had cut to the right length. Vise screws and bench dogs are available from mail-order tool suppliers.

Make sure you choose a dense hardwood and that the wood is properly dried. We use maple because it is extremely hard and durable and is the least expensive in this area. When cutting up the stock, cut the longest pieces first. Cut them all 1 in. longer than the final dimension and at least ¼ in. wider to allow for ripping and joining. It is best to purchase rough lumber, joint and thickness-plane it rough, and then plane the whole top to final thickness after it is glued. If a thickness planer isn't available, buy the lumber planed and

align carefully during gluing. I suggest not using pieces wider than 4 in. in the top because of possible warpage, but when rough-cutting this lumber, allow an extra inch of width overall for ripping and joining. We use 8/4 stock (that is, 2-in.-thick) for everything except pieces #18 and #8, which are from 5/4 stock. For the heavier pieces, which finish 2¾ in. by 4 in., we glue up two pieces of 8/4 because in this area it is almost impossible to find properly dried lumber of that thickness. You can bricklay or stack these pieces if you're short on lumber. We use Titebond yellow glue for all the glued sections.

C Wedges lock tenons in base subassembly.

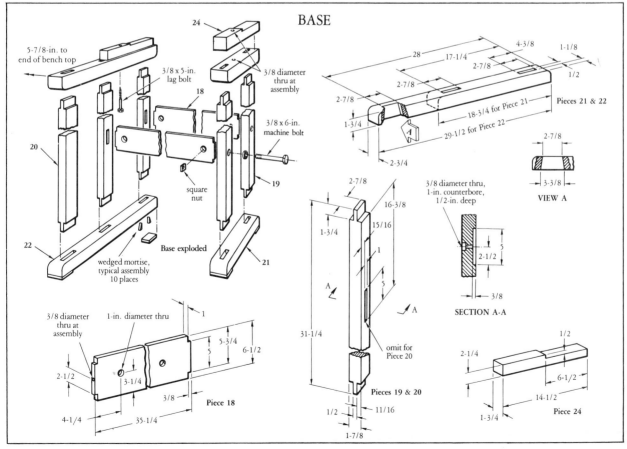

D *Radial-arm saw cuts dados for bench dogs. Note second dado in saw fence: indexing stick spaces each cut from the one before.*

E *Plywood board keeps the parts of the right-hand vise square during glue-up; middle piece is #5, the bench end-piece, included here for clarity.*

F *Scribe and fit runner pieces #15 and #17.*

G *The completed vise, from below.*

Many students have found it best to start assembly with the base. Assembling the base first eliminates many pieces, making things less confusing when the vise is to go together. If you wish, you may round over the edges of the base pieces and radius the ends of the feet. The way you handle these details, along with your vise corners and handles, will give your bench a personal touch. Sand all pieces before gluing. When wedging the tenons, be sure to hammer evenly on both wedges and don't overhammer or the wood will split (photo C). After the wedges are in, check the sections for squareness. At this point you can remove the clamps because the wedges will hold everything in place. Clean off all the excess glue while it is still wet and you will have little finishing work. After the glue dries, saw the excess off the wedges and plane the top bearers (#21 and #22) even and flat. Drill the bolt holes in the uprights (#19), then clamp the base parts together to drill into the stretchers (#18).

In making the bench top, we use splines between the pieces to make gluing up easier. It isn't a bad idea for strength either, because of all the hammering that will take place on the top surface. A spline should definitely be used between pieces #1 and #3, to help align the front piece flush with the rest of the top. We use a dado head to cut the grooves for the splines but it could be done with a shaper, a hand router or a plough plane. The bench top is glued and planed before piece #3 with the bench dog slots is added. We use the dado head on the radial arm saw to cut the bench dog slots, with a stop to keep the spacing and the angle consistent (photo D). It could be done instead with a router, a saw and chisel, or a router plane. The top step of the slot is chiseled out by hand at the very end. Cap piece #2 is added afterward, with a brad in each end to prevent the piece from sliding over the length during gluing. Don't use too much glue or it will be necessary to do a tedious clean-up inside each bench dog slot. After the front piece is attached, the top is sawn to length and width. The tongues at each end can be made with a shaper, circular saw, hand router or rabbet plane.

The lengthwise cut for the right-hand vise must be parallel to the front of the bench top, and the crosswise cut precisely square to it. These can be done on a band saw, or with a circular saw or hand saw. For making the groove for the right-hand vise to ride in, you can use a hand router or chisel it out. The accuracy of this groove is very important because it will determine how smoothly your vise works.

As mentioned previously, none of the end-cap pieces is glued. For this reason it is essential that the holes for the bolts be drilled very accurately, or else the bolts will not go in squarely. Therefore I suggest drilling the holes through pieces #4, #5 and #7 on a drill press or with a doweling jig. At the same time, drill the hole for the vise in piece #7. After the holes are drilled, the end-cap pieces (#4 and #5) are clamped in place with filler #6 inserted. The holes are then continued into the bench top. The best way to do this is to use an extra-long drill bit, or a bit on an extension. If you don't wish to invest in the bit, you can cut a dado and let the bolt ride in that. The same procedure should be followed on piece #18, the under-frame stretchers. If you do use a dado and wish to close up the groove, you can glue in a piece to conceal the bolt. However, this isn't necessary because the nut will nestle in the shoulder of the right-angled hole, pulling the bolt in tight. In our benches we inset the vise hardware brackets flush, but this certainly isn't crucial.

TOP

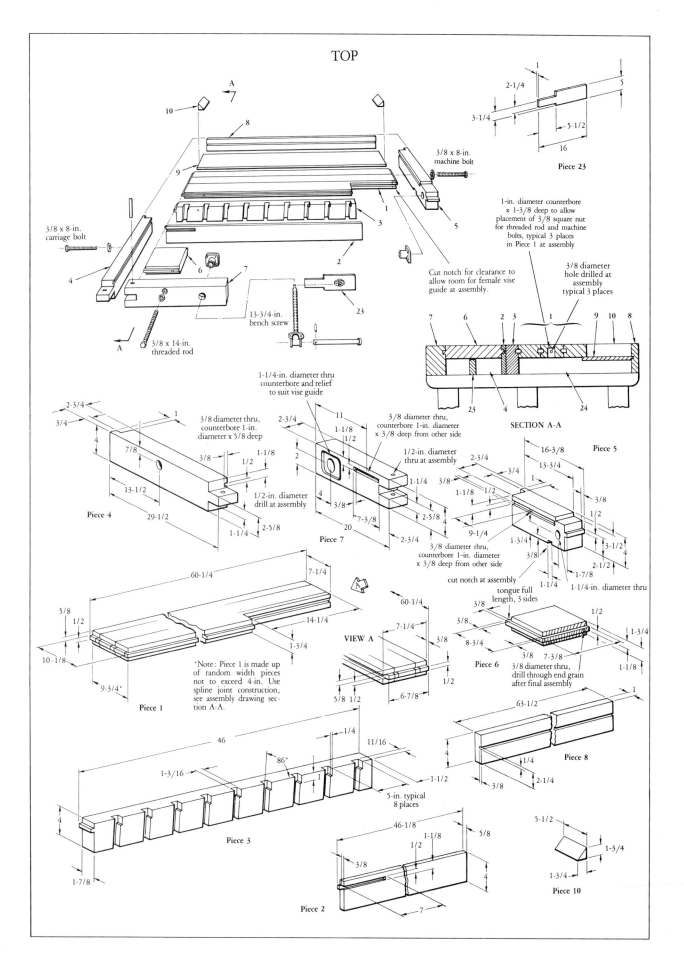

Piece 23

1-in. diameter counterbore
x 1-3/8 deep to allow
placement of 3/8 square nut
for threaded rod and machine
bolts, typical 3 places
in Piece 1 at assembly

3/8 diameter
hole drilled at
assembly
typical 3 places

3/8 x 8-in.
machine bolt

3/8 x 8-in.
carriage bolt

Cut notch for clearance to
allow room for female vise
guide at assembly.

13-3/4-in.
bench screw

3/8 x 14-in.
threaded rod

SECTION A-A

Piece 5

1-1/4-in. diameter thru
counterbore and relief
to suit vise guide

3/8 diameter thru,
counterbore 1-in. diameter
x 3/8 deep from other side

1/2-in. diameter
thru at assembly

3/8 diameter thru,
counterbore 1-in.
diameter x 5/8 deep

1/2-in. diameter
drill at assembly

Piece 4

Piece 7

3/8 diameter thru,
counterbore 1-in. diameter
x 3/8 deep from other side

cut notch at assembly

tongue full
length, 3 sides

1-1/4-in. diameter thru

Piece 6

3/8 diameter thru,
drill through end grain
after final assembly

*Note: Piece 1 is made up
of random width pieces
not to exceed 4-in. Use
spline joint construction,
see assembly drawing sec-
tion A-A.

Piece 1

VIEW A

Piece 8

5-in. typical
8 places

Piece 3

86°

Piece 2

Piece 10

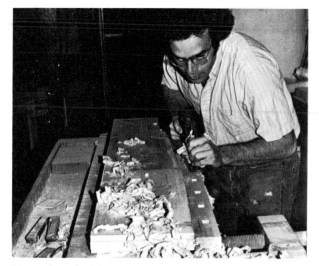

H Leveling the top.

1 Face piece of left-hand vise swivels to grab irregular work.

QTY.	PARTS #	T	W	L	COMMENT
1	#1	1¾"	9¾"	60¼"	Bench top
1	#2	⅝"	4"	46"	Cap piece
1	#3	1⅞"	4"	46"	Bench top
1	#4	2¾"	4"	29½"	Left end cap
1	#5	2¾"	4"	16⅜"	Right end cap
1	#6	1¾"	7⅜"	8¾"	Filler
1	#7	2¾"	4"	20"	Left vise
1	#8	1"	4"	63½"	Back apron
1	#9	½"	7"	59½"	Tool tray; plywood
2	#10	1¾"	1¾"	5½"	Corner block
1	#11	2¾"	4"	12"	Right vise jaw
1	#12	2¾"	4"	11"	Right vise
1	#13	1⅞"	3½"	20"	Right vise
1	#13A	⅝"	3½"	20"	Right vise
1	#14	½"	5"	18½"	Right vise
1	#15	¾"	1¼"	18¾"	Right vise guide
1	#16	1"	2¾"	5½"	Right vise guide
1	#17	½"	1½"	15"	Right vise guide
2	#18	1"	6½"	35¼"	Stretcher
4	#19	1⅞"	2⅞"	31¼"	Legs with mortise
1	#20	1⅞"	2⅞"	31¼"	Leg without mortise
2	#21	1¾"	2¾"	18¾"	Base right
2	#22	1¾"	2¾"	29½"	Base left
1	#23	¾"	5"	16"	Left vise jaw
2	#24	1¾"	2¼"	14½"	Filler

LUMBER: 50 board feet of 8/4-in. maple
10 board feet of 5/4-in. maple
one 8 x 60-in. piece of ½-in. Baltic birch plywood

HARDWARE: four ⅜" x 6" machine bolts
two ⅜" x 8" machine bolts
one ⅜" x 14" threaded rod (or bolt)
two ⅜" x 5" lag bolts
two 7" bench dogs with heavy springs
(1" x ⅝" knurled face, ⅞" x ⅝" shank—
we use Ulmias)
one bench screw: 1¼" dia. x 20¼" overall length
(you might have to cut this to fit)
one bench screw: 1¼" dia. x 13¾" long
(with swivel end)

Now comes the most difficult part of assembly—the right-hand vise. It is advisable to make the tongues on the pieces all slightly oversized and carefully fit them into their grooves. It is essential that every part of the vise be completely square. We use finger joints in the corners but if you are only making one bench, you might find it faster and more satisfying to hand-cut some large dovetails. When gluing the vise pieces together, cut a piece of plywood to the exact dimension of the inside rectangle of the vise. Clamp the vise pieces around this piece so the vise will have to end up square (photo E).

The vise should be glued and fitted and all the holes drilled for the hardware before cover piece #14 is added. The hole for the bench screw is drilled in the endpiece, #11, and from there guided into piece #5, with #5 bolted in place. It might be necessary to chisel a little notch into the bench top to make room for the screw's bracket, but such a notch is invisible. The bench has to be flipped upside down for the fitting of the guides. The notches should be scribed off the runner pieces and carefully routed or chiseled out by hand (photo F). Countersink all the screws so that they don't interfere with the vise travel. Piece #17 should be screwed down first and then the other guides set in place. Take the time to make all of these fit right. Fitting the vise will drive you crazy at times, but be patient and worry about one section at a time and eventually it will all fit just right. When the vise is working properly, the cover piece, #14, is added. It is set into pieces #11 and #12, so suitable recesses must be chiseled out. If you want to get a little fancy you can undercut the edges so that the effect is almost like one large dovetail. A complementary angle is cut on the edges of #14 and the piece is glued. Be sure to glue only to the moving parts of the vise and not to any of the stationary parts of the bench top. Drill up from the bottom through the bench dog slots to locate the tops of the slots and finish chiseling them out.

Piece #8 is screwed onto the back of the bench after it receives a groove to support the plywood for the tool trough. The plywood is screwed directly to the underside of the bench top and is further supported by the filler pieces (#24), which secure the top to the legs. Screw in the two corner blocks (#10) from below to make the trough easy to sweep out.

After the bench is completed, the top should be hand-planed and belt-sanded level (photo H). All the edges should be eased off slightly, or "broken," to minimize chipping out when something hits against an edge.

All the places on the underside of the right-hand vise where wood is running against wood should be coated with a paraffin-turpentine mixture. Melt the paraffin in a can or pot, remove from heat, then add a tablespoon or two of turpentine per block of paraffin. Paint the pieces liberally with the mixture to protect them and help them to function smoothly. Do not oil any of these pieces.

At completion, the rest of the bench and especially the work surface should be completely penetrated with raw linseed oil. This will take several hearty coats. At least once a year the bench top should be resurfaced. This is done by scraping it down, releveling it, and again soaking it with oil.

Four small pieces should be added under the legs so that the bench rests on four points. The thickness of these pads can serve as an adjustment for the final bench height. The height is up to you, but one rule of thumb is to stand up straight with your arms straight down, then stick your thumb out level. It should land right on the bench top.

Now your bench is completely finished and looks so beautiful you hate to use it. If you take good care of it, working *on* it and not *into* it, it should stay like that for years. ☐

Tage Frid is professor emeritus of woodworking and furniture design at the Rhode Island School of Design.

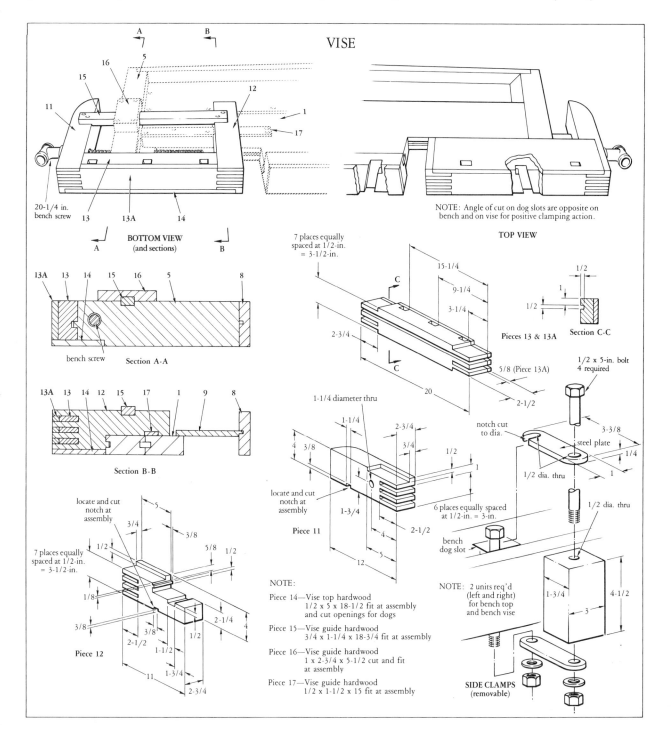

VISE

NOTE: Angle of cut on dog slots are opposite on bench and on vise for positive clamping action.

BOTTOM VIEW (and sections)

TOP VIEW

Section A-A

Section B-B

Pieces 13 & 13A

Section C-C

Piece 11

Piece 12

NOTE:
Piece 14—Vise top hardwood
1/2 x 5 x 18-1/2 fit at assembly and cut openings for dogs

Piece 15—Vise guide hardwood
3/4 x 1-1/4 x 18-3/4 fit at assembly

Piece 16—Vise guide hardwood
1 x 2-3/4 x 5-1/2 cut and fit at assembly

Piece 17—Vise guide hardwood
1/2 x 1-1/2 x 15 fit at assembly

NOTE: 2 units req'd (left and right) for bench top and bench vise

SIDE CLAMPS (removable)

A Shoulder Vise and Clamping Dogs
Attachments make a table a workbench

by R. J. Silvestrini

Tage Frid's workbench (see pages 20 through 25) offers two features I had long sought—a shoulder vise with its jaw unobstructed by the usual screw and guide bars (it can grip irregular objects, as well) and a tail vise with a traveling dog. My workbench has a radial arm saw mounted on one end of it and I don't have room for another bench in my shop. Therefore, instead of building a copy of Frid's workbench, I chose to adapt these two features to the bench I already had.

After studying Frid's plans, I decided that the shoulder vise could be made separately and then attached. But the tail vise was a different story. I wanted its traveling dog so I could hold long workpieces on my bench, but I really didn't need the vise jaws, and besides, my radial arm saw was sitting right where these would go. I resolved this dilemma by doing away with the vise part of the system and rigging a traveling dog in a sliding, screw-driven housing. This mechanism, together with a row of dog holes, could be mounted on the edge of my bench top in one long unit. I decided I would make all of these components—the shoulder vise and the bench-top clamping system—detachable. This way, if I wanted to switch to another bench later on, they could easily be removed from the old and mounted on the new.

For the shoulder vise, I followed Frid's design, making changes as necessary for fit. I used an acme-threaded bench screw (available from Woodcraft Supply Corp., PO Box 4000, Woburn, Mass. 01888) for the vise jaw. To hold the cantilevered arm in place and keep it from being pushed outward as the vise is tightened, I used a ½-in. threaded rod, which is passed through the arm and spacer block and secured by a captured nut let into the top of the bench.

I departed from Frid's design when making the row of dog holes and the moving housing that opposes them. Instead of cutting the slots in a solid strip as Frid does, I cut a lot of parallelogram-shaped spacer blocks (angled 4° off the perpendicular so the dog would be canted appropriately) and sandwiched them between two strips 3 in. wide and as long as the bench. Each block is 4⅟₁₆ in. wide, and to make the holes, I spaced the blocks 1⅝₁₆ in. apart. The little slots in the front of each hole (Frid chisels these in by hand) which accommodate the head of the dog, I easily cut by elevating the blade on my radial arm saw and using a 3-in. high fence.

I designed the sliding dog housing after having looked at a drawing of a similar one made by David Powell of Leeds Design Workshops in Easthampton, Mass. While his uses a lot more hardware, I made mine with a minimum of metal parts by connecting two spacer blocks with a pair of wooden bars. These bars serve also to guide the housing as it travels, riding in grooves cut into the two strips that form the back and face sides of the dog unit. These grooves should be long enough to allow the slide to travel about 7½ in., approximately 1½ times

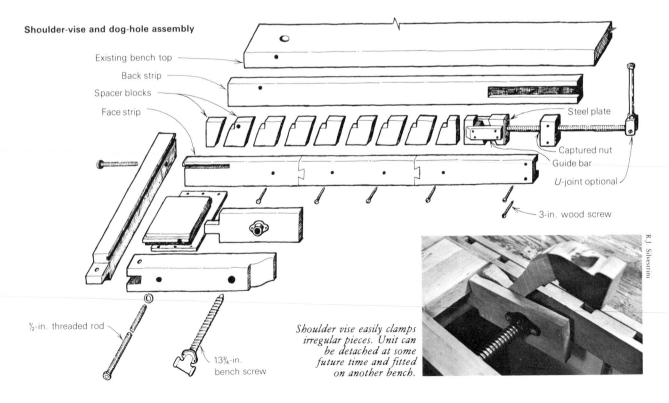

Shoulder-vise and dog-hole assembly

Existing bench top
Back strip
Spacer blocks
Face strip
Steel plate
Captured nut
Guide bar
U-joint optional
3-in. wood screw
½-in. threaded rod
13¾-in. bench screw

Shoulder vise easily clamps irregular pieces. Unit can be detached at some future time and fitted on another bench.

R. J. Silvestrini

the distance between dog holes. The threaded rod is attached to the slide by means of a metal plate, which is drilled in its center to receive a ⅛-in. bolt. The threaded end of this bolt is epoxied into a hole drilled in the end of the ½-in. threaded rod. Before attaching the plate to the slide with wood screws, the slide must be counterbored to accommodate the head of the ⅛-in. bolt.

The last piece of the slide assembly to make is the block that holds a ½-in. captured nut in which the threaded rod turns to advance or retract the slide. Once all the pieces are cut, the spacer blocks are glued to the back strip. Then the face strip is attached. I made a separate face strip to be attached only with screws to cover the part of the unit that's involved in the slide mechanism. This gives me access to the guts of the thing if it needs tuning or repair. When the system is complete, it's affixed to the edge of the bench top with 3-in. wood screws that are countersunk into the face strip. □

R. J. Silvestrini is president of an industrial equipment distribution company in Huntington, W. Va.

Wooden Vise

by G. Barry Ellis

The jaws, the screw, the guide rods and the handle of early vises were all made of wood. Modern vises like the one I will describe here have a metal screw, nut and rods, which you can buy from catalog supply houses or find used in a second-hand store. The jaws must be strong and durable. Many species of wood will work, but I think green ash, maple, beech (the traditional choice) and pecan are best. The size and shape of the jaws will depend on your requirements. Most European vises have relatively shallow throats and thick jaws, a combination that produces great clamping pressure and is suitable for use with bench-top clamping systems. If, however, you need large holding capacity in a vise with only moderate clamping pressure, then a wooden-jaw vise modeled after North American steel vises will do the job.

The jaws need to be a matching pair. On my vise they are 12 in. long, 6 in. wide and a full 2 in. thick. For proper alignment, the two jaws should be clamped together when drilling the holes for the screw and the guide rods. I use ½-in. black pipe for the guide rods and standard pipe nuts for attaching the rods to the front jaw. This requires threading the pipe 2 in. along its length on the front end and about ¾ in. at the back where it screws into the drag bar, a horizontal piece of wood or metal that holds the trailing ends of the guide rods and screw in alignment. The length of the guide rods is determined by the length of the screw you use and by how they are attached to the front jaw and to the drag bar. If you make

Wood-jaw vise with steel bench dog, above, can be made with standard hardware items. The front jaw is attached to the guide rods by two pairs of pipe nuts. Rear view of vise, right, shows how guide rods are affixed to drag bar by means of pipe flanges. Braces dadoed into rear jaw provide added strength and stability.

your drag bar out of wood, you can fit it with threaded flanges and screw the guide rods into them as shown above. Keep in mind that the two guide rods should be slightly higher than the screw to prevent a workpiece from resting on an oily screw. And when you attach the rods to the front jaw by means of two pairs of nuts, you must recess the two nuts on the inside of the jaw so the vise will close completely.

The rear jaw of the vise can be secured to the edge of your bench with lag bolts or with machine-thread bolts screwed into barrel nuts let into the bench top from underneath. In either case, you must counterbore the rear jaw for the bolt heads. For extra strength you can dado the backside of the rear jaw to receive a pair of braces that fasten to the underside of the bench. The addition of a bench dog is easy once the vise is affixed to your bench. Just bore a hole directly above the screw (or several of them if you want to use more than one dog at a time) into the top of the front jaw. For the dog I use a steel pin with a head on it and file a flat on one side of the head where it will contact the workpiece. Another hole bored in the side of the jaw holds the dog when it's not in use. □

G. Barry Ellis, of Calgary, Alta., is a workshop specialist who writes for Canadian newspapers.

Post-and-Spar Lumber Rack

by Richard Starr

The storage rack I designed for the junior-high-school woodshop where I teach consists of four units like the one in the photo below, set on 4-ft. centers. Each unit has three oak spars, through-mortised and pegged into 6x6 fir uprights. The 40-in. spars are tapered to add capacity to the next lower storage area and neatness to their appearance. The mortises were chopped very tight, and each spar was driven in with a sledge hammer. There is a ½-in. shoulder at the top and bottom of each tenon.

The uprights of the rack are mounted against a concrete-block wall, but not sup-

Post-and-spar lumber rack has large capacity and great inherent strength. Wedge-shaped strips added to top edges of spars cant the load backwards, reducing the likelihood of lumber falling off the rack accidentally.

ported by it. Their main strength comes from tying them into the rafters of the building using the little cleats shown in the drawing. The cleats are cut from 2-in. oak, open-end mortised into the upright and pinned with a 1-ft. dowel. Carriage bolts hold the cleats to the rafters. Before being erected, the bottom end of each 6x6 was nailed to a 2x6 block, then the 2x6 was nailed to the concrete floor. This locates and stabilizes the bottom end.

The advantage of a cantilevered woodrack is that you can approach it from three sides. It is easy moving wood around to find the one piece you need and quick to load up with new material when it arrives. The capacity of this thing is enormous. If you load it with 16-ft. boards to a depth of about 26 in. per shelf (compensating for the taper in the spars), you get about 5,550 bd. ft. Of course it's less if you sticker your wood, but more if you allow for overhang over the ends of the thing, which are 16 ft. apart. We've never fully loaded the top shelf, but with the bottom two spars loaded solid with pine, there is no sign of flexing in the uprights or in the spars. I'm sure the rack could be loaded to the brim with unstickered hardwood, if the building itself could take it. If the rack were to hang in a frame building, I'd think over the scantlings of the entire structure. □

Richard Starr lives in Thetford Center, Vt.

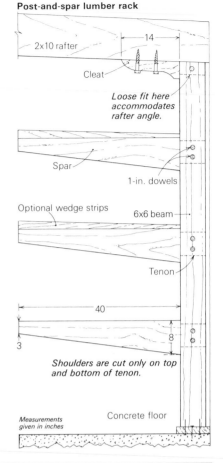

Post-and-spar lumber rack

2x10 rafter · 14

Cleat

Loose fit here accommodates rafter angle.

Spar

1-in. dowels

Optional wedge strips · 6x6 beam

Tenon

40

3 · 8

Shoulders are cut only on top and bottom of tenon.

Measurements given in inches · Concrete floor

Double-Top Workbench
Design increases workspace and clamping capability

by Ramon Sanna

With its tail vise and shoulder vise, the Scandinavian-style cabinetmaker's bench (see pages 20 to 25) offers a number of ways to hold a workpiece, and its design is well suited to most shop operations. But for those of us who like to have a lot of room on our benches—room for project parts and for tools—a larger work surface is desirable. Without sacrificing any of the clamping features of the Scandinavian bench, I designed mine with two tops, four rows of dog holes, a center tool well and three vises. This gives me a work surface that's a full 28 in. wide, in addition to an out-of-the-way place to keep all the hand tools I'm using at a given time.

Each top is glued up from five pieces of 8/4 maple, three boards for the work surface and two for the aprons. Edge-joined with ¾-in. thick splines, each top surface measures 11 in. wide, just right for being surfaced to 1¾ in. thick on my Parks 12-in. planer. The aprons are also splined to the underedges of the tops, which gives them a finished thickness of

4¼ in. The center aprons are rabbeted on their bottom outer edges to receive the tool tray, which separates the tops and provides a 6-in. wide well between them (see drawing). Finally, each end of the bench is fitted with a facing board 28 in. by 4¼ in. These facing boards are joined to the bench tops with ¾-in. thick splines and are best attached by bolts and barrel nuts, one pair for each apron, two pairs for each top. The counterbores for the bolt heads can be plugged. When the tandem top is finished, it's mounted onto a single base frame.

Instead of using the conventional rectangular bench dogs, I bored two rows of ⁵⁄₁₆-in. diameter holes in each top and counterbored the undersides of each hole ²⁵⁄₆₄ in. to accept a ⁵⁄₁₆-18 short-prong T-nut. These are available from the Sharon Bolt and Screw Co., 60 Pleasant St., Ashland, Mass. 01721 (#TN-355Q). Using horizontal counterbored bench stops made of pine (see photos), I can securely hold workpieces of almost any size and shape by bolting the bench stops into any

Right, Sanna's workbench with three vises, tool well and storage shelf beneath is spacious and sturdy. The bench and tail-vise jaws have a total of 56 dog holes, each containing a T-nut. Tail vise, below left, clamps board to bench top. Stops are bolted into place rather than just slipped into holes. Both tail vises, below right, can hold a single long piece, or with stops on both vises, they can become part of a four-point clamping system.

Section through bench top

Facing boards are bolted onto each end of bench top and held firmly by barrel nuts let into underside of top. All other parts are splined together, except for tool tray, which is glued into rabbets.

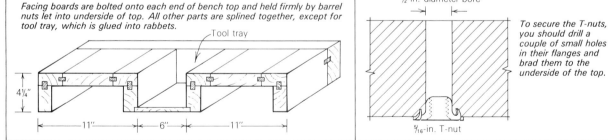

Tool tray

4¼"

11" — 6" — 11"

½-in. diameter bore

To secure the T-nuts, you should drill a couple of small holes in their flanges and brad them to the underside of the top.

⁵⁄₁₆-in. T-nut

of the 56 *T*-nuts in the two tops. These serve also as hold-downs for jigs and other fixtures.

The two tail vises, also bored and equipped with *T*-nuts, can be used as part of the bench-stop system or as woodworking vises. Because they are both on the same end of the bench, I can use them together to clamp a long board edge up, something the Scandinavian bench won't do at all. Rather than making a shoulder vise of the kind Tage Frid recommends, I got an ordinary woodworker's vise with a steel dog and mounted it on the front of the bench (opposite the end with the tail vises). I can use the dog in conjunction with the bench

stops or use the vise to hold long cumbersome pieces like doors.

Since my tool well is in the middle of the bench, I can work on both sides of my bench and always be within easy reach of my tools. Though it takes more time to bolt the stops into place than it does to slip a dog into its slot, I find this disadvantage to be offset by the increased versatility and firm clamping capability of the bench-top system. The more I use my bench, the more I am convinced that it's the most important tool in my shop. □

Ramon Sanna, of Madison, Wis., is an amateur woodworker.

Three leg vises and three rows of dog holes give Schuldt's bench large holding capability. Side view of leg vise, right, shows threaded rod, pivot foot and steel strap stiffener.

A Softwood Workbench
Leg vises keep it versatile and affordable

by Ted Schuldt

A few years ago when I was beginning to get involved with woodworking as a hobby, I was awed by those $600 European workbenches sold by the purveyors of fine woodworking tools. I wished I could afford one but knew I would have to find a substitute. Someday I may build a hardwood bench such as the one described by Tage Frid (page 20), but until then I'll get by well enough with a bench made of common materials from a straightforward design that you can adapt to suit yourself.

Before determining the dimensions of your bench, evaluate your needs and the size of your shop. I chose a length of 60 in. because of space restrictions and a width of 27 in. to provide enough workspace to assemble casepieces. After determining the required dimensions, begin by making the bench top.

All the wood used in this bench is fir, readily available at any lumberyard. The bench top is made of 2x4s set on edge. Take extra care in selecting the pieces for the top. They should be straight, and the edges that will be the top should be as free of knots as possible. Most dimensioned lumber has rounded edges, so rip off enough of the edge to get the corners square to provide for a smooth, flat surface when the boards are glued up. Select the two best 2x4s in which to cut

the bench-dog slots. Set a dado head for ¾-in. depth and ¾-in. width and cut parallel dadoes 3 in. apart at an angle of 86°. Also space a short row of slots across the width of the bench near one end. Slant the holes toward the vise to force the dog into the slot when it's under pressure.

Before gluing up the top, drill holes in each of the 2x4s for the two threaded rods used to reinforce the top. I glued up the 2x4s in pairs, then in fours, then in eights, then I added one more to make two halves each of nine pieces.

Then I took the two halves to a high-school woodshop and ran them through a thickness planer. You could plane these by hand, but I took the more expeditious way to the end result. With the two halves completed, run two ½-in. Redi-Bolt threaded rods through the predrilled holes to join the two halves of the top and to reinforce the glue joint. Mortise out enough of the outside pieces to countersink the washers and nuts of the rods. As the top dries from the 17% moisture content of kiln-dried dimension lumber, the nuts will have to be tightened. Depending on the length of your bench, you may want to install a third or fourth rod.

Next work on the legs. In positioning the legs, the center of the legs must line up with the center of the bench dog slots. Chop through mortises in the 4x4 legs for the stretcher tenons

Photos: Ted Schuldt; Illustration: Ric Lopez

and the vise positioners. I cut these by drilling holes at opposite corners of the mortise and cutting out the waste with a
saber saw to within 1/32 in. of the line and cleaning up with a
chisel. Now, drill a 13/16-in. hole for the vise screw in three of
the legs and mortise out just enough to countersink a 3/4-in.
nut at both ends of the hole. Also drill for a 1/2-in. draw pin
for each mortise in the leg. Cut tenons on the stretchers, fit,
drill holes for the draw pins 1/8 in. off center to pull the tenons
into the joint and then glue up the leg assembly and pin the
tenons with 1/2-in. birch dowels.

To fasten the top to the legs, drill a 3/8-in. hole down
through the top into the end rails in four places. Drill a 1-in.
hole to intersect the above hole and set into it a cylindrical
"washer"—a short piece of pipe or electrical conduit. This
will keep the captured nut from indenting the wood. Countersink the bolt in the top enough to cover the head with a
wood plug. Now come the leg vises. I made mine out of 2x4s
stiffened by two 1/8-in. by 3/4-in. steel straps screwed into
grooves on their edges. If I had it to do over again, I would
make the vises out of 4x4s. Make the vise positioner (pivot
foot), and fit it onto the end of the vise so it will pivot on a
1/2-in. dowel pin. The vise screw is 3/4-in./10 Redi-Bolt
threaded rod. It comes in 36-in. lengths, so each vise screw is
12 in. long. Screw the rod into the two nuts mortised into the
leg and use it to line up the hole in the vise for the screw, then
bore it to a 1-in. diameter. The nut nearest the vise must be
restrained from coming out as the vise is tightened. This is
done with a retainer made of steel straps filed to allow the rod
to pass through. The retainers are screwed to the leg. The nut
on the other side can be secured with a piece of 1/8-in. hardboard because it's under no stress.

With the vise screw and vise in place, drill 1/2-in. holes in
the pivot foot so that the leg is perpendicular to the bench
top at jaw spacings for common thicknesses of lumber (3/4 in.,
1 1/2 in., 2 1/2 in., 3 1/2 in.) or whatever spacings suit your needs.
Placing the holes too close together, however, will weaken the
pivot foot, which takes considerable stress as it keeps the vise
jaws as parallel as possible. I glued sandpaper to the jaws of
one vise but it did not significantly improve its holding
power. The bench dog slots can now be drilled and chiseled
out in the end grain of the leg vise if you use a 4x4; but if you
use a 2x4, make the slot using a dado cut into the end of the
2x4 and glue a 2x4 block to the back of the leg to house the
slot. Again, incline the slots at 86° toward the bench top to
ensure proper clamping dynamics.

A handle can be made for the threaded rod by screwing a
1/2-in. T-pipe fitting onto it. Secure this by drilling a hole
through the T and the vise screw and pin them together with
a nail or hardened steel pin. The pitch of #10 threads makes
for slow going, but I can get the holding power I need using
my hands on the T without using a long handle for leverage. I
pinned the threaded rod just on the inside of the vise jaw so
that the jaw opens when the rod is loosened.

I made bench dogs in two sets of four out of some scrap oak
flooring. One set sticks 1/2 in. above the bench top, and the
other sticks up 1 in. for larger pieces. I drive the bench dogs
in with a rubber hammer and out by using a short rod and
hammer from underneath the bench. I don't mind doing this,
but if the idea of driving the dogs in and out sounds cumbersome to you, you may want to dimension them to an easy fit
and equip each with a bullet catch to hold it in place. The tool
tray is held on by two lag bolts, and a support for long pieces

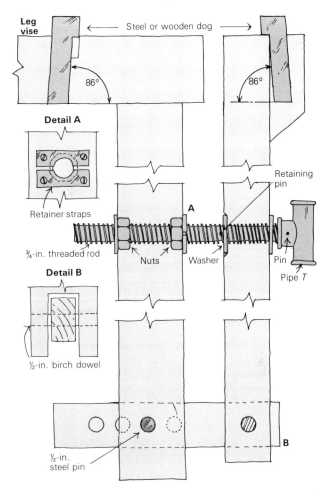

Bill of materials		
Quantity	Length	Item
1	12 ft.	4x4 fir
13	10 ft.	2x4 fir
2	4 ft.	1/2-in. birch dowels
1	3 ft.	3/4-in. threaded rod w/nuts and washers
2	3 ft.	1/2-in. threaded rod w/nuts and washers
4	4 in.	3/8-in. hex bolts w/nuts and washers
3		1/2-in. T-pipe fittings
1	5 in.	1-in. pipe or conduit (sawn into four 1-in. lengths)
2	2 in.	1/4-in. lag bolts and washers
2	3 ft.	1/8-in. by 3/4-in. steel strap
1		qt. yellow glue

of lumber is made using 3/4-in. dowel in a 2x4 screwed to the
legs of the bench.

This bench has given good service for two years now. I have
not had the courage to bear down on any of the vises just to
see how much it takes to break one. But none has ever failed
to hold a workpiece firmly. Fir might not be the best material
for a bench top, but it's inexpensive and can be resurfaced
easily with a hand plane and scraper. The bench is very heavy,
and this gives it good stability when all my weight is put into
planing a piece. It is versatile too, but best of all it would cost
less than $100 to build today (1980 prices). □

*Ted Schuldt, a minister and amateur woodworker, lives in
Toledo, Wash.*

Island Bench
Storage with dogs and drawers

by Dwayne J. Intveld

I've accumulated quite a selection of tools over the years, but when I was setting up the basement workshop in my new home recently, I found my tools to be poorly organized and my bench—a knock-up affair of plywood and 2x4s—in dire need of replacement. I decided a bench should be my first project, so I set out to design one to suit my needs.

I've always admired European-style benches for their solidity, clamping flexibility, and beauty. But since my shop is small, my new bench would have to function as both work surface and storage cabinet. I needed a large surface for assembly, and I also wanted to be able to work on all four sides. The design I settled on is an island-type bench which has the bench dogs that make European benches so versatile.

Construction of the bench is straightforward. The base carcase consists of a framework of 2½-in.-sq. maple rails and stiles mortised and tenoned together. I used ¼-in. maple plywood for panels in the base, letting them into grooves in the various frame members. I installed three ¾-in. fir plywood dividers inside the carcase—this breaks it into four compartments. I used three of these compartments for drawer banks, and installed a door on the fourth to provide storage for tools too bulky to fit in drawers.

I dovetailed the drawers together, using maple for the fronts, pine for the sides and backs, and hardboard for the bottoms. I chose the size and number of drawers to suit what would be stored in them. Before the drawers were assembled, I cut a series of vertical dadoes ¼ in. wide by ¼ in. deep so I could adjust the dividers in the drawers later. I used metal drawer slides for all the drawers except the top ones, which are too shallow; these ride on wooden slides.

The fourth compartment, accessible through a door at the end of the bench, has a shelf set on adjustable metal standards let into the frame legs and divider panel. On the opposite end of the bench, I installed a pegboard that's useful for hanging miscellaneous tools.

The bench top overhangs the base on the vise side so that dust and chips will fall through the two rows of bench-dog slots to the floor instead of into the drawers. I made the top of 1¾-in. hard maple ripped into strips 2½ in. wide and glued up, but a commercially-made maple block top could also be used, if you can find one the right size. To avoid a lot of tedious clean-up work, I glued up the top in three pieces, ran the sections through a surface planer and then glued them together, leaving only two glue lines to clean by hand. For bench-dog holes, I dadoed slots in two 3½-in. wide pieces of maple and glued these (edge up, and with a narrow section of bench top in between) to one long edge of the bench top. With the top glued up and trimmed to length, I routed grooves into the ends of the bench top and attached end caps with bolts.

My Sears vise isn't equipped with bench dogs, so I made an adapter block that screws to the vise jaw and accepts two dogs. Two inches of lost vise opening seemed like a small price to pay for the greater clamping range of the dogs. A sprayed lacquer finish protects the bench from moisture, dirt and spills.

Dwayne J. Intveld, of Hazel Green, Wis., is a design engineer for a construction equipment manufacturer. Photos by the author.

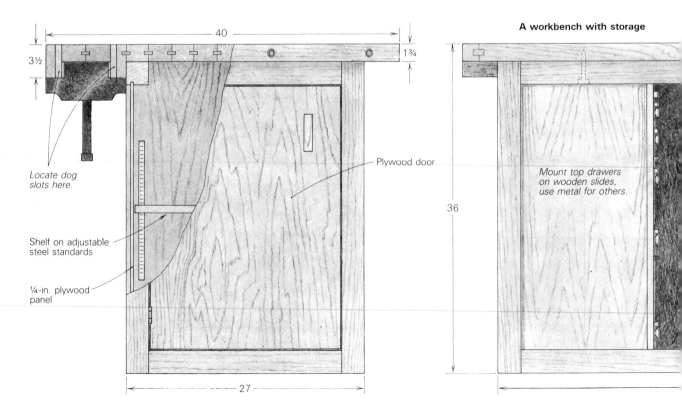

A workbench with storage

40

3½

1¾

Locate dog slots here.

Plywood door

Shelf on adjustable steel standards

¼-in. plywood panel

Mount top drawers on wooden slides, use metal for others.

36

27

Workers with limited shopspace need to make use of every nook and cranny, and Intveld's island-style bench does just that. A large, maple-block work surface is mounted over a frame-and-panel cabinet that has 18 drawers—plenty of storage for tools and supplies. Carcase frame is made of 2½-in.-sq. members mortised together and paneled with ¼-in. plywood. Intveld modified his Sears vise, shown at lower left, by attaching a maple block that will mount two European-style steel bench dogs. Dog slots in the bench stop should be spaced no farther apart than the maximum throw of the vise. And they should be located beyond the edge of the bench so debris will fall to the floor instead of into the cabinet. The bench's end compartment, below, has a plywood door and adjustable steel standards for a shelf, but it could be fitted with drawers instead. A rack on the door stores easy-to-lose items like arbor wrenches, saw throats and other small tools.

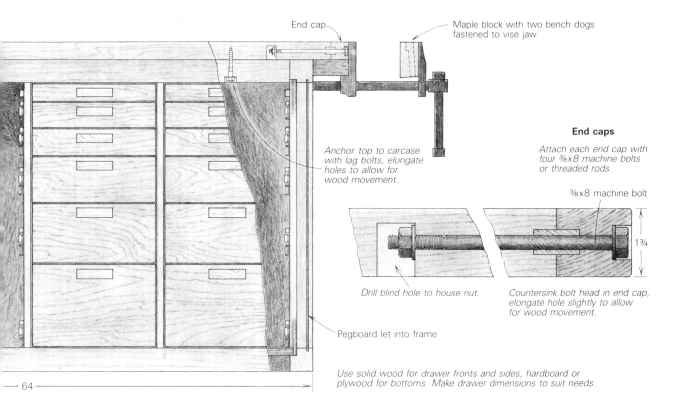

End cap

Maple block with two bench dogs fastened to vise jaw

Anchor top to carcase with lag bolts, elongate holes to allow for wood movement.

End caps

Attach each end cap with four ⅜x8 machine bolts or threaded rods.

⅜x8 machine bolt

1¾

Drill blind hole to house nut.

Countersink bolt head in end cap, elongate hole slightly to allow for wood movement.

Pegboard let into frame

Use solid wood for drawer fronts and sides, hardboard or plywood for bottoms. Make drawer dimensions to suit needs.

Basic bench with accessories (left to right): bench hook, pivoting front jaw pad for vise, flush-mounted Silex #13 adjustable aluminum bench stop, Record #52½ 9-in. by 4-in. vise with quick release, ½-in. thick particle board hooked wedge with rails, shooting board and bench jack.

Workbench
Ingenious ways to hold the work

by Donald Lloyd McKinley

EDITOR'S NOTE: Donald Lloyd McKinley, who teaches woodworking and furniture design at Sheridan College near Toronto, spent the year starting August 1976 in Tasmania. He came home with a remarkable workbench, incorporating several ingenious work-holding systems, which he describes in the following text and photo captions. The bench was made of "Tasmanian oak," the local trade name for several species of eucalyptus. Its overall dimensions are 72 in. long by 36 in. wide by 36 in. high.

Base: *Eucalyptus regnans*, total weight 90 lb.
  Legs: 2 @ 2⅛" × 3⅞" × 34" (rear)
        2 @ 2⅛" × 3⅞" × 34⅜" (front)
End rails: 4 @ 1⅞" × 3⅞" × 36"
  Long rails: 4 @ 1⅞" × 3⅞" × 52¼"
Top: *Eucalyptus obliqua*, weight with vise 190 lb.
    1⅞" thick × 36" wide × 72" long
  Accessories: Huon pine *(Dacrydium franklinii)*

As a furniture maker/woodworker your workbench is the most important piece of furniture you'll ever make or own. At its simplest a workbench is a table—an elevated surface that supports and accommodates an activity at a comfortable height. In principle, a chopping block, if you want to split kindling or billets, is a workbench because it elevates and supports the workpiece for the task at hand. Fitted with vises and securing devices, the usefulness of the workbench is wonderfully increased. It is as basic as the tool. If you can't hold the workpiece, you can't do the work.

Ends of the basic frame parts, arranged in groups of four, in the relationship they will have when assembled. The annual rings form a diamond toward the center of the bench. This may not be important to many people, but it is a perception and an arrangement that is possible and pleasant to be in charge of. The front legs are ⅜ in. longer than the rear legs, to fit locating sockets in the bench top (shown in the photo at right). Joints were roughed out on a radial-arm saw. Bevels were cut using sharp chisels and gauge blocks.

From top to bottom, left, the end rail, leg and long rail at the top-front-left corner of the bench, partially assembled. The notch in the top edge of the long rail tenon (partly visible) will coincide with the bridle in the leg. Thus the interlocking lower edge of the end rail will draw the long rail shoulders snug against the leg. The joint assembled, right. The gap at the top of the leg mortise is due to the shrinkage in width of the long rail, when the bench was transported from humid Tasmania to the dry Canadian winter.

End rail, leg and long rail assembly

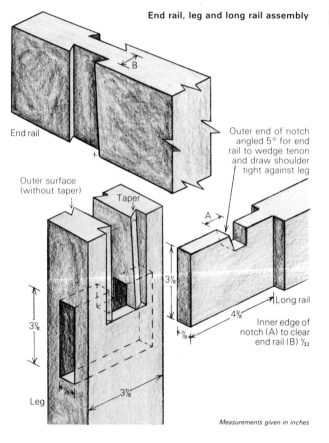

End rail

Outer end of notch angled 5° for end rail to wedge tenon and draw shoulder tight against leg

Outer surface (without taper)

Taper

A

3⅞

3⅞

Long rail

4⅜

⅞

Inner edge of notch (A) to clear end rail (B) 1/32

⅞

3⅞

⅞   3⅞

Leg

Measurements given in inches

Photos: Donald Lloyd McKinley

Top, the tilting vise, at an angle appropriate for coopering. The vise mounting block is assembled from scraps of eucalyptus and held to the bench with two standard door hinges, their barrels let into grooves safely below the surface. The arm (1½ in. by 2 in.) that extends from the vise mount is simply clamped to the 2x4 huon pine diagonal brace for intermediate angles. For frequently used angles, a hole may be drilled through both arm and brace and a dowel inserted to lock that position. Above, the bottom side of the bench top is mortised only at the front to accept the front leg extension. This keeps the front edge of the top in alignment with the front of the under-structure, but allows the top to expand freely and contract rearward as it exchanges moisture with the atmosphere. The arm of the tilting vise mount is also shown.

I made this bench in Hobart, Tasmania, Australia, at the start of my year as state resident designer-craftsman in wood. The wood had been adequately dried for use in humid Hobart, but has predictably shrunk in Canadian winter dryness. The tapered-dovetail bridle joints at the ends of the legs have been lengthened by 3/16 in. to restore self-locking rigidity in their contact with the end rails.

The dimensions given are "as-finished" rather than "as-is" and were reasonable finished dimensions from the rough stock dimensions available in Tasmania. The proportions have proved structurally satisfactory. I believe the finished dimensions could be safely reduced to 1¾ in., as typically yielded from 8/4 rough stock. Equivalent domestic North American woods would be red oak for the base and white oak for the top. Eucalyptus is almost invariably quartersawn and

for the stability required of this floating top, quartersawn stock is essential.

I had a number of basic objectives (and personal preferences) when I designed the bench:
—rigidity and solidarity in use (increased load tightens joints in the base);
—compactness for easier storage or shipping (assembly and disassembly with minimum tools);
—slab top (no tool trough to fill with shavings or reduce usable surface area);
—top overhang or clearance from base for ease of clamping workpieces flat on the bench top (i.e., for mortising);
—vise end of top overhanging the base structure (to permit the mounting of a standard Record #52½ vise);
—layout for right-handed user.

An adjustable bench jack made of huon pine supports the right end of a long board. This reduces deflection and the need for overtightening the vise to stop an unsupported board from twisting down. The bench jack simply hooks over the long front rail. Two cleats straddle the rail, and the jack may be slid anywhere along the bench. The cleats and foot support are placed so that the face of the jack is the same distance out from the bench top as the fixed jaw of the vise. The support block adjusts vertically in the notched slot: A quarter-turn clockwise from horizontal allows it to be slid up and down or removed. The two lag screws in the block are set off-center by one-half the amount of the quadrant-notch interval, to double the number of height positions simply by removing and inverting the block.

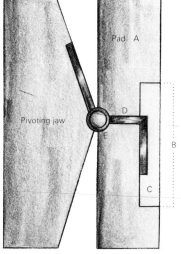

A pivoting block fitted to the front jaw pad of the vise allows it to hold tapered work without stress and without crushing the wide end of the work, left. The pivoting block removed from the vise, right. A butt hinge fastened to the back of the pivoting block has one leaf bent at 90°, which slides into a corresponding slot in the front pad of the vise.

Here's one way to make the front jaw pad: A) Start with complete pad, B) dado out the area marked against the vise jaw itself, C) glue back in a piece the shape of the unshaded area, D) saw a slot in the face of the pad, and E) shape a half-round to accept the hinge knuckle.

angles may be sawn. In addition, extra length on the right side of the back cleat may be used to clamp on stops for repetitive cuts.

A shooting board is primarily used to true end grain on the work. The type shown at right is very similar to the bench hook. The workpiece is held against the back cleat in the same way, but instead of sawing on the board, plane along its right edge, using a regular smoothing plane that has been laid along its right side. Take care that the cutting edge of the blade is at 90° to the right side of the plane. This will ensure that the end of the workpiece will be planed square vertically.

Squareness, looking down on the work, depends on the front face of the back cleat being perpendicular to the edge of the shooting-board base. A rabbet plane could destroy squareness in this direction since the whole edge of the board would be planed away. A regular bench plane will not cut closer than about 3/16 in. to its side. This means that the lower edge of the board remains true and will continue to guide the plane.

It's wise to break in the shooting board by planing along the whole length of its edge, front-to-back. Otherwise, a small taper might result at the front edge of a wider-than-usual workpiece. Of greater importance is using essentially the same amount of blade projection each time. If the board edge and back cleat have been deeply rabbeted by previous heavy cuts and you then use a shallow setting, the workpiece must project beyond the back cleat for the blade to engage it. This invites tear-out when the plane blade leaves the unsupported back edge of the work.

Once you have a bench, a bench hook is one of the most useful accessories for cutting small parts that you can have. The work is held against the back cleat with your left hand. This pushes the bench hook and its front cleat against the edge of the bench top, immobilizing the whole setup. Long pieces may have additional support by keeping a bit of stock the same thickness as the hook base to slide under the overhang.

The bench hook prevents tear-out as the saw teeth pass through the back and bottom of the workpiece, because the fibers at the back and bottom are supported. As sawcuts widen in the bench hook and give less support, a new cutting position along the back cleat and base should be established. The arrows on the back cleat locate screws, and serve as a reminder not to cut there. As with a miter box, other

The hooked wedge with bench-fixed rails. When force (as from planing) is applied to the workpiece in the direction of the arrow, the work contacts the hook of the wedge. The work and the wedge then move together in the direction of the arrows, and are forced against and confined by the converging rails. Right, the same workpiece on edge, wedged in place by a half-inch thick set of parts. The work is easily disengaged by tapping back on the hook end of the wedge.

This version of the hooked wedge is my answer to the inadequacies of a commercial product. About 20 years ago I bought a Stanley bench wedge designed around a flanged tapered plate of bent steel. Its various problems included an inside radius where the flanges were bent—unfortunately, the workpiece needed a matching radius and was abused to this condition whether you wanted it or not. Its fixings to the bench necessitated a recessed area into which the work would teeter under pressure of the plane, it would only accept pieces narrower than 3 in., and a plane could be devastated by unwarily working a thickness down to the height of the metal flange. It was still a good system, so I worked it through several generations over the years, and finally abandoned the use of metal altogether to arrive at the parts shown here. It is a versatile, inexpensive, easily made and installed device that does some of the work-holding better than anything else I've used.

The rails are made by gluing and wedging dowels into ³⁄₁₆-in. hardboard or ½-in. particle board. The dowels plug into pairs of holes on the bench top. The width of work that can be held is limited only by the width of the bench itself. The hooked wedges are made of the same materials—thus you can safely plane into the wedge and rails. A suitable taper is about 1 in. in 4 in., or 15°. I sometimes find it useful, with a few strokes of the plane, to readjust the edges of the wedge or rails to a bevel, thereby shifting the pressure higher or lower on the part held (especially if the part also has a bevel).

The most versatile narrow setting seems to come from a combined width of hook and wedge (narrow end) that will just pass through the gap between the converging ends of the rails. A really narrow hook (much less than ½ in.) can cause concentrated pressure and some marking where it contacts the end of a softwood workpiece.

The last batch of rails I made, in thicknesses from ⅛ in. to 1 in., has the dowels located off the centerline to provide three increments of space for each set of bench holes. This is accomplished by turning one or both rails end-for-end in the holes.

I am well aware of the carpenter's pinch block, that is, two converging strips or two converging cuts in a single block nailed to floor, bench or sawhorse. It is quick to make and use, and usually no more shoddy than the work it holds. However the pinch it exerts on the end of a soft workpiece may be unacceptable, justifying the trouble of making a hooked wedge to match the converging strips, thus distributing the pressure over a larger area. Obviously the nature of the gripping edges can be altered by applying felt, rubber or sandpaper to match the task at hand. □

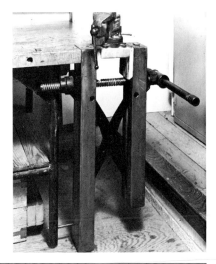

McKinley's primary bench since 1958, top left, has been this pipe-frame construction salvaged from a ceramics factory. Its amenities include tool storage above and below, and two unusual vises: the Emmert Roto-Vise, left, and a scissors-section leg vise of unknown manufacture, right. You can't buy either vise because neither is being made any more, but both have features worth study and imitation in shop-built versions. The Emmert vise, bottom left, made in Waynesboro, Pa., until about 1965, houses its single screw in a cast beam, which rotates through 360° as shown here. The whole vise tilts up and down through 90°, which inspired the tilt modification shown on the Tasmanian bench. Its front jaw also swivels about 5° to hold tapered work—another feature transferred to the standard vise on the Tasmanian bench. Right, leg vise with 3-in. by 5-in. maple jaws has cast-steel scissors that ensure parallelism at any opening. Eyes at the top end of the scissors rotate freely on ⁵⁄₁₆-in. bolts, while the lower ends rise as the scissors spread riding in a groove plowed in the jaws. The bottom of the groove is faced with a strip of ⅛-in. by 1-in. strap iron to prevent wear.

The replaceable basswood jaw pads can be inverted, whereupon they project above the uprights and their angled ends give more access to fine work. In this photo, the leg vise holds a square fir block carrying a small metalworker's vise.

Holding the Work
Shaving horse and low bench

by John D. Alexander, Jr.

EDITOR'S NOTE: The post-and-rung chair at right is one of the basic seats that for centuries has kept Western man off the ground. It is light, rugged and beautiful. The vertical posts are white oak, the horizontal rungs and the back slats are hickory, and the seat is woven from the supple inner bark of the hickory tree. The chair is not hard to make, when you know how—which is explained in the book *Make a Chair from a Tree: An Introduction to Working Green Wood,* by John D. Alexander, Jr. (The Taunton Press, Inc., Box 355, Newtown, Conn. 06470, 1978, paperback, 128 pp.).

The key to making a post-and-rung chair is working the wood green, as it comes off the tree. Green wood is relatively easy to cut, bore, shave and shape. As it dries, it hardens and shrinks. In chairmaking, the posts are shaped green, dried a little, then mortised to accept the rungs, which also are shaped green. But the rungs are well dried, then tenoned a hair oversize. When the tenons are driven home, they take on moisture from the post wood, expand tightly in their mortises, and then the whole joint dries to equilibrium with the atmosphere. It shrinks tightly together. A few further subleties—the post mortises interlock, the tenons are shouldered, notched and flattened for a dovetail effect and the grain direction of all the parts is carefully orchestrated—make a joint that just won't come apart.

Alexander is a Baltimore lawyer who has spent more than a dozen years investigating old tools and chairs and figuring out how they were used and made. This article is taken from his chapter on working surfaces and holding devices.

A chopping block is necessary. In the woods, use the stump of the tree you are harvesting. The stump, cut off immediately above the roots, makes a good block for the shop. Its flared, curved wood is not good for much else. Tall and short blocks, side by side, make it easy to hew out long back posts, because they can be shifted from one block to the other. A white oak, elm, locust or catalpa block will last outdoors for a long while, but use whatever is available. Work in a cleared area, with no one in the plane of travel of the hatchet head.

You need a low workbench and a shaving horse, although the shaving horse can be modified to serve as both. I'll describe the low bench first. The standard cabinetmaker's bench is not as useful for chairmaking as a bench that is low, narrow and heavy—a bench that can be moved, sat upon and battered.

The body of a low bench is a heavy slab. Split a slab between three and five feet long out of heavy hardwood. White oak is best both for weight and for resistance to weathering. Work while the wood is still wet. Make the slab anywhere between two and five inches thick and between nine and sixteen inches wide. The bench should be low enough and narrow enough to be straddled comfortably, either standing or sitting. When you sit astride the bench, your legs should be comfortable. Fixed dimensions are not important—make the bench fit yourself and your task. You will spend a lot of time at this bench, so design it carefully. The important thing is a flat top. If no logs are available, use heavy planks or 2x4s glued face-to-face.

The bench posts taper up into the bench surface. It is easier to cut and adjust them if the posts come right through the slab. If you don't have a tapered reamer for making conical mortises in the slab, tapered rectilineal mortises and tenons chopped out of the green wood with a heavy chisel will also do a good job. Don't permanently secure the posts in the slab because they will swell and shrink throughout the life of the bench. If the movement of the wood makes the posts project above the slab, trim them off. If they become loose, drive a wedge alongside them.

Make the posts from wood that isn't good enough for chairs. Taper them to fit the tapered mortises. Drive them home. Building the bench is a good introduction to wet woodworking in general and to post and slab construction in particular. You will learn how to hew, chisel and bore wet wood. Almost no mistake is fatal with this bench. The harder you pound on it, the tighter it will become.

When moving the bench, be careful that one of the heavy posts doesn't fall out and smash your foot. I wasn't. I have never taken the time to put in stretchers.

What you have made is the ancestor of the common Wind-

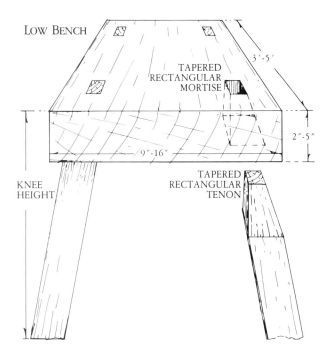

LOW BENCH

TAPERED
RECTANGULAR
MORTISE

3'-5'

2"-5"

9"-16"

KNEE
HEIGHT

TAPERED
RECTANGULAR
TENON

The low bench should be heavy and about knee height, so it can be locked between the knees whether the maker is sitting or standing. It is made of split green wood or from scrap lumber. Tapered pegs driven into round holes in the bench, right, hold work for boring or mortising. A wedge locks the pieces in place.

sor chair. Your bench (also called mare, horse, buck or trestle) allows you to align your body with your work. The bench puts the work at waist rather than at your chest. You can sit down at and on your work, which is a big help. Once you are sitting on the bench or standing astride it, locking it between your knees, you, the work and the bench become one mechanical system—if you can secure the work to the slab.

To secure work for boring or mortising, drive three or four square tapered pegs into round holes in the bench. Lay sticks between the pegs and lock them in place with a wooden wedge or wedges. Space the holes and pegs so that posts can be held down singly and in matching pairs. The simplicity of this holding system was hard to accept until I tried it. It was the last method I tried.

You can also use screws as holding devices. Wooden screws of ⅞-in. or 1-in. diameter are more than strong enough. Because permanent handles get in the way, make the screws with large heads and drill holes through them. You'll always

have rung rejects (factory seconds) lying around to put into the holes for handles.

Hold-down yokes are fastened to the bench top by boring a hole through the middle of the slab to accept the wooden screw bolt. I don't tap vertical holes in the bench, but use a wooden screw bolt from above the slab and a wooden lever nut from below. A deep-engagement pipe clamp also works, with the pipe running through a hole in the bench and the screw beneath the bench. Run the pipe up through a hole in the hold-down yoke and screw a threaded pipe flange or sleeve on the top end. Protect your tools by covering with wood any metal projecting above the bench so metal doesn't strike metal.

I use the English style of shaving horse, also called a bodger's bench, cooper's shaving bench or shaving brake. It holds posts, rungs and slats for drawknifing and shaving. The crossbar on the horse securely locks the workpiece in place. The shaving horse is a perfect holding device: The harder you

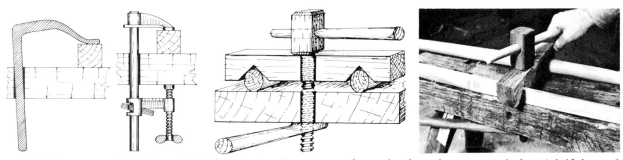

More holding systems (left to right): the holdfast, the pipe clamp, the hold-down yoke. A holdfast works by spring action. A tap at its knee jams it against the sides of a hole in the bench. A pipe clamp can be run through a hole and tightened underneath the bench, but

cap the metal with wood to protect tool edges. A hold-down yoke will secure matching posts side by side. It is tightened by a square-headed wooden screw fitting loosely through the bench into a wooden lever nut below.

The Small Workshop   **39**

pull the tool toward you, the harder your feet push the lever arms away from you. The crossbar is thus forced down on the workpiece.

The horse design I use allows more adjustment than some versions, and it makes the horse adaptable for various tasks. My horse has two horizontal parallel beams, like a lathe, rather than a solid slab. The work surface is nailed (with deeply countersunk nails) to a tiller that fits between the beams. Pegs driven through the sides of the beams and the tiller adjust the surface to any angle or height. I made my shaving horse from scrap hardwood lumber. White oak is excellent, but almost any wood will do. Of course you can split the parts out of green wood.

The shaving horse crossbar is square in cross section. Its round ends friction-fit into the side lever bars. Thus the crossbar can rotate and will always seat squarely on the work. One surface of the bar is notched to hold square-sectioned sticks corner up.

Shaving-horse dimensions depend on the worker. The height and size of the bench should allow the worker's heels to rest on the ground while his toes touch the lever foot bar.

To make a shaving horse double as a low bench, mount a heavy plank on the beams. You'll find a separate low bench a help, but you can get started without one. If you make both a horse and a bench, or two benches, make them the same height, so they can double as sawhorses or be used to hold larger pieces of work laid across them.

Because the work surface is adjustable, the shaving horse has a variety of other uses. I hold sharpening stones or tools with it: both my hands are free to control sharpening pressure and angle.

Take time to make a tool box or rack. Tools get lost easily, and edges become nicked and ruined in the mess. The rack must be easy to move from one work area or bench to another. I have a rack made of sticks with tapered ends (conical tenons) jammed into mortises that are bored and taper-reamed through post-wood rejects. The rack is bound together by a toggle rope. A twist or two on the rope adjusts for dimension and design changes.

Now we are ready to make a chair. ☐

SHAVING HORSE

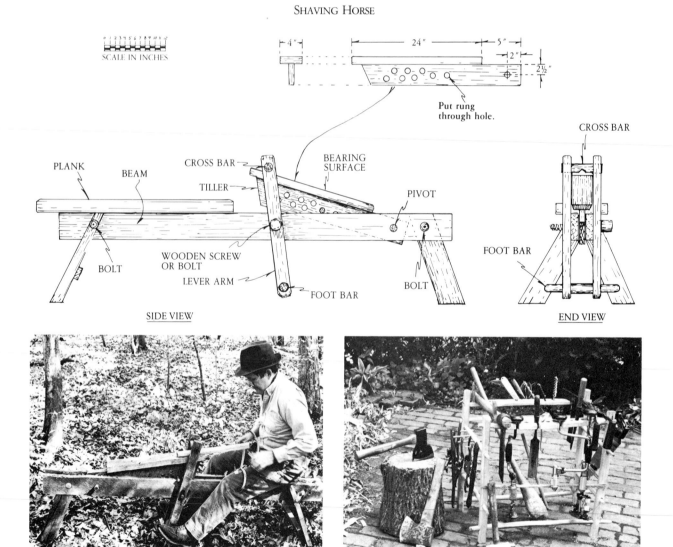

This style of shaving horse is light enough to be toted into the woods for drawknifing split sticks right where the tree is felled.

A post-and-rung tool rack can be made quickly from spare and rejected chair parts, bound together with a toggle rope.

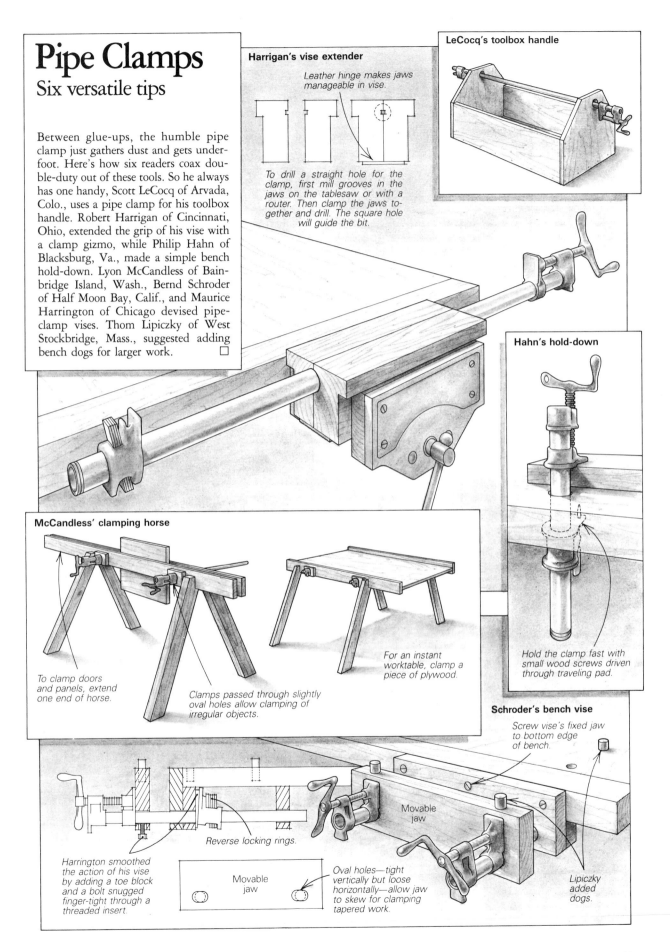

Pipe Clamps
Six versatile tips

Between glue-ups, the humble pipe clamp just gathers dust and gets underfoot. Here's how six readers coax double-duty out of these tools. So he always has one handy, Scott LeCocq of Arvada, Colo., uses a pipe clamp for his toolbox handle. Robert Harrigan of Cincinnati, Ohio, extended the grip of his vise with a clamp gizmo, while Philip Hahn of Blacksburg, Va., made a simple bench hold-down. Lyon McCandless of Bainbridge Island, Wash., Bernd Schroder of Half Moon Bay, Calif., and Maurice Harrington of Chicago devised pipe-clamp vises. Thom Lipiczky of West Stockbridge, Mass., suggested adding bench dogs for larger work. □

Harrigan's vise extender

Leather hinge makes jaws manageable in vise.

To drill a straight hole for the clamp, first mill grooves in the jaws on the tablesaw or with a router. Then clamp the jaws together and drill. The square hole will guide the bit.

LeCocq's toolbox handle

Hahn's hold-down

Hold the clamp fast with small wood screws driven through traveling pad.

McCandless' clamping horse

To clamp doors and panels, extend one end of horse.

Clamps passed through slightly oval holes allow clamping of irregular objects.

For an instant worktable, clamp a piece of plywood.

Schroder's bench vise

Screw vise's fixed jaw to bottom edge of bench.

Movable jaw

Harrington smoothed the action of his vise by adding a toe block and a bolt snugged finger-tight through a threaded insert.

Reverse locking rings.

Movable jaw

Oval holes—tight vertically but loose horizontally—allow jaw to skew for clamping tapered work.

Lipiczky added dogs.

Sawhorses
Basic design adapts to several workshop tasks

by Sam Allen

"**Y**ou can judge a man by his sawhorse" was a remark made often by a carpenter I once knew. When he was foreman on a job site, he would have job applicants build a pair of sawhorses. The one who built the best pair got the job. A craftsman who takes pride in his work wants his tools to reflect that pride. But what usually happens with sawhorses is that a temporary pair gets thrown together for use on a particular job, then becomes a permanent fixture in your shop. Why not take time now to build a sturdy, good-looking pair of sawhorses that you can be proud to own?

Construction—To build a basic pair of sawhorses you'll need one 8-ft. 2x6, three 8-ft. 1x6s plus a few 1x6 scraps for braces. Fir or pine is the usual choice because of its strength and light weight. All operations in sawhorse construction can be performed with hand tools, but power tools make the job faster and easier.

Start by cutting two 42-in. long pieces of 2x6 for the saddles. Some people prefer to use a saddle 48 in. long, but the 42-in. length is handier for working on doors and still gives plenty of support to a 4x8 sheet of plywood. Next cut eight legs 28 in. long from the 1x6 stock. Once the sawhorses are assembled, the legs will be trimmed to give an overall height of 24 in. Taper the legs on one edge starting full width at a point 8 in. from the top and tapering down to 3½ in. at the bottom. This makes the horse lighter and more stable.

When the legs are done, cut the gains (notches) in the saddle to receive them. This is probably the most critical part of making sawhorses. The gains are cut on a compound angle, and much of the strength of the sawhorse depends on a good fit. Use a steel square to mark the angles. Make the first mark 3½ in. from the end of the saddle. Place the square on the edge of the 2x6 so the 3-in. mark on one leg and the 12-in. mark on the other line up with the face corner of the 2x6, and

With legs of pine and saddle of fir, sawhorse is both sturdy and attractive.

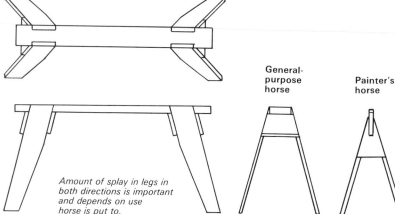

Amount of splay in legs in both directions is important and depends on use horse is put to.

General-purpose horse

Painter's horse

Left, legs are sawn flush with saddle after they're secured in place and braces are attached. You can add a central slit, above, for ripping boards of any length using a handsaw.

Photos and Illustrations by the author

scribe a 4:1 (75°) slope. Line up a 1x6 leg with this slope and use its opposite edge to make a second mark. This gives you the lengthwise slope of the leg. Now determine the spread of the legs across the width. There are two dimensions in common use. For a sawhorse used in house framing, the spread should be 14 in., as this allows it to be carried between studs that are on 16-in. centers. A 20-in. spread is better for finish work and shop use because of the added stability.

Mark the gains for this angle on top of the 2x6 by scribing a line ¾ in. in from the edge between the two marks previously made. On the bottom make a line that will vary according to the spread you choose. For the 14-in. spread, it should be ½ in. in from the edge; and for the 20-in. spread, ⅜ in.

Using a handsaw, cut along the marks on the edge of the 2x6. Stop cutting when the teeth touch the lines on the top and bottom of the 2x6. Now make parallel sawcuts about ½ in. apart between the first two cuts, stopping at the top and bottom lines also. Use a chisel to clean out the gain. Cut the leg braces from the leftover pieces of 1x6. Hold a piece in position and mark the angles of the legs on it, making sure the legs are spread to the correct degree and the angles are equal. Use this as a pattern to cut the rest of the braces. Bevel the top of each brace so it will fit flush under the saddle. After the braces have been fastened with glue and nails, trim the legs flush with the top of the saddle using a handsaw.

With the horse standing on a flat surface, measure the distance from the top of the saddle to the ground. Set a scriber for the difference between this measurement and 24 in. Scribe around each leg to get a cutting line that will allow the legs to sit flat. Chamfer and sand all the corners and edges to avoid possible slivers and cuts, then finish with oil.

Lowboy—A short sawhorse (usually about 12 in. high) called a lowboy is often used in cabinet shops for elevating furniture and cabinets to a convenient working height. It's especially useful when fitting drawers and cabinet doors. Sometimes a 2x8 is used for the saddle to give a larger area of support to the cabinet.

Ripping horse—If you do a lot of ripping with a handsaw, you'll appreciate this horse. A 1-in. wide slot is cut in the center of a standard sawhorse saddle. Stop the slot at the point where the legs attach so the joint won't be weakened. To use this sawhorse, place the board to be ripped on the horse with the cutting line over the slot and the end of the board about 8 in. from the slot end. Put the sawblade through the slot and start ripping. When the blade reaches the end of the slot, move the board forward and begin ripping again.

Painter's sawhorse—When you're painting something supported on sawhorses, invariably some of the paint will drip down the edge of the work and land on the saddle of the sawhorse. Then it seeps between the saddle and the work and leaves a mark on the back of the object. If the object being painted has two sides that show, a door for example, this is not good. A narrow point of contact between the work and the sawhorse will help solve this problem.

Make the painter's sawhorse out of 1x6s. The saddle is a 1x6 turned on edge. On top of the saddle nail a ¾-in. by ¾-in. strip, which can be changed whenever it gets coated with a lot of paint drips. To reduce further the point of contact with the work, the top strip can be beveled so that only a

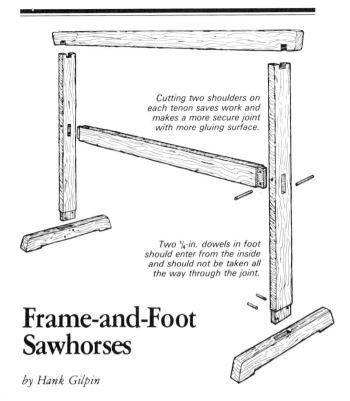

Cutting two shoulders on each tenon saves work and makes a more secure joint with more gluing surface.

Two ¼-in. dowels in foot should enter from the inside and should not be taken all the way through the joint.

Frame-and-Foot Sawhorses

by Hank Gilpin

For supporting cabinets and carcases while you're working on them, for laying out cuts in long boards and for various other jobs around the shop, here's a sawhorse (basically a frame on two feet) that is light and strong, yet stores easily without taking up a lot of space. I made mine out of red oak (only because I had a large quantity on hand), but you can make them out of almost any wood you choose. All the pieces are 1⅓₁₆ in. thick and 2½ in. wide, except for the foot, which is 1³₁₆ in. wide. The uprights are through-tenoned into the feet and secured with glue and a couple of ¼-in. pegs. To receive the stretcher, I chopped through-mortises in the uprights. The tenons, all of which I cut long to use the same saw setting, were trimmed to length after assembly. They are pinned also with ¼-in. dowels, though wedges would do as well. Both of the uprights and the saddle member are notched to make a secure double-lap joint, which can be pinned or not.

These horses can be made quickly and in quantity with a minimum of materials and fuss. I have a couple dozen of them. They travel well, taking up much less space than conventional four-leg horses, and they nestle together neatly when not in use. □

Hank Gilpin makes cabinets and furniture in Lincoln, R.I.

small point is left on top. However, this may be undesirable if the underside of the work has been freshly painted, because the point will cut into the paint.

Because of the narrow saddle, you can't cut gains for the legs. Cut the ends of the legs to the appropriate angle so they can be butted against the sides of the saddle. Notch the leg braces so they will extend part way up the saddle.

Padded saddle—If your sawhorses are to be used with finished pieces, you can avoid scratches by padding the saddle. A strip of carpet is one of the best pads. Glue it down or fold it over the edges and tack it to the underside. □

Sam Allen builds furniture in Provo, Utah.

Small Workbench
A simple and versatile design

by R. Bruce Hoadley

Wet sand anchors outdoor bench.

Everyone knows a workbench should be rugged and massive, "the bigger the better." But some years ago I set out to build a firm yet semiportable stand for teaching and demonstrating. The little workbench that eventually evolved is now an indispensable part of my workshop. At first glance it looks like a traditional sculpture stand, and one might hastily conclude that it is too small, too frail and too tippy to be of general use to the woodworker—it simply doesn't look like a workbench. However, it does offer some noteworthy advantages.

First, it is tall. Most benches are 36 in. high or lower, but many—if not most—hand operations are more comfortable at a higher level. For me (I'm 6 ft.), a 42-in. bench makes all those little jobs like letting in an escutcheon plate, carving out a fan, or cutting a dovetail, much easier.

For woodcarving, a top surface of 12 in. by 12 in. is ideal: small enough to work all around, yet large enough to handle a sizable sculpture. For general woodworking the dimensions can be increased to about 16 in. by 18 in. (as shown). Getting much larger subtracts more than it adds.

Making the top in two halves minimizes warping. High-density hardwoods such as oak, birch, maple and beech about 1½ in. thick are suitable. A one-piece top of 1-in. hardwood plywood might also do nicely. Cross support cleats should also be hardwood and the top should be fastened with heavy wood screws, lag screws or carriage bolts. Be sure fasteners are well counterbored below the surface. On my first model I set the screws flush with the surface and frequently hit them with carving chisels until I finally set them deeper.

The dimensions given here are only suggestions and can be modified for each person's specific needs.

The key feature of the top is plenty of clamping edges all around. The middle area has holes to stick C-clamps or quick-set clamps up through. Making the top surface in two halves with an ample slot down the middle adds to this versatility. A carving screw can be put anywhere along the slot, or the slot can be widened in places for clamps. Any number of holes or recesses can be added to accommodate your favorite vise, bench stop or holddown.

A vertical apron on one side might be bothersome to the carver, but helpful to the cabinetmaker for clamping stock to work on edges. Put rows of holes in the apron for support pegs.

The base frame must be stable and rigid, and 2x4's or similar lumber will do nicely. Splaying the legs adds stability but is not absolutely necessary. I try to make the frame with as much unobstructed interior space as possible and with a bottom shelf as low as possible for piling weight on. The first bench I built is at home, and I weigh it down with bricks and stones because I happen to have them: bricks in the cellar shop, stones when I move the bench to the garage or backyard to carve in the summer. Lead would be ideal ballast.

Behind our little summer house on Cape Cod, my favorite carving place, I have another bench, built from wood recycled from the town dump. I enclosed the entire bottom assembly with plywood and once it was set in location, filled it with sand for ballast. Then I slowly poured in as much water as the sand would absorb. The bench has been in place for four years and is now settled in rock solid. Occasionally I water it. A plastic trash bag keeps the top dry when the bench is not in use.

At the laboratory where I work, I have a third bench, as a teaching aid and for research setups. To weigh it down, we pile the base with assorted scrap metal.

This mini-bench will never replace traditional workbenches, but it might well be a good first bench for the woodworker with limited space. Once you've built and used such a bench, complete with your favorite accessories and modifications, you'll understand why it's the "teacher's pet." □

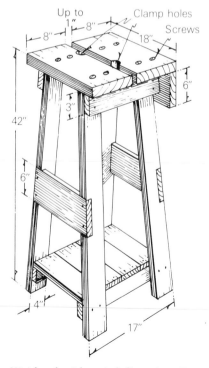

Up to 1"
Clamp holes
Screws
8"
8"
18"
42"
3'
6"
6"
4"
17"

Mini-bench with typical dimensions: Base frame of 2x4's supports hardwood top.

R. Bruce Hoadley, a carver, teaches wood technology at the University of Massachusetts at Amherst.

The Set-Up Table

An old door makes an adaptable, low work surface

by Henry T. Kramer

Someone starting out to equip a home workshop must be made of stern stuff if, after totaling the cost of all the needed tools, he doesn't give it up and turn to ocean racing or something else closer to his budget. The set-up table—which is nothing more than a well-placed, plainly dressed work surface—won't replace expensive power tools, but it can ease the pain by allowing you better use of hand tools.

The set-up table is a triple threat. It serves as an ordinary worktable, it's an aid to setting up and assembling, and it makes working with hand tools a positive joy. (It also offers a safe retreat for the dog when he comes to visit.) It's not intended to replace the typical workbench, but after you've used both for a while, don't be surprised if you favor the set-up table for its simplicity and ease of use.

The top of my present set-up table is a 1¾-in. solid-core door, 36 in. by 80 in., which was given to me by a friend. I finished it with a synthetic varnish (awful stuff, but tough as the back of a shooting gallery) and then waxed it. One can't avoid dropping glue on the table occasionally, but the surface is so smooth that a fingernail will get the glue right off.

I made a base of rough 4x4s and pine lumber. I doweled the base together, even though I know that some good and true men are on record against dowels—in this table, they're strong enough and quick to make. The top rests on the tops of the legs and is fastened to the rails with blocks and screws.

I made my table 28½ in. high, but you can build yours to suit you. For best leverage when using hand tools, the set-up table should be lower than the typical workbench. Height ought to be a function of your height, specifically, about ¾ in. less than the height of your fingertips with your arms at your sides—give or take a fingernail. This is very close to the ideal sawhorse height, making the table suitable for handsawing, boring with a brace and bit, and use with other hand tools.

Depending on the size of your shop, a set-up table may be as long as you want, but 80 in. is enough for me. When deciding on width, remember that you'll often want to be able to reach comfortably beyond the midpoint. Thirty-six inches is right for me. If you've got arms like an ape, make it wider. The most important feature of the set-up table is that the top overhangs the base on all sides by at least 5 in. This overhang gives you plenty of room to clamp work and tools to the table—without the vises, bolt heads or drawers of the typical workbench getting in the way.

The set-up table ought to be located as centrally in the shop as possible, and you should be able to get around all four sides of it. Because the table is lower than the work surface of most major machine tools, it shouldn't interfere with long boards passed through them. Put the table on the off-feed side of the tablesaw and you can clamp a roller table to it when you're cutting long stock.

As a jack-of-all-trades work surface, the set-up table is hard to beat. You can clamp portable tools such as vises,

A set-up table, a universal shop work surface, could hardly be simpler. Here, Kramer uses a brace and bit with his work clamped to the table with a hand screw. Size can vary, but the height ought to be less than that of a conventional workbench.

grinders and miter boxes to the table, and then stow them away on a shelf underneath when they aren't needed. For assembling large jobs such as big frames and cases, the set-up table offers plenty of space for clamps, tools and glue bottles—all the stuff that always gets knocked off small benches during the heat of glue-up.

But the nicest thing about the table, I find, is that it's just plain easier to use hand tools with the work clamped to the table. Everything doesn't have to be done on a big power tool just because it's there and it cost so much. Besides, it's more pleasant to see what you are doing and to do it right, because once you start a cut with a power tool, you are committed to finishing it whether it works out well or not.

It's surprising how many words it takes to describe how useful such a simple thing can be in the home workshop. It is this very simplicity and universality that appeals to the person who works wood for fun and doesn't take himself or his work too seriously. If you plan and build a set-up table, you'll be amazed at how it will change your work habits.   □

Henry T. Kramer is a retired reinsurance specialist and an amateur woodworker in Somerville, N.J.

Stairwell Workshop

Making do with what you have

by John Burrowes

"Well, it looks as though the only place I can have my shop is on the stairwell in the hall," I said with a laugh. I sat myself down on a trunk to share a cup of coffee while we looked over our third-floor apartment. It was a nice old Pennsylvania farmhouse, but this seemed a lot like an attic.

It was true that I had never had a shop of my own, and it was also true that I had three orders to fill as soon as I could. Two of the orders were from customers and the other was from my wife, who sat across from me on the other trunk looking wearily at the rows and rows of clothes and dishes, and furniture and shoes and records and books, and three boxes of tools. The children were running from room to room, happy to be in a new setting.

The next morning I went to two lumberyards where I got the boards and the beams for the furniture I was going to make, and I begged a 4x6, 4 ft. long. Without the faintest idea how I was going to find a place to do the job, I brought all these materials home. As I climbed the stairs with the 4x6

under my arm, it occurred to me that the stairs would actually make a fine shop. I bored a 1-in. hole toward the end of the 4x6 and another hole through the middle. I took an old bench screw, saved for just such a moment, and installed it with a board and a spacer stick for a jaw, in the center hole. The hole on the far end was placed over a dowel fitted in an old hole where some fancy spindles had formerly been part of the stairwell. Here was my bench with hold-down, firmly stretched across the stairwell, and I, standing on the fourth step, was at a perfect working height. I got out a board and a plane and started to make some shavings. They rolled down the steps and out of my way. Not that I wouldn't have to clean them up eventually, but they were not under foot. On the flat of the board I could plane only half of its length at one time, but I couldn't have reached the full board anyway. I drilled another hole through the 4x6 so it could be rotated 90°, and in that position, with a wooden brace clamped to stabilize the other end of a long board, I could easily plane the long edges. I had one power tool, an old-fashioned ¼-in. drill to which I could attach a grindstone when I needed to sharpen my tools. I set my tool box along the crude railing of the stairwell where I could reach it and where it would keep the children from tumbling into the stairwell. Next to it was a box full of all the hardware I had saved through my years of apprenticeship and teaching.

As I sat down to the task of sharpening my tools, I discovered another advantage of working in a stairwell, for there on the top step like two python rock snakes sat my oldest children, watching me and fiddling with the vise. This turned out to be the most sociable of all the shops I have ever worked in, sometimes disadvantageously so because neighbors would want to come up the stairs, or my wife with wet laundry in her

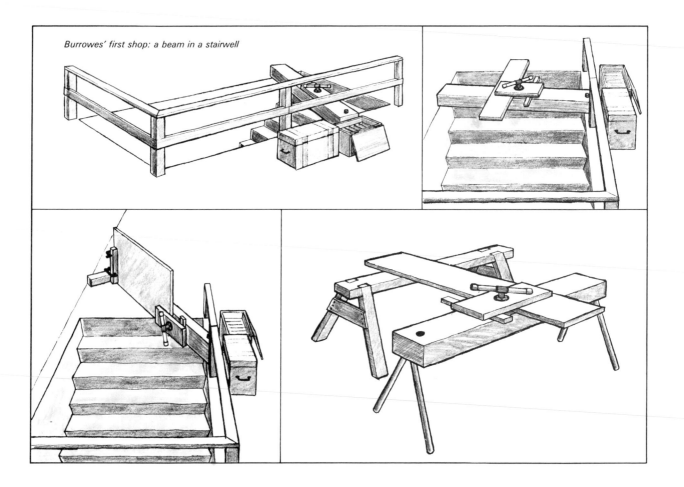

Burrowes' first shop: a beam in a stairwell

hands would want to go down. But one swing of the 4x6 on its dowel pivot, and traffic could move as usual.

Since my 4x6 with bench screw could be slipped off its dowel at any time, I soon found that on nice days I wanted to work outside, under the trees. So I bored a slanted 1-in. hole in a 2x4 and, holding the 2x4 over the bottom of the 4x6, bored four symmetrically angled holes for 1-in. dowels. This made my 4x6 into a "vise-horse" with a bench screw in the middle of its crosspiece. Then I made the 2x4 into another horse, 6 ft. long and nice and squat. With the saw horse at one end and the 4x6 on its dowel legs at the other end, I could work big pieces of wood outdoors. When things began to rock too much, I just drove stakes into the ground. It was clumsy when thunderstorms arose, but in fair weather the summer's work proceeded with pleasant dispatch.

Toward the end of the summer I came to my biggest assignment, a black walnut table 4 ft. wide and 10 ft. long. I could barely manage the boards to glue them together on their splines, and I had to do that outdoors on a clear day. I could have handled the gluing on the stairs, but then I wouldn't have been able to fit the tabletop down the stairwell. I was glad to have figured that out before trying it. The hardest part of the job was cutting housings all the way across the width of the table for the crossbraces for each pair of legs. I attached my little electric drill to a dovetail router bit. I carved out a piece of 4x4 that would hold the drill at just the right height, then clamped a fence onto the table so I could run the cutter the whole width. I knew that routers are supposed to run at thousands of RPM, and I knew the dovetail bit was not designed to be used this way, but necessity is the mother of adaptation and compromise. With frequent pauses to let the drill cool and gentle pressure to gain an inch now and then, I made a beautiful housing joint—after about two hours. The dovetail tenons I had cut slipped in with a snugness that quite surprised me.

Even with hand tools there is constant alternation between courage and caution. Like a sculptor or a surgeon, a woodworker must be able to strike the material at the right point so that it splits in the right way. With good materials, he must have that sense of care that makes it often happen just the way he wants it. Experiences like these taught me that there are no tools that will take a man out of these problems. No fancy benches or fancy shops can ease the burden of sensing the way a given piece of wood can be used.

Since then I don't know how many times I have been approached by people who want to know what power tools are absolutely necessary, or how to get started making things of wood. The answer is so simple that people have a hard time believing it. There are no essential power tools and there are no necessary pieces of equipment. If you need a clamp, go buy one. If the work needs a sharp saw, get a saw file. You can always find a need for more tools, but the essential beginning is so simple that you can always afford to start. I did not learn from my first shop that power tools are not needed, but I certainly learned that you would do well to get a good drawing board long before you buy a table saw. The drawing board will give you a clearer notion of what you want to accomplish and how. I have always found that the best means to speed is not having to do the job over again. After 30 years I still find that extra deliberation and a slower pace are the best way to save time. Sometimes the pace is set by the rhythm of hand tools, which allow me time to think and to feel both the texture and the proportions of the work. Now I sit in a large shop with all kinds of equipment and a huge bench, and in the middle of that bench is the same old bench screw installed much as it was in the 4x6 vise-horse. It reminds me that although we have moved many times, my shop has never been closed since that time in the stairwell. ☐

Which Three?

One man's opinion on the basic workshop

by Robert Sutter

Open the big double doors to my cabinetmaking shop in Rye, New York and you'll see an array of woodworking machinery. Right up front, where it's handy, is a ten-inch table saw and next to it, a thirteen-inch thicknesser. In a side aisle squats a heavy-duty, long-bed nine-inch jointer. Scattered about the shop where they fit in best are several sanding machines and an overarm router. And if you nose around a bit, you'll find a drill press and a two-spindle dowel borer.

In the center of the shop towering over all the other machinery is a twenty-inch bandsaw. It will cut through a 13-inch thick piece of hard wood. A heavy gauge one-inch blade will fit it comfortably. The upper and lower guides on this saw hold the blade firmly to make an unwavering cut. I have used my bandsaw to cut everything from a tiny Dutchman for a repair to a monster bowsprit for a forty-two foot schooner.

Once in a while I wonder which of these sweat-saving machines I'd choose to carry with me were I suddenly to be transported to a desert island and I could bring only three.

Now this is not as idle a thought as it may seem, especially for those who are just starting to build up a power workshop. In other words, if we are limited by money or space to three stationary machines, which should they be?

First choice: the band saw

My choices would be the band saw, jointer, and 6 by 48-inch industrial floor-mounted belt sander. With these three machines (and a boxful of hand tools) my aim would be to be able to accomplish almost anything in the way of classical joinery and cabinetmaking.

Now before you snort, "Doesn't he know that the tilt-arbor table saw is the heart of any shop?" stop and ask, "Who says so?" Consider that the circular saw was invented in 1810 by Sister Tabitha Babbit of the Harvard Shakers. And fine furniture was being made for a long time before that, using frame saws which could cut wood from log to finished shape.

For those unfamiliar with it, the frame saw is a wooden rectangular frame holding a narrow blade stretched the long dimension of the rectangle. Its teeth are oriented perpendicular to the plane of the frame. To use it, one straddled the board to be cut with the saw, which was moved up and down by grasping the side of the frame. It was a big job to rip a long board—so much so that water power was harnessed to it as early as the 17th century.

A band saw is really an outgrowth of the frame saw with the narrow, hooped blade now in tension around two rubber-tired wheels. It will rip or cross cut depending upon the relationship of work piece to blade, just as the circular saw will. But the thinner band saw blade makes a smaller kerf, hence wastes less wood. Unlike the circular saw, the band saw will cut curves. It is safer to use for ripping thick wood because kick back is not possible. You can also cut very small pieces with greater safety.

What a band saw won't do

Now there are certain things a band saw will not do. It will not cut boards wider (or longer, depending on which way you are cutting) than its throat size—say 14 inches. But how many times does that happen compared to trimming off less than the 14 inches? And how easily could those odd occasions be handled with a hand saw?

If your band saw is of rugged enough construction to accept a wide, heavy-gauge blade, you can resaw thick lumber into thinner boards. But plane a one-inch board to one-half inch and you leave another one-half inch board on the floor as shavings.

I know the bandsaw does not always cut as straight a line as the circular saw. Do as the old timers did: Cut oversize and plane to exact dimension. Just be sure your bandsaw has provisions for a rip fence and grooves for a miter gauge to help guide cutting.

Now I'm not against table saws—I use mine constantly. What I am against is a table saw that is not heavy enough to do the different kinds of work it is meant to do. The kind of table saw I have in mind costs over $600; for a lot less, you can buy a good serviceable band saw. And later on, when you get more money or more room, get the good table saw you want. At that point you'll want a band saw anyway, and you'll already have it!

Second choice: the jointer

I would bring a jointer to my desert island because planing irregular edges and surfaces (left by a bandsaw) is what jointers do best. You should purchase a jointer with the biggest capacity you can afford, limited solely by your purse and the size of your shop. Not only will this tool square and smooth edges and faces of planks, but it will also dimension rough lumber, remove warp cupping and twist, taper legs and rabbet edges—a truly versatile tool.

For all its usefulness, however, the jointer is the only one of the three power tools chosen for which hand tools can be easily substituted. Careful manipulation of a hand-pushed 24-inch jointer plane will produce beautiful smooth, square edges suitable for gluing up. A jack plane and smoother plane will clean up the face of a board in short order. If you need a true face for gluing, then take a few swipes with the jointer plane to finish the job.

If you do choose to go the hand plane route, buy the best hand planes you can; wood or metal is up to you. A set of jointer, jack and smoother planes will set you back over $100, unless you make them, so consider your choice in this light.

Third choice: the belt sander

My third choice, an industrial quality stationary belt sander, will square cross cuts as well as sand edges and surfaces. Of course you can do this by hand, but considerable skill and patience is required.

When purchasing a sander, I recommend the 6 by 48-inch size rather than the 4 by 36-inch since belts for the former are easier to obtain. Make sure that the platen against which the belt runs is rugged. It will be the determining factor in getting a good result. Most sanders can be operated in either vertical or horizontal positions: the former for edge grain with table and mitre gauge which should be included as standard equipment, the latter for sanding surfaces and edges against a fence, likewise standard equipment. Open garnet cloth belts in grits 60 and 100 give good wear and sufficient variety for most work.

In case you're wondering, portable belt sanders are alright for flat surfaces, but almost impossible to hold square on narrow edges. Stationary disc sanders are fine for end grain, but death on faces and edges where they will leave scratches and gouges galore.

Smuggle in a router

That completes my triumvirate. But there is one other tool I'd like to take to this desert isle if I could smuggle it in somehow. It is the indispensible, all-purpose, hand-held electric router. A router rated under 7/8 horsepower will not be capable of the full range of tasks this versatile tool can perform. I prefer rack and pinion depth settings and a micrometer fence for accurate and easy control. It will help if you substitute a 12 by 5 by 1/4-inch piece of plexiglass for the black bakelite base that comes attached to the router. Since plexiglass is transparent, you can see what is going on, and the longer base adds stability. I use plain steel router bits in preference to carbide tipped ones, for carbide can only be kept sharp with an expensive diamond hone. Get used to honing your bits each time you use them, as dull ones tend to chip, splinter, and burn the work.

The router will cut grooves and rabbets both straight and circular. It will bore clean, flat-bottomed holes and trim overhanging edges flush. With its help you can make mouldings and shape edges, set locks and hinges, and make lap, mortise and tenon, finger and dovetail joints. It is a versatile tool, the uses of which are as broad as experience and imagination permit.

Finally, for those who still have trouble swallowing the band saw over the table saw, maybe it will go down easier with a portable contractor's saw for difficult occasions. But someday do get a table saw. And thank you, Sister Tabitha. □

Q & A

Machine oil—*Oil distributors in my area know nothing about machine oil. Machinists tell me not to use hydraulic oil because it is too crude. How does non-detergent machine oil vary from non-detergent motor oil? Where can I buy machine oil in quarts?* —Melvyn J. Howe, St. Paul, Mo. Lubricating oils cling to a surface without running off because they have a tackiness not found in automobile engine oils. Some special oils used on die-stamping presses feel almost like thin molasses. Gun oil, available at sporting goods stores, and sewing-machine oil are good machine oils. South Bend Lathe, 400 W. Sample St., South Bend, Ind. 46623, sells machine oil in quarts; a minimum order is required. McMaster Carr Supply Co., PO Box 4355, Chicago, Ill. 60680, supplies machine oil in gallons. —*Lelon Traylor*

Mobile-Home Woodshop

by Anthony Wheeler

Few can afford to build a shop, but a house trailer affords a good solution to the one or two-man business or to the serious hobbyist. Since the house trailer is somewhat mobile, it allows for changes in residence or even for the building of a new shop while already having a completely functional one. The cost can be as low as $5/sq. ft., with internal alterations kept to a minimum; a fixed-foundation building of equal size would run $10 to $12/sq. ft. Most trailers are designed with windows on one side, good for solar heating. The basic shape of a trailer accommodates long stock, and even plywood can be maneuvered in trailers 12 ft. or 14 ft. wide. The longest trailers are 950 sq. ft. (14 ft. by 70 ft.), with low ceilings; thus the size and variety of the equipment that can be used is limited.

I live on rented property out in the country, where a 1974 Shultz 14-ft. by 70-ft. house trailer has become an extremely functional shop for about $7/sq. ft. It had been damaged in a fire. In hunting it out, I saw other trailers ranging from a 1965 10-ft. by 50-ft. for $600 to a 1976 14-ft. by 70-ft. with expanded living room for $7,600. My fire-damaged trailer cost $5,000 (this may have been high), plus $2,000 to lay a new plywood floor, replace interior walls with drywall, replace over half the windows, rewire for power-tool equipment and fluorescent lighting, repair the ceiling and put in bench areas.

An extra-heavy block base was constructed to spread the trailer's weight over soft earth. The location required blocking one end up about 5 ft., and once skirted, this space has provided a good storage space for lumber. All of these details can increase the cost of setting up this type of shop.

The long narrow shape of the trailer is well suited to a cabinet shop. My shop is laid out so that work moves in one direction, from the front door as rough stock to the finishing room in the rear. The first and largest room (13 ft. by 30 ft.) is devoted to wood storage and power-tool work. A narrow storage area here will hold approximately 15 to 20 sheets of plywood and 100 bd. ft. of lumber. The power tools include a 10-in. table saw, a 12-in. band saw, a jointer, a panel saw and a Shopsmith. The table saw and Shopsmith are on casters so they can be moved when working on odd-size stock. The panel saw's proximity to the lumber storage area saves work. The Shopsmith has been an adequate tool thus far. For this room I made a large router table that can be stored vertically when not in use.

The second room (13 ft. by 20 ft.) is the bench room and is separated from the first room by a large sliding door, which reduces dust flow. This room contains a woodworking bench and an auxiliary bench and is where final assembly and gluing are done, and all carving. The adjacent area includes an office, converted from the bathroom, a gas furnace and a woodburning stove. The last room is used for wood finishing, stained-glass work and storage. I plan to install a large bank of sunlamps to improve finish results. Once a piece is finished it makes a single trip back through the shop and out to the customer. There is really no place to store completed work. □

Tony Wheeler, of Nevada, Iowa, is a self-taught professional woodworker. All prices are 1980 estimates.

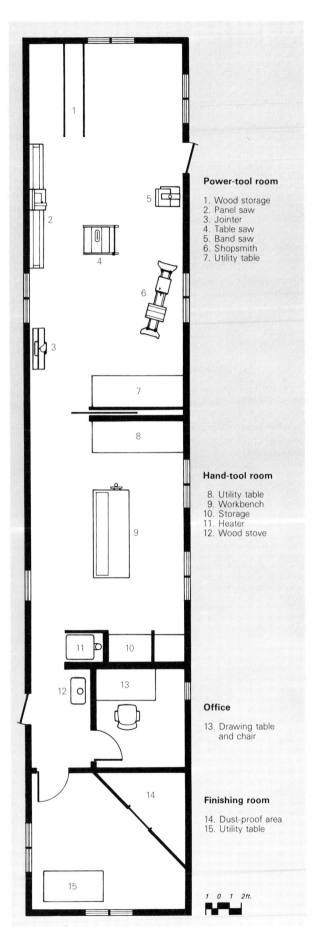

Power-tool room

1. Wood storage
2. Panel saw
3. Jointer
4. Table saw
5. Band saw
6. Shopsmith
7. Utility table

Hand-tool room

8. Utility table
9. Workbench
10. Storage
11. Heater
12. Wood stove

Office

13. Drawing table and chair

Finishing room

14. Dust-proof area
15. Utility table

Wooden Bar Clamps
How to make these essential tools

by Tom Gerson

For edge-joining boards and gluing up frame or leg/rail assemblies, sturdy and stable bar clamps are indispensible. The trouble is that a really good bar clamp can cost upwards of $40, depending on its length, and to equip a shop with a couple dozen of these could mean a thousand-dollar investment. Many woodworkers try to get by with pipe clamps, but though these are comparatively inexpensive, they are cumbersome and the pipes bend easily, their jaws wobble, and they never seem to want to lie flat and steady on your glue-up table. Give one a nudge and it will fall over.

The solution is to make your own bar clamps. Shown here are some very practical and inexpensive homemade bar clamps that have been in use for nearly ten years and are still going strong. Their bars are flat and stable, their jaws stay consistently perpendicular to the bars, they sit flat on a table and they will not easily flop over. These clamps consist of a rectangular-section hardwood bar, a headstock which houses a nut for a threaded rod, a movable front jaw powered by the rod and an adjustable rear jaw whose bit and bridle allow it to be secured at 1-in. intervals along the bar.

The bar—Material for the bar can be any strong, close-grained wood. The clamps shown here are of cherry and maple. You can use the same wood to make the other parts of the clamp. The stock must be dimensioned 1¼ in. thick, 2 in. wide and as long as you choose, though you should increase the sectional dimensions for clamps longer than 24 in. The half-holes along the bottom of the bar are bored by clamping two bars together, bottom to bottom. Using a ⅜-in. machine spur bit in the drill press, bore exactly through the line of juncture between the two beams. Spaced 1 in. apart, the half-holes will provide plenty of rear-jaw adjustment.

The headstock end of each bar must be grooved on both sides. Plow these grooves ¼ in. wide and ⅛ in. deep so that the top of the groove is about ¼ in. below the top edge of the bar. The grooves should be at least 8 in. long, which gives the movable jaw about a 4-in. lateral run after the headstock side plates are attached. Within reasonable limits, the dimensions of the grooves can vary, depending on the diameter of the pins that will ride in the grooves; but I wouldn't make them any deeper than ¼ in., nor any wider than ⁵⁄₁₆ in.

The headstock—The headstock is just a small block of wood 1¼ in. thick by 1½ in. wide by 2½ in. long. Its job is critical, and you must take care to do precise work when making it. It's bored along its length to house the tightening screw for the movable jaw, and mortised across its width to capture the nut for the screw, which can be made from Allthread or from a ⅜-in. by 8-in. hex bolt, or square-head bolt. An ordinary ⅜-in. hex nut or square nut can be fitted into the mortise, but you will get greater thread length, and therefore less wear and longer life for the threads, by using threaded connectors. The connectors come in 2-in. lengths, and can be cut in half to yield two nuts. Acme (square) threaded rod and nuts can be used in place of Allthread.

Drill a ⅜-in. pilot hole through the length of the headstock to accommodate the screw. Accuracy in boring this hole is important, as any deviation from the true axis is going to be magnified when the screw is fully extended. Skewing can cause the movable jaw to bind on the bar. The hole must be centered in the thickness of the block and ⅝ in. above the bottom edge where it joins the bar. The ⅝-in. measurement is about right for gluing up panels and frames up to 1¼ in. thick, assuming that it's best for the screw to be centered in

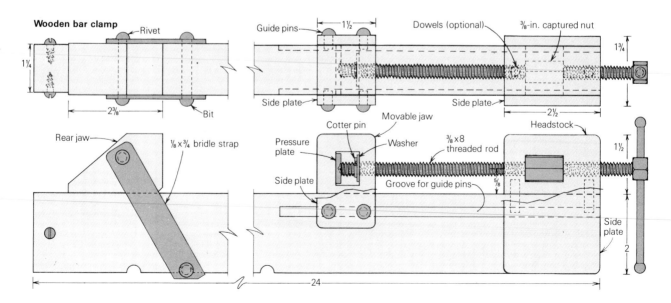

Wooden bar clamp

Rivet

Guide pins — 1½

Dowels (optional)

⅜-in. captured nut

1¾

1¼

2⅜

Bit

Side plate

Side plate

2½

Rear jaw

⅛ x ¾ bridle strap

Cotter pin

Pressure plate

Movable jaw

Washer

⅜ x 8 threaded rod

Headstock

1½

Side plate

Groove for guide pins

⅝

Side plate

2

24

the thickness of the stock being joined. For clamping thicker stock, you might want to make several clamps whose tightening screws are ¾ in. to 1 in. above the bar.

Next cut the mortise for the captured nut. It's easier to cut the mortise all the way through the block, making it square top and bottom and centered on the axis of the bore. It should be just wide enough for the nut to fit snugly, and tall enough to house the nut and prevent it from turning. If you use a threaded connector you can secure it in the mortise by filling around it with epoxy putty (but not at this point in the process). The mortise should be positioned somewhat forward of the middle of the headstock since clamping pressure will be exerted toward the rear, and more wood is needed there to support the nut or connector. Mortising complete, ream the hole using a ²⁵⁄₆₄-in. twist drill; this will keep the screw from dragging when you use the clamp.

Now glue the headstock to the bar. You can reinforce the joint with a couple of short ⅜-in. dowels if you want, but they are not really needed. Make sure that the sides of the headstock are flush with the sides of the bar. The side plates are now glued in place and will tie the headstock to the bar, strengthening the entire structure. When these are glued on, the nut is forever sealed up, so be certain to have the screw in place before gluing on these plates.

The movable jaw—First dimension a block 1½ in. square by 1⁵⁄₁₆ in. wide (¹⁄₁₆ in. wider than the bar, for clearance). Like the headstock block, the movable jaw is bored and mortised, but in this case the hole stops in the mortise. The mortise accommodates a pressure plate against which the screw bears as the clamp is tightened. Made from a piece of hacksawn and filed ⅛-in. thick steel strap, the pressure plate is counterbored slightly with a ½-in. twist drill. The lead end of the screw is rounded, either by filing or turning in a metal lathe, to nest neatly in the counterbore. Epoxy the pressure plate against the rear wall of the mortise.

A thin washer, slipped over the screw on the inside of the mortise and retained by a cotter pin, prevents the screw from backing out of the jaw on retraction. Having fitted the hardware, shave off the bottom of the jaw about ¹⁄₃₂ in. so it will be free to slide along the bar.

Make a pair of side plates 1½ in. wide by 2¼ in. long by

¼ in. thick and temporarily clamp them to the sides of the jaw so that they are flush at the top and overhang at the sides ¾ in. Now mark the centers for two bores on the bottom edge of each plate so that the holes will line up precisely with the grooves. Remove the plates, bore them, and glue them in place, inserting wax paper under the jaw to keep glue off the bar. The guide pins can be made from rivets or from carriage bolts sawn to the proper length and dressed lightly with a file for a sliding fit in the grooves; the jaws should not wobble. Fitting done, epoxy the guide pins in the holes.

Provide for fitting a crank handle to the tail end of the screw by sweat-soldering a hex nut onto the threads, and drilling a hole through both the nut and the rod. You can make the handle from a 30d common nail or any other mild-steel bar stock. I turned the knobs on the ends of the handle from brass, but aluminum or wood would do as well. An acceptable alternative would be to thread the ends of the handle a few turns and screw a small hex nut on either end.

The rear jaw—This part can be made in any shape that suits the builder's eye, but it must be ¹⁄₁₆ in. wider than the bar. The two bridle pieces are made from ⅛-in. by ¾-in. steel or aluminum strap, and are riveted to the jaw at such an angle to allow it to be tilted forward and moved along the bar. If the angle of the bridle is too steep, you can't tilt the jaw, and if it's too shallow the metal straps will cut across the front face of the jaw and bite into the workpiece.

The rivets shown here are made from ¼-in. steel rod. To prevent the straps from marring the bar when I peened the rivets, I turned a small shoulder on the rods to hold the metal clear of the wood, and bored the holes in the bridle the size of this minor diameter. If you don't have access to a metal lathe, you can attach the bridle to the jaw with a stove bolt or carriage bolt. The bit (the rod engaged by the half-holes) can also be a carriage bolt.

A couple of coats of lacquer will finish the project, and keep glue squeeze-out from adhering to the jaws and bar. Besides saving money, these clamps are lighter than pipe clamps or metal bar clamps, and I find them handier to use. □

Tom Gerson is a retired accountant who makes furniture, taxidermy panels, and bootjacks in Stillwater, Minn.

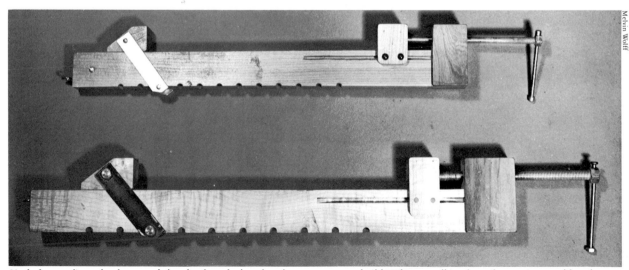

Made from ordinary hardware and clear hardwood, these bar clamps are easy to build and serve well in place of expensive metal bar clamps.

Wood-Thread Clamps

They're strong, handsome and cheap to make

by Richard Showalter

Author's tub of clamps.

During the six years I've been making my living as a woodworker, I've lived in a small town in Oregon, fifty miles from the closest city. The markets for the expensive children's toys I make are still farther away and it became obvious very early that shipping and packing were going to play an important role in the way I make my livelihood. Because of this, I became interested in the potentials of wooden screws for making my work collapsible and more easily shipped. I bought a wooden threading tool and began making my own screws. They did everything I had hoped in making my work more portable and added to the value of the toy as well.

The most important spin-off has been the manufacture of wooden clamps. My shop is now equipped with a wonderful variety of them. They are fitted to my own hand, suited to my particular needs and esthetically pleasing to me by virtue of their materials and because they were fashioned in my own shop. The financial benefits are not to be despised either—it would cost hundreds of dollars to duplicate the number and range of clamps now at my disposal.

The scale you work on will determine the size clamps you need. If you want to make clamps corresponding to Jorgenson hand screws in the 8-in. to 12-in. range and want to buy only one threading set, the best size is 7/8 in. This makes a screw

heavy enough to handle the strains of most applications, but still slender enough to be in proportion to a comfortable handle. One-inch screws make the clamp a little clumsy and the extra strength seems unnecessary. Wooden screws rarely strip. Most hand-screw clamps fail—when they do—by breaking at the center hole in the unthreaded jaw. If you work on a smaller scale, making instruments or doing similar, delicate work, the 1/2-in. and 3/8-in. sizes will make little hand-screw clamps as well as luthier's clamps.

Clamp jaws may be made from nearly any hardwood. (I've even made acceptable clamps using yew, technically a softwood but a very dense and springy one.) Clamp jaws flex considerably in use and should be free of knots, bark inclusions and wind shakes. The slightest fault will be magnified by the stress of use.

The finished width of the jaw should be at least double the diameter of the screw. A clamp using 1/2-in. screws should have jaws at least 1 in. wide. Jaws should be as thick as or slightly thicker than they are wide. These tolerances are critical for large clamps. Obviously, adding more width and thickness increases the strength of the clamp, but in the larger sizes also increases the weight and clumsiness of the tool and ruins its feel. In the smaller sizes bulking up the measure-

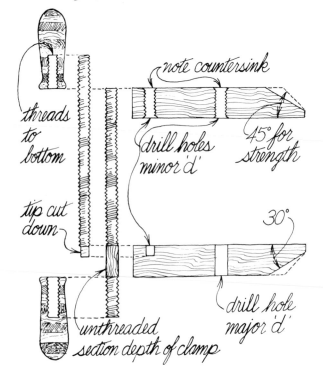

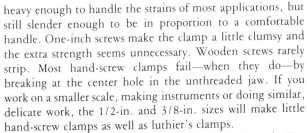

Wooden hand screws may be made in almost any size, with jaws and handles shaped to fit particular types of work.

ments can provide a valuable safety margin and does not make them too clumsy.

Surfaces of jaw stock should be square and parallel. Clamp the jaws together during drilling so the surfaces will mate when the clamp is finished. Holes should be drilled with a drill press or doweling jig. Any skew to these holes will cause the finished clamp to bind in a way that cannot be corrected. The middle hole should be centered from end to end of the clamp. A 12-in. jaw will have its middle screw 6 in. from either end. The rear hole should center 1 in. from the back edge of the jaw in large clamps, 3/4 in. in smaller ones.

Because the tap raises a small curl of wood as it enters and leaves the stock, I use a Forstner bit 1/8 in. larger than the hole I'm drilling and drill a countersink 1/8 in. deep in the top surface of the clamp jaw that will be threaded. (The other jaw is not threaded.) I then use the proper-size bit to drill the two holes to be tapped, stopping the bit when the point breaks through. Using the breakout hole as a guide, I switch back to the larger bit and drill the same 1/8-in. deep hole on the opposite surface. The same result may be achieved by leaving the stock 1/8 in. oversize and planing or jointing to dimension after it has been tapped.

Holes in the piece of jaw stock that is not tapped should be located by allowing the point of the bit—remember, the jaws are clamped together—to break through. The middle hole in the untapped jaw should be drilled the same diameter as the screw, e.g., a 1-in. hole for a 1-in. screw. The rear hole in the unthreaded jaw should extend one-third of the way through the piece of stock, and should be the same diameter as the hole in the threaded jaw before it's tapped, e.g., for a 1-in. screw the hole is 7/8 in. If this hole is too shallow the clamp

Holes in upper jaw are countersunk with Forstner bit before drilling through and tapping. Rear hole in lower jaw is blind.

falls apart in use; if it's too deep the clamp will be weak.

I put a 30° slope on the front of the jaws. If you are going to use your clamps to apply very heavy pressure most of the time, the angle should be increased to 45°. This extra material in the nose makes the clamp stronger. It is amazing how such a small change in dimensions will affect the clamp's feel.

I plane or joint a bevel on the two upper edges of each jaw, but this is cosmetic. In use clamps are often laid in piles and banged around, and the bevel keeps them from looking chewed up quite so soon.

No sandpaper, by the way, should be used on any piece until after it is completely threaded. Small pieces of abrasive will cling to the work and dull thread cutters. Although they

Threading Tools

A user's evaluation

I presently have in my workshop taps and screwboxes for threading in 1/2-in., 3/4-in. and 1-in. sizes. The best commercially available threading tools I've found are made in West Germany (there is no brand name on them) and were formerly sold by Woodcraft Supply. Woodcraft has since begun manufacturing its own version of this tool in this country. My 3/4-in. tool is a Woodcraft product but I like the West German one better because its screwbox handle is fixed to the box with a full-length metal tang, headed over at the end. The Woodcraft handle is attached to the screwbox by a coarse screw threaded into end grain—a poor woodworking practice. The handle constantly unscrews itself in use if you are left-handed, as I am.

The most serious fault of the Woodcraft tool is that the screwbox cuts only a fair thread. The West German tools I have leave a small portion of the original dowel surface intact at the crown of the thread; the Woodcraft tool brings the thread to a sharp crown that makes the threads very delicate.

Frog Tool in Chicago still carries the West German imports and I would advise buying from them.

Marples, which, ordinarily makes excellent tools, markets a threading set whose 1/2-in. model I found unsatisfactory. The die consists of a wooden box with a metal cutter, the traditional way in which this tool has been made. The tap is cast metal, not machined tool steel. The thread it cuts is sharply crowned and overfine, with too many threads to the inch. The only way I found to make it produce any sort of screw was to cut the wood off to length as it emerged from the box. This inefficient pro-

cedure limits the number of things that may be done with the tool. The Marples tap is also very fragile. (My difficulty with this tool is not unique. I spoke with a high-school shop teacher who had purchased the Marples sets in all sizes and was unable to make them perform as they should.)

Brookstone Co. markets a threading set in three sizes, made by Conover Woodcraft of Parkman, Ohio. This is almost an excellent tool. Both tap and screwbox produce a clean thread and the tools are attractively priced. But at three inches the shank of the tap is simply too short.

Finding adequate doweling can be almost as difficult as finding a satisfactory screw set. Stanley used to market a hand-cranked dowel maker, and expensive lathe-powered tools are still available. Commercially available doweling is usually birch or hard maple and very seldom truly round. Variations in moisture content during manufacture and storage often produce doweling that is oval in cross section. For the same reason, much doweling is not straight either. Always check doweling for straightness, piece by piece, before buying it.

Woodcraft Supply sells sizing blocks for doweling that consist of a piece of tempered tool steel with accurately sized circular holes. Doweling is driven through them with a mallet to remove excess stock and bring it back to round. These blocks do not include sizes over 1/2 in., however. I have made sizing blocks for larger sizes by detempering a piece of automobile leaf spring and having a machine shop drill appropriate holes, countersunk on the underside. If you do this, have two holes drilled for each size, one the exact size and one 1/32 in. smaller. The reason for this is that the West German tap and screwbox are made on metric lathes that only approximate U. S. sizes. The "1-in." tool, for example, is made for 2.5-cm doweling. A true inch is 2.54 cm. The undersized holes allow you to make appropriate adjustments. Also drill two small holes in the plate so you can fasten it to a bench top. And don't forget to retemper the metal. —R. S.

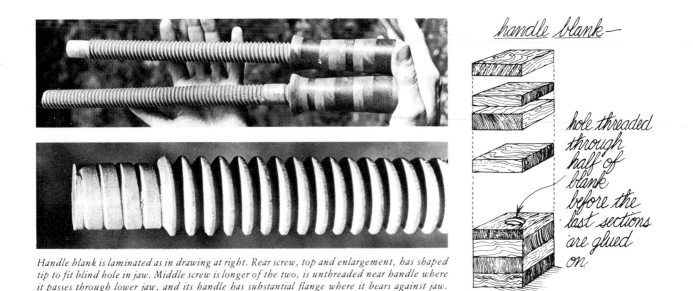

handle blank—

hole threaded
through
half of
blank
before the
last sections
are glued
on.

*Handle blank is laminated as in drawing at right. Rear screw, top and enlargement, has shaped
tip to fit blind hole in jaw. Middle screw is longer of the two, is unthreaded near handle where
it passes through lower jaw, and its handle has substantial flange where it bears against jaw.*

can be sharpened again, extreme care must be used to make
the tools perform properly and you will wish to do it as
seldom as possible.

The two holes in the threaded jaw should be tapped next.
The tap needs to be backed off one-quarter of a turn every
two turns to break the chip and help keep the nose clear of
impacted shavings. The tap should turn freely, without much
resistance. If the tap becomes difficult to turn, removed stock
is probably packing up in its nose. It should be backed out
and the chips and shavings removed. For this purpose I use a
heavy piece of Bakelite plastic that I have sharpened to a
point. A copper or brass rod about 4 in. long and sharpened
to a long point will work well too. Steel should not be used;
sometimes considerable force is necessary to clear chips from
the nose hole and it is easy to slip and damage the cutters.
Packing is worst in threading blind holes where there is no
place for removed stock to go but the bottom of the hole.

If you find yourself using all your strength to turn the tap,
something is wrong. The tap should be backed out and the
trouble located. I keep a small lump of beeswax on my bench
and after tapping the first hole in a piece of work I run the
beeswax over the tap. Friction makes the tap warm, and the
beeswax flows on nicely and eases the work. I then stick a
small piece of rag or cotton in each tapped hole and drip
Danish oil into it until it is saturated. Remove the rag in an
hour or so, after the thread is thoroughly soaked. It is not uncommon in use for some glue to drip on the wooden screws. If
a drip gets inadvertently turned into the tapped hole in the
jaw while the clamp is being adjusted, the oil will keep it
from adhering and freezing the clamp. Danish oil also
strengthens the threads. If you try your clamp while the oil is
wet it will make an ear-splitting squeal with every turn. The
squeal disappears as soon as the oil is dry.

After the initial tapping, even with a well-sharpened tap,
stresses in the wood and compression caused by the tapping
process cause the sides of the hole to expand slightly over a
period of two or three days. This can make the screws bind. It
is not critical in hand-screw clamps, which can always be
taken apart and retapped, but in other applications—
C-clamps and bar clamps where the tool cannot be taken
apart after assembly—stock should be set aside and retapped
after a few days. Take care to start the tap in the same track as

for the first threading. Only a very small amount of material
will be removed in the second tapping but it will make a great
difference in how smoothly the finished tool will turn. If the
clamp still binds, rethreading the screw will help.

The jaws of the clamp can be scraped or sanded to final
surface finish. I oil and wax my clamps. Besides making them
more attractive, wax keeps glue drips from sticking.

Screws should be made from dense, close-grained wood
that is free from knots. I've successfully used beech, cherry,
pear, apple, dogwood, black walnut, yew and myrtle. I own
an antique clamp that has ash screws, but I've had poor
results with both ash and oak, though these woods tap well
and make good clamp jaws. I have successfully used oak stock
taken from root balls rather than the trunks of trees.

There are two methods of making screws and their handles.
The standard way is to turn both handle and screw from one
piece. I don't have a lathe so I make handles and screws separately. The only difference is that in the lathe-turned method
the rear screw cannot be threaded all the way to the shoulder
of the handle—it has to be slightly longer to compensate.

Because taps cannot be used in end grain, I laminate
handle blocks by alternating blocks of wood according to
grain, sometimes as many as seven or eight for each handle.
This is a good use for scraps. I laminate half the length of the
handle at a time, drill it through and tap it, then glue on
three or four blocks to finish the blank. This allows the screw
to bottom out in the hole made for it. If the handle is glued
together completely and then tapped, the screw will not fit in
the portion of the hole left unthreaded by the nose of the tap.
This void in the handle will be weak.

When I first started making clamps I drilled a hole the
diameter of my screw stock in my handle, inserted the
unthreaded end of the middle dowel with a liberal dose of
glue and put another, smaller dowel across the handle to
secure it. This didn't work because the middle handle under-
goes great stress. All of these original handles eventually
broke their pins and glue joints and had to be redone in the
way I am describing.

I turn handles by removing the appropriate tap from its
handle, chucking it in the drill press and screwing the blank
onto the tap. With the drill press running, I shape and finish
them free-hand with a Surform and sandpaper. The handle of

the middle screw should have a good flange of very hard wood at the bottom, where it will bear against the clamp jaw. This flange should be at least 1/8 in. wide all around and well-supported. The handle above it shouldn't be thinned too drastically. The rear handle is under much less stress and need have no flange. Of course very nice handles can be made without turning—simply cut them into hexagonal shapes.

The two screws that fit into the handles aren't identical. The middle screw should have an unthreaded section the depth of the unthreaded jaw. If this section is threaded the clamp jaw tries to ride down the spiral when the clamp is turned two-handed, and it gives a galloping effect to what

should be a smooth rotation. If your doweling is accurately sized you will have to scrape or sand this unthreaded portion to get it to fit the hole and turn smoothly.

The tip of the rear screw should also be sanded or shaped to fit its socket in the unthreaded jaw. Shallow grooves showing the bottom of the threads should still be there when the fit is proper. The accuracy of the fit in these holes makes the difference between a sloppy and a tight clamp.

On large clamps I make the screws long enough to open the jaws 9 in. I rarely use the clamp opened this far because flex in the center screw cuts down on the pressure that may be applied. Occasionally, however, it has been nice to have this

A Dowel Maker

by Trevor Robinson

Because commercial dowels are made only in birch, beech or maple, and large diameters are expensive or hard to get, it is useful to be able to make your own with the simple tool shown here. Properly sharpened and set, the tool turns easily around a square length of hardwood, cutting it smooth and round in a single pass.

The body of the tool is made from a block of hardwood about 2-3/4 in. square and 7-1/2 in. long. First locate and bore a hole

Dowel maker, top, is made of one block of wood cut into two parts, bottom. Note rounded heel of cutter—it just grazes finished dowel.

the diameter of the desired dowel. Then on the lathe a conical depression is turned to meet the hole so that about an inch of cylindrical bore remains. For a 1-in. dowel, the mouth of the cone is 2-1/8 in. wide; for other dimensions the cone should allow the square of wood to enter about 1/2 in. before it encounters the cutter. This means that the large diameter of the cone is about twice the small diameter. The next step is to drill the holes for the four screws that will fasten the two sections together. By drilling them before sawing the block; alignment is automatic. Two saw cuts separate the clamping section from the main block. Mating channels are then chiseled along the inner faces of the two pieces to hold the cutting blade, which is just a saw kerf thicker than the resulting channel. Thus the cone remains smooth, and the screws hold the blade tightly.

Blades can be made from old files. The file should first be annealed by heating red-hot and cooling slowly. Then a suitable length can be cut off and shaped. Before the final sharpening the cutter should be retempered by heating red-hot, quenching, and reheating to 475° F (light-orange oxidation color) before you do the last quench.

The position of the cutter is very important for getting a smooth dowel. The heel end of the cutting edge should just graze the surface of the finished diameter so that the dowel is a snug fit as it comes through. Waxing the bore will make it go more easily. The square of wood to be cut should be just slightly larger than the diameter of the dowel—about 1-1/16 in. square for a 1-in. dowel. It helps to chamfer off the four corners at the leading end of the piece to get it started without splintering. Then the wood can be held vertically in a vise and the tool turned without forcing it down. With a sharp, properly positioned blade the weight of the tool is enough to keep it moving along the wood.

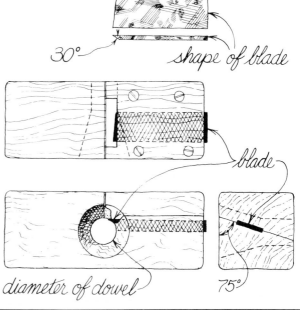

30° shape of blade

blade

diameter of dowel 75°

Modified tubing cutter propels dowel through German screwbox.

capacity. If you make both screws 14 in. long from handle flange to tip, you can shorten them until they feel right.

When threading doweling, you can insert it in a bench vise and turn the die round and round the dowel. If the wood you are using is brittle or of small diameter, however, the dowel may twist, cracking the threads. If this happens, hand-hold the dowel and turn the die around it. The flex then takes place in your wrist. Large doweling, 3/4-in. diameter and up, can be hand-held successfully without undue fatigue. Smaller sizes are difficult to grip and your hands are liable to cramp. I have modified a small tubing cutter by removing the cutting wheel and reshaping the bottom jaw into a doweling holder to help thread small screws.

To glue screws to the handles, drip glue into the hole; don't coat the screws with it. If possible, try not to get any glue on the threads in the upper half of the hole. Most of the holding is done by the threads on the screws; the glue is only to keep them from turning off the handles. Too much glue can cause the screw to freeze before it seats because frictional heat rapidly sets the glue. Turn the handles on slowly and evenly without stopping until you feel them seat. It is best to turn the screws in dry first and mark them when they are fully seated. This allows you to stop when you should. The screw provides a lot of mechanical advantage and it is easy to pop the end off the handle. Too much glue and this mechanical

advantage can produce a hydraulic effect, causing the end to come off or the sides to rupture.

The design of the C-clamp I am about to describe is from an article in *USSR* magazine describing a contemporary Soviet woodworker's shop. I've seen a similar clamp in a 17th-century print of a French cabinetmaker's shop.

Wooden C-clamps are bulkier than their metal counterparts and because of the center brace look deeper than they should to someone used to metal clamps. The center brace in the Russian clamp was made from a piece of brass rod threaded for a nut at either end. I use a wooden brace because I have a suitable small threading set.

The three parts of the clamp body are held together by mortise and tenon joints. If you are using a wooden screw for the center brace, make up the upper and lower jaws of the clamp body first and thread the holes. Screw the small-diameter dowel through the holes and then measure for the long piece that will form the spine of the clamp. If you are using a metal rod, all three pieces may be made at the same time, to arbitrary measurements. With a metal rod it is possible to draw the rod down to the dimensions of the clamp; with a wooden rod, clearance in the mating threads can result in play of 1/16 in. in the length of the spine piece.

The threaded hole in the clamp jaw that will receive the main screw should be made slightly less than 90° to the axis of the jaw. Two or three degrees is enough. There is a certain amount of spring in the clamp that, because wood is flexible, cannot be eliminated. If the hole is drilled at the logical 90° angle, the clamp will spring under pressure and tend to slide off the work. This is true not only for the C-clamp but for wooden bar clamps as well.

Handles for these clamps can be made in either of the ways described earlier.

Since the hole in the upper jaw will not be accessible when the clamp is assembled, all C-clamp parts should be set aside for two or three days and the upper jaw hole rethreaded. The screw assembly should be attached to the upper jaw before gluing the spine and lower jaw to this piece.

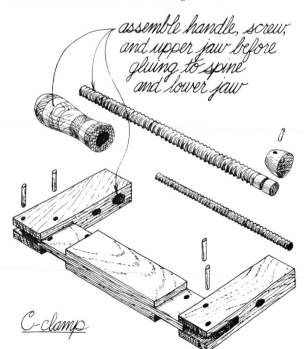

assemble handle, screw, and upper jaw before gluing to spine and lower jaw

C-clamp

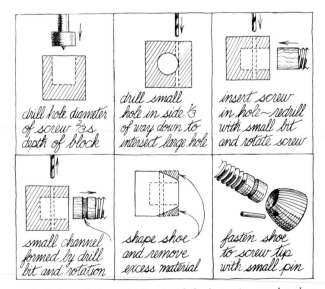

drill hole diameter of screw ⅔s depth of block

drill small hole in side ⅓ of way down to intersect large hole

insert screw in hole—redrill with small bit and rotate screw

small channel formed by drill bit and rotation

shape shoe and remove excess material

fasten shoe to screw tip with small pin

Basic C-clamp, left, can be fitted with freely turning wooden shoe, above. Shoe is made of toughest available wood—author starts with square chunk of hardwood root and drills across the grain, not into end grain. Shoe will break if tip of screw isn't cut truly square. For delicate work, surface shoe with scrap of leather.

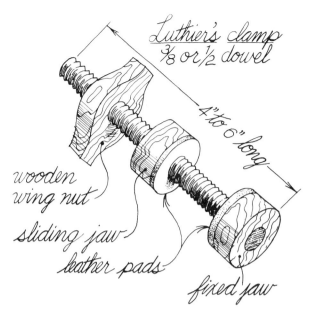

Luthier's clamp
⅜ or ½ dowel
4" to 6" long

wooden wing nut
sliding jaw
leather pads
fixed jaw

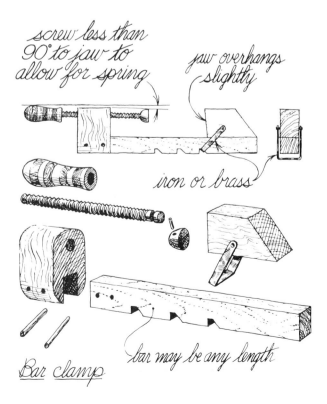

Screws of C-clamp, top, and bar clamp are slanted to allow for flex.

Bar clamps, because they must adjust to material of greatly varying widths, cannot have a center brace. Consequently, they must be more massive. The jaw of the clamp that takes the screw is fixed and heavily made. Again, depress the angle of the screw hole a few degrees from square to allow for spring. The adjustable jaw of the bar clamp should also be slanted a few degrees for the same reason. The bar that secures the adjustable jaw of the clamp can be made from iron or 1/8-in. sheet brass cut to shape and bent with heat.

Luthier's clamps can be made using 1/2-in. or 3/8-in. threaded dowel. The wooden wing nut shown in the drawing

above has numerous applications in clamps and other kinds of woodworking using wooden screws.

Gang clamps for marquetry should be easy to make using the protective tip described for the C-clamp, although this application is outside my personal experience.

By making threaded holes in the tips of the jaws of a standard hand-screw clamp you can increase its possible applications. Different mandrels can be made to screw into the tips, to produce deep engagement clamps or clamps specially tailored to shaped work.

The action of wooden clamps, like all wooden machinery, improves with time. Small mechanical irregularities wear to accommodate one another and the combination of wax, oil, heat and pressure forms bearing surfaces like glass.

I have described the assembly of a single clamp. Obviously it will always be a more efficient use of drill and saw setups to make a number at once. I have a box under my bench where I save likely pieces of material. When it begins to overflow I take a day off and make a batch of clamps. I try to make clamps using all the woods that pass through my shop. This allows me to show wood samples to visitors and it keeps a variety of wood in front of me. The choice of wood for a piece I am making is often suggested by the clamps I am using.

Once you have been through the process you will find you can easily make five or ten clamps a day. □

screw less than 90° to jaw to allow for spring
jaw overhangs slightly
iron or brass
bar may be any length
Bar clamp

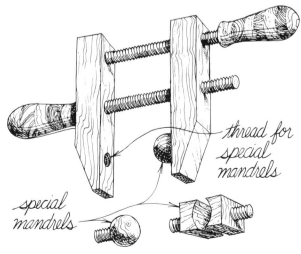

thread for special mandrels
special mandrels

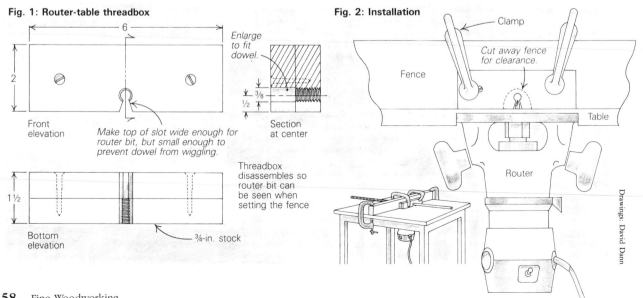

Threading Wood

1. A router-table threadbox

by Andrew Henwood

I have always found setting up a hand threadbox to be a fussy and time-consuming business. It has often taken me an hour or more of shimming the cutter in and out, up and down, and back and forth to get it right. Moreover, I was completely stymied recently when I tried to put 12 threads per inch on a ⅜-in. dowel. I spent half a day reducing a quantity of good dowel to round rubbish. Try as I might, I was getting all root and no crest.

I was unwilling to admit defeat. I wanted to make some little wooden clamps for delicate work, and I had put considerable time and effort into making a metal tap that did a dandy job of threading the hole. The tap wasn't going to be much use by itself.

I figured that to succeed I would have to use a high-speed cutter, so I decided to build a threadbox with a router to do the cutting. I managed to produce an acceptable thread on my first attempt, within an hour of the time I'd gotten the idea. I'll show you how to do it, then you can adjust dimensions to suit your own taps.

Take two squared scraps of close-grained hardwood, as shown in figure 1. Screw the pieces together face to face. Don't use glue—you will need to take the pieces apart again as you make the threadbox, and also when you set the router bit. Drill through both pieces with a 9/32-in. bit (the pilot size of my tap). Now take the two halves apart and enlarge the hole in the front half to ⅜ in. Thread the hole in the back block, carefully cleaning away the wood frayed by the entry of the tap. Refasten the halves together and cut out the keyhole slot across the bottom, giving it a good flare in order to provide clearance for chips and room for the router bit.

Next chuck a 60° V-groove bit in your router, and mount it under a router table. Make a cutout in the fence so the dowel can pass through, then set the fence loosely a couple of inches behind the bit. To adjust the fence, first disassemble the threadbox. Take the back (tapped) section and center it so that the bit is exactly in line with the first crest of thread. You can judge this most accurately if you adjust the height of the bit until it matches the contour of the thread. The threadbox will work best if the crest just enters from the surface at the left-hand side of the keyhole, so you should plane the block down a little to achieve this. Now place the block so that its front face is just a hair behind the point of the router bit. The back half of the threadbox is now correctly aligned, and you can use its position to set the fence on the table. Hold the back part of the threadbox down firmly while you snug up and secure the fence. Mark the position of the block on the fence so you can reorient the threadbox after it's been assembled.

Screw the two halves of the threadbox together again and clamp the whole unit to the fence, centered over the bit. Raise the router bit until the point is fractionally above the minor diameter of the threaded portion. Switch on the router, insert a dowel into the pilot hole, and rotate it clockwise as you apply pressure to push the dowel in. As soon as a turn or two of dowel is engaged in the tapped section, it will self-feed as you turn it.

A few pointers that may help: Make darn sure you provide a positive way to remove the waste, otherwise it will jam up in the thread behind the bit and wreck the work (my router vacuums the waste down through the keyhole slot). Also, I find that I get a better thread that is less likely to crumble if I

Fig. 1: Router-table threadbox

6

2

Front elevation

Make top of slot wide enough for router bit, but small enough to prevent dowel from wiggling.

1½

Bottom elevation

¾-in. stock

Enlarge to fit dowel.

⅜

½

Section at center

Threadbox disassembles so router bit can be seen when setting the fence

Fig. 2: Installation

Clamp

Cut away fence for clearance.

Fence

Table

Router

Drawings: David Dann

first dip the dowel in Watco oil or mineral spirits. Don't be in too much of a rush when feeding the dowel—in my enthusiasm I tried mounting the dowel in a brace for fast and easy turning, but I found that too much speed rips the crest off the thread. Feeding with the fingers lets you feel what's going on. I've found that it's a good practice to chamfer the end of the dowel for easy starting. The results will readily reveal whether the bit should be raised or lowered for the desired depth of cut. If the dowel won't feed, you have only to nudge the fence a trifle forward or back.

I can just barely stand the noise of routers, even with earplugs. I much prefer the quiet, crisp sound and feel of a hand threadbox as it slices its way around a dowel. But all in all, I don't suppose I ever would have gotten twelve threads on a three-eighths stick that way.

Andrew Henwood is an airline pilot and furnituremaker living in Georgetown, Ont.

2. A commercial threader

To speed production on a line of threaded novelty items, Beall Tool Co. (541 Swans Rd. N.E., Newark, Ohio 43055) devised a threadbox that clamps to the base of a router. Shown here as a wooden prototype, it is manufactured in reinforced plastic, with interchangeable leadscrew inserts (three sizes to fit the taps included). You attach the threadbox to a router, center and adjust Beall's three-flute V-groove bit, then simply screw a dowel into the wider end of the leadscrew. As the thread is cut, it automatically follows the leadscrew's pattern. The device costs about $130 (1983); it is likely that more leadscrew sizes will become available, and eventually left-hand threads too. —*Jim Cummins*

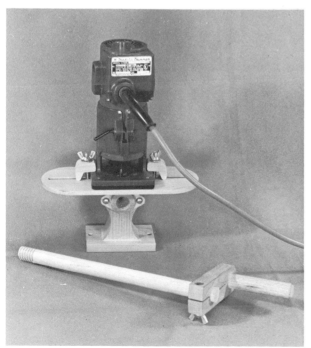

Any standard router attaches to J&J Beall's dowel threader.

3. Versatile threadbox cuts inside *and* outside threads

by Robert J. Harrigan

I needed some wood threads, and had in mind a jig for one size. After a while at the drawing board, however, I came up with a tool with interchangeable guides and thread sizes to fulfill all of my threading needs. All you really need to start making one is a tap and a matching threaded rod. The tool shown cuts outside threads up to $3\frac{5}{8}$ in. and inside threads up to $2\frac{7}{8}$ in. Some chipping occurs with ring-porous hardwoods such as oak, but it doesn't affect the action of the threads.

The key to the threadbox is the threaded feeder rod inside the box (figure 1, next page). When you turn the handle at the back of the box, the workpiece rotates and advances past the cutter. The feeder rod affects only the coarseness or fineness of the thread, and has nothing to do with the diameter of the work you are threading. Change the feeder rod to suit the job. As a general rule, use fine threads on containers, and coarse threads when you are making clamps, so they will tighten up faster. A different guide disc is needed each time you change the diameter of the work, but you can make as many sizes as you need. Use plywood for the guide discs—you end up with a rounder hole than if you had used solid wood.

The large photo on the next page shows the threadbox cutting an outside thread. I'm using a Weller model 601 motor tool. It rides in a track on the front plate that allows coarse adjustment of the cutter; fine adjustment is done with a machine screw that runs through an aluminum block. It's important that the work fit the guide disc precisely. If the holes and the work are slightly oval, the errors will double and the thread will show it.

To cut inside threads, you reposition the tool on an auxiliary plate that holds the tool in a horizontal position. Here also the work moves past the cutter as you turn the handle. The depth of the threaded section is limited by the length of the fly-cutter's shank, but a lot of thread would just be a nuisance on a container anyway.

When you want to make a long threaded dowel, such as for a clamp, tap a threaded disc to support the dowel as it comes out the front of the box. The bottom left photo on the next page shows an extension plate I made to hold the extra disc. There is a rear extension plate also, which can be used to make dowels longer than the box. Use a scrap when you set the thread depth, and increase it little by little until a nut fits right. The dowel will chip when you take a series of light cuts like this, but when the depth is set correctly, you'll get a clean cut with one steady pass. Use the tap to thread the holes in the clamps. If you are working oversize threaded dowels, such as for a press, and you don't have a tap big enough to match

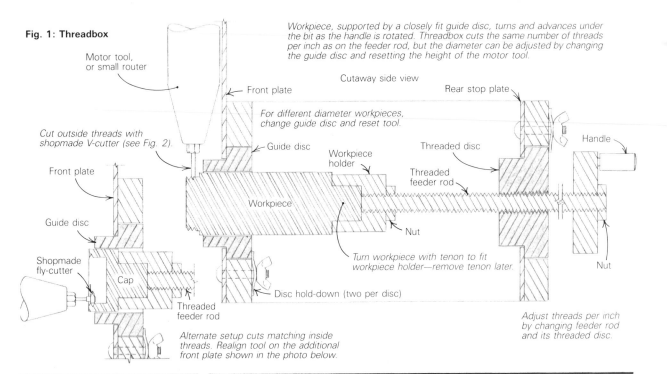

Fig. 1: Threadbox

Motor tool, or small router

Cut outside threads with shopmade V-cutter (see Fig. 2).

Front plate

Guide disc

Shopmade fly-cutter

Cap

Threaded feeder rod

Workpiece, supported by a closely fit guide disc, turns and advances under the bit as the handle is rotated. Threadbox cuts the same number of threads per inch as on the feeder rod, but the diameter can be adjusted by changing the guide disc and resetting the height of the motor tool.

Cutaway side view

Front plate

For different diameter workpieces, change guide disc and reset tool.

Guide disc

Workpiece holder

Workpiece

Threaded feeder rod

Nut

Turn workpiece with tenon to fit workpiece holder—remove tenon later.

Disc hold-down (two per disc)

Rear stop plate

Threaded disc

Handle

Nut

Adjust threads per inch by changing feeder rod and its threaded disc.

Alternate setup cuts matching inside threads. Realign tool on the additional front plate shown in the photo below.

To cut inside threads, the motor tool is mounted on an auxiliary aluminum plate. Instead of the V-groove cutter that makes outside threads, a fly-cutter is used. The length of the threaded section is limited by the length of the bit's shank, but a container doesn't need many threads. Below, a front extension supports and indexes longer work.

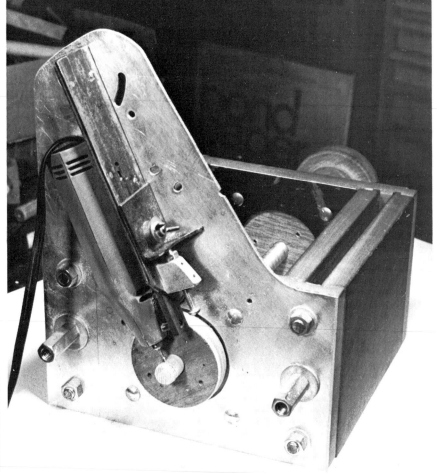

In cutting outside threads, as the rear handle is turned, the work advances according to the pitch of the threads on the feeder rod inside the box. For adjusting to different diameters, the motor tool slides in a track; depth-of-cut is set with a fine-adjustment screw.

Harrigan's threadbox makes threads in various sizes.

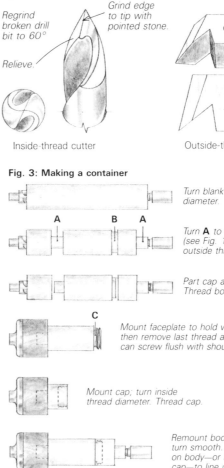

Regrind broken drill bit to 60°

Relieve.

Grind edge to tip with pointed stone.

10°

Inside-thread cutter

Outside-thread cutter

Fig. 3: Making a container

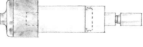

Turn blank to guide-disc diameter.

A   B   A

Turn **A** to holder diameter (see Fig. 1); turn **B** to outside thread diameter.

Part cap and body. Thread body.

C

Mount faceplate to hold work on lathe, then remove last thread at **C** so cap can screw flush with shoulder.

Mount cap; turn inside thread diameter. Thread cap.

Remount body with cap; turn smooth. Trim shoulder on body—or bottom of cap—to line up grain.

Turn body cavity, screw on cap, turn to final shape and sand.

the threads, simply make an inside-threaded plug that fits the dowel. Glue it, just as you would an embedded nut, where you need it.

I make my own V-groove cutters from broken drill bits $\frac{1}{32}$ in. wider than the thread pitch. I grind the end to 60°, then sharpen inside the cutting flutes with a pointed stone held in the Weller, using angles as shown in figure 2. Relieve the back of the cutting edge as you would a normal drill bit. I make fly-cutters from pieces of lawnmower blade—any high-carbon steel will do—screwed or bolted onto an arbor that fits the tool. You can buy high-speed bits instead, but they are bulky and won't cut as close to a shoulder.

To make a container, it helps to visualize the steps involved. Figure 3 shows how I do it. The most tedious step is turning the outside diameter so that it fits the guide disc. I use the disc itself as a gauge—I hang it over the tailstock center, and size the work from that end, turning off the lathe and sliding the disc along to check the fit.

When you turn the tenons that will fit into the holder inside the threadbox, it's better to turn them small rather than too large. You can always build them up with a turn or two of masking tape for a tight fit.

To avoid chipping, cut the body threads in one pass. When they are done, turn off an unthreaded neck below the threads on the body—if you don't, the cap won't screw on all the way. When making the cap threads, take a series of light cuts. You will find that you can remove the cap from the threadbox to check the fit without changing the cutter setting. Put a little more thread in the cap than you think you will need. This extra length will allow you to trim the bottom of the cap down later, so that the grain on cap and body will match when the cap is screwed tight.

When you turn out the end grain from the cavity, secure the blank to the faceplate with a couple of nails through the tenon for more support. □

Robert J. Harrigan has a stained glass and woodworking shop in Cincinnati. Photos by the author.

Truing dowels

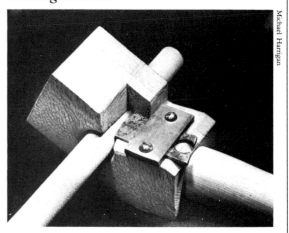

Michael Harrigan

This lathe tool trues a dowel to exact size. Taper the entrance hole to the finished dowel size at the end of the blade, and relieve the blade's cutting edge at the corners to prevent the work from binding. —R.J.H.

Lumber Grading
A guide for the perplexed

by William W. Rice

Typical grade stamps of the Western Wood Products Association (top: Douglas fir, sugar pine) and the Northeastern Lumber Manufacturers Association (right: Eastern white pine, balsam fir). Stamps indicate the association mark, the species, the mill, the grade and sometimes the relative dryness.

When I hear a woodworker exclaim, "How can that board be a Select? It has a knot as big as your fist!" I sympathize with his frustration. But I also know that he, like many, is confused about commercial lumber grading. A bewildering assortment of grades confronts the buyer. There are different standards for hardwoods and for softwoods, and the rules make exceptions for certain species like walnut.

Lumber grading is a way of evaluating the usable lumber in a board. It takes into account the number, size and degree of defects, and the number and size of clear pieces that will remain when the defects are cut away. But not every project needs a perfect board 12 ft. long. Once a cabinetmaker learns his way through the intricacies of the grading system, he will be able to select the most suitable lumber for the job at hand. He may well find that he can cut the size pieces he needs from No. 1 Common as well as he could from Firsts and Seconds—at considerable saving.

As far back as the early 1700s the need for classifying lumber by grades was recognized. Originally, appearance was the primary requisite, but with increased knowledge about wood properties and methods of utilization, lumber grades now also take into account strength characteristics and yield potential. Modern lumber-grading rules provide standards for the manufacture of the same product by different mills. They also serve as common specifications both buyer and seller can use to determine that full value is received and sold.

In the United States, the American Lumber Standards Committee (ALSC) of the Department of Commerce is responsible for general establishment and administration of lumber grades. Application and enforcement of specific grading rules are the responsibility of various lumber inspection associations. For example, the California Redwood Association has jurisdiction over member mills and dealers handling redwood, and the Western Wood Products Association monitors the standards for several West Coast species, including ponderosa pine and Douglas fir. Some other associations are the Southern Pine Inspection Bureau, the Northeastern Lumber Manufacturers Association and the National Hardwood Lumber Association. Altogether there are about 15 associations that oversee the grading of wood products; each is represented on the American Lumber Standards Committee and all operate under its certification. Grading rules are voluntary standards set by the lumber industry through the ALSC, not dictated by the government.

Lumber grading is judging the surface quality of boards with respect to established standards, which are different for softwoods and hardwoods. Softwoods are graded from the best face, usually as surfaced material, and it is assumed that the piece will be used as is, without further manufacturing. Select and Common softwood boards are graded for appearance from the best face, while dimension lumber and timbers are graded for strength by inspecting all four surfaces, with

the poorest surface determining the grade. Hardwoods are graded in the rough, from the poor face, and it is assumed that each board will be cut into clear-face parts. Softwoods are generally grade-stamped, hardwoods are not. Both softwood and hardwood grading rules describe the poorest piece permitted in each grade. Softwood Select and Common grades specify a moisture level of 15% or less. There is no moisture-content rule for hardwoods, and generally grading is done while the lumber is green, unless buyer and seller make special arrangements.

Softwood grading

Softwood species most often used for cabinetry and furniture are Eastern white pine and the western pines: sugar, Idaho white, ponderosa and lodgepole. Other species used include Douglas fir, Englemann spruce, Sitka spruce and Western larch. Eastern white pine is graded under the rules of the Northeastern Lumber Manufacturers Association (NELMA). The others are graded under the rules of the Western Wood Products Association (WWPA) and/or West Coast Lumber Inspection Bureau (WCLB). Upper grades are designated Select or Finish and usually are further separated by the letters B, C, and D to indicate descending quality. The exception to the rule is Idaho white pine (IWP), which carries the grade names Supreme, Choice, and Quality in place of B Select, C Select and D Select respectively.

Lower lumber grades are called Commons, and quality within this category is designated by the numbers, 1, 2, 3, 4, 5—with the highest number assigned to the lowest grade. But Idaho white pine Commons carry the names Colonial, Sterling, Standard, Utility and Industrial, with Colonial corresponding to 1 Common, and so on.

While grade descriptions may vary slightly from one softwood association to another, in general each grade describes the type, size and number of defects permitted in the worst board in that grade. For example, the WWPA grade of B and Better Select (B & BTR) for all species permits on the best face: light stain (blue or brown) over not more than 10% of the face; small (1/32 in. deep by 4 in. long) season checks, one at each end of the board or 3 or 4 if away from the ends; very light torn grain (1/64 in. by 3 in.); two sound, tight pin knots (1/2 in. dia.) *or* slight traces of pitch *or* a very small pitch pocket (1/16 in. by 3 in.); very slight cup (1/16 in. in an 8-in. wide board); very light crook (1/4 in. in an 8-in. by 12-ft. board). In addition to the above, the poor face may have wane (bark) 1/4 the thickness by 1/6 the length of the piece.

As another example, a Premium (No. 2 Common) Eastern white pine board graded under NELMA rules could contain on the best face: medium surface checks (1/32 in. by 10 in.);

Bill Rice teaches lumber grading in the wood science and technology department at the University of Massachusetts.

red knots (2¾-in. dia. in 8-in. wide boards); sound pith; medium pitch (⅙ the width by ⅓ the length of the piece); short splits; medium stain (not affecting a paint finish); one knothole (½-in. dia. in a 6-in. wide board); one ¼-in. wormhole for every 6 lineal feet of board. The poor face could have all that plus wane ½ the thickness by ¼ the width by ¼ the length of the board.

At first glance the reader might think that anything goes as far as defects in a board. In practice the grader exercises judgment about the number allowed and seldom, if ever, do all the permitted defects occur in a single board. In fact, there may be some pieces in a pile that would make the next higher grade except for one unacceptable defect. For example, a perfectly clear board with too much wane on the reverse face grades as C Select instead of B, or a No. 3 Common board misses the No. 2 Common grade because of one oversize knot. The softwood grade is stamped on each piece when it leaves the mill, although retail lumber dealers often cut long boards into shorter lengths and in the process lose the stamp. Inspection by the association quality-control people ensures that the grade is correct on at least 95% of the pieces.

Hardwood grading

Except for specialty grades such as Factory and Shop or Furniture (NELMA), softwood grading depends on the grader's experience and good judgment and assumes lumber use in full widths and lengths. In contrast, hardwood grading is based on the assumption that the boards will be cut into furniture parts ranging from 2 ft. to 7 ft. long, and that each part should have a clear face. The grade of individual boards is related to the yield of clear parts as determined by a mathematical system called the Cutting Unit Method. In addition, hardwoods are always graded from the poor face.

While there are rules similar to softwood rules for grading hardwood timbers and framing, they are seldom applied commercially. For this reason hardwood grades are usually considered to be furniture grades. There is only one association, the National Hardwood Lumber Association (NHLA), responsible for the grading of native hardwoods as well as many imported foreign and tropical species. Hardwood grading rules define standard requirements for all hardwood species and, in addition, spell out modifications that apply to individual woods. A cabinetmaker who understands the general rules will usually be able to purchase any hardwood species on grade without major problems. An exception might be walnut which, because of the decreasing size of the available trees, has required a number of adjustments.

The standard grades assigned to hardwoods are Firsts, Seconds, Selects, Numbers 1, 2, 3A and 3B Common, and Sound Wormy. Firsts and Seconds are usually combined into the one grade of Firsts And Seconds (FAS). Sound Wormy is essentially No. 1 Common with an allowance for wormholes. As with softwood grades, the more defects in a board, the lower the grade. However, in grading hardwoods the concern is for the yield of clear material, not the number of defects.

A grader spends only 10 or 15 seconds inspecting each hardwood board. In that time, he determines its width, length and surface measure (area in square feet); selects the poor face; visualizes a series of clear face cuttings on the surface; determines the percent of clear material available; and assigns a grade based on board size, number of cuttings, percent of clear area and defect or species restrictions.

The heart of this grading operation is the determination of clear material available and this is done by the Cutting Unit Method. A cutting is a portion of the board that can be obtained by crosscutting, ripping, or both. A cutting must be

Minimum Grade Requirements for Hardwoods

Grade	Minimum Board Size width	length	Conversion Factor (% clear face)	Minimum Size of Cuttings	Maximum Number of Cuttings for Board SM
Firsts	6″	8′-16′	11xSM (91⅔%)	4″x5′ or 3″x7′	1 for SM 4′-9′ 2 for SM 10′-14′ 3 for SM 15′ or more
Seconds	6″	8′-16′	10xSM (81⅔%)	4″x5′ or 3″x7′	1 for SM 4′-7′ 2 for SM 8′-11′ 3 for SM 12′-15′ 4 for SM 16′ or more
Selects	4″	6′-16′	11xSM (91⅔%) 10xSM (83⅓%)	4″x5′ or 3″x7′	1 for SM 2′-3′ 1 for SM 4′-7′ 2 for SM 8′-11′ 3 for SM 12′-15′ 4 for SM 16′ or more
No. 1 Common	3″	4′-16′	9xSM (75%) 8xSM (66⅔%)	4″x2′ or 3″x3′	1 for SM 2′ 1 for SM 3′-4′ 2 for SM 5′-7′ 3 for SM 8′-10′ 4 for SM 11′-13′ 5 for SM 14′ or more
No. 2 Common	3″	4′-16′	6xSM (50%)	3″ x 2′	1 for SM 2′-3′ 2 for SM 4′-5′ 3 for SM 6′-7′ 4 for SM 8′-9′ 5 for SM 10′-11′ 6 for SM 12′-13′ 7 for SM 14′ or more

The chart gives the minimum requirements a board must meet to merit a particular grade. In general, a high-grade board is relatively long and wide and a high percentage of its area is free of defect. The clear lumber in a high-grade board must be obtainable in relatively few and large cuttings.

To grade a board, first note its dimensions—they will eliminate some grades immediately. For example, a board that is only 5 in. wide cannot be a First or Second. Next, note the board's surface measure (SM)—its area expressed in square feet. Mentally lay out the largest clear cuttings that could be obtained by straight ripping and crosscuts, and measure each cutting in inches of width and feet of length (cutting units). Then total the number of cutting units available, and count the number of cuttings necessary to obtain the total. The last two columns give the minimum size of a cutting and the maximum number of cuttings allowed for each grade.

The percentage of clear face required for each grade can be found by dividing the number of cutting units by the area of the board, but instead, lumber graders use a conversion factor, which is given in the third column of the table. The surface measure of the board multiplied by the conversion factor gives the minimum number of cutting units required for the grade.

For example, the smallest board that can be a First is 6 in. wide and 8 ft. long, or 4 ft. surface measure. If this board were perfect, it would contain 48 cutting units. It must contain its surface measure times the conversion factor of 11, or 44 cutting units, to be graded a First. This much clear lumber must be obtainable in one cutting.

The two examples on page 64 show how lumber is graded. The diagrams were derived from real boards, but the defects that determined the grade were too small to reproduce photographically.

parallel to the edges of the board. Further, a cutting must be clear of all defects on one face and it must be of a certain minimum size, depending on the grade to be assigned to the board. Based on the surface area of the board, each grade specifies the maximum number of cuttings that can be used in determining the grade. Note that grading does not consider the thickness of the board, only the surface area. The grader visualizes the various cuttings, but does not actually make the sawcuts. How the buyer ultimately cuts the board may not coincide with the grader's visualization. What is important is that the yield of clear material is mathematically available in specified cuttings and therefore anyone check-grading the inspector should arrive at the same grade.

The mathematics of the Cutting Unit Method are relatively

EXAMPLE 1: RED OAK BOARD

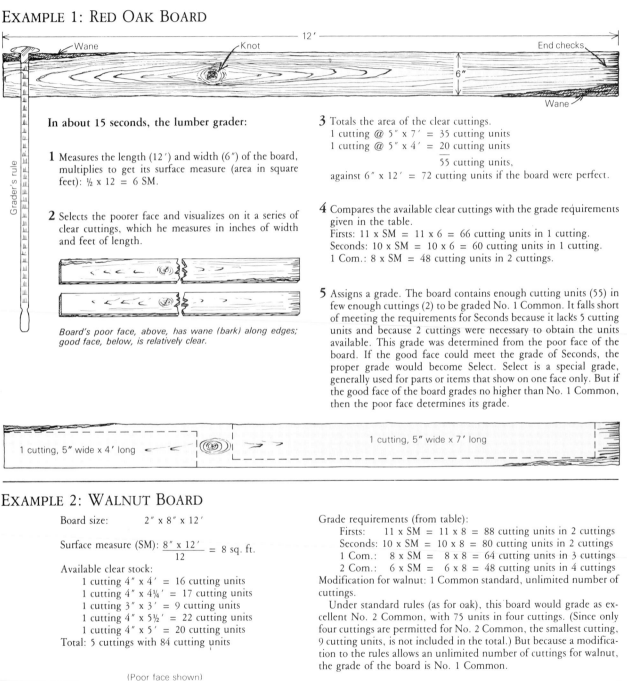

In about 15 seconds, the lumber grader:

1 Measures the length (12´) and width (6˝) of the board, multiplies to get its surface measure (area in square feet): ½ x 12 = 6 SM.

2 Selects the poorer face and visualizes on it a series of clear cuttings, which he measures in inches of width and feet of length.

Board's poor face, above, has wane (bark) along edges; good face, below, is relatively clear.

3 Totals the area of the clear cuttings.
1 cutting @ 5˝ x 7´ = 35 cutting units
1 cutting @ 5˝ x 4´ = 20 cutting units
                          55 cutting units,
against 6˝ x 12´ = 72 cutting units if the board were perfect.

4 Compares the available clear cuttings with the grade requirements given in the table.
Firsts: 11 x SM = 11 x 6 = 66 cutting units in 1 cutting.
Seconds: 10 x SM = 10 x 6 = 60 cutting units in 1 cutting.
1 Com.: 8 x SM = 48 cutting units in 2 cuttings.

5 Assigns a grade. The board contains enough cutting units (55) in few enough cuttings (2) to be graded No. 1 Common. It falls short of meeting the requirements for Seconds because it lacks 5 cutting units and because 2 cuttings were necessary to obtain the units available. This grade was determined from the poor face of the board. If the good face could meet the grade of Seconds, the proper grade would become Select. Select is a special grade, generally used for parts or items that show on one face only. But if the good face of the board grades no higher than No. 1 Common, then the poor face determines its grade.

1 cutting, 5˝ wide x 4´ long   1 cutting, 5˝ wide x 7´ long

EXAMPLE 2: WALNUT BOARD

Board size: 2˝ x 8˝ x 12´

Surface measure (SM): $\frac{8˝ \times 12´}{12}$ = 8 sq. ft.

Available clear stock:
1 cutting 4˝ x 4´ = 16 cutting units
1 cutting 4˝ x 4¼´ = 17 cutting units
1 cutting 3˝ x 3´ = 9 cutting units
1 cutting 4˝ x 5½´ = 22 cutting units
1 cutting 4˝ x 5´ = 20 cutting units
Total: 5 cuttings with 84 cutting units

Grade requirements (from table):
Firsts: 11 x SM = 11 x 8 = 88 cutting units in 2 cuttings
Seconds: 10 x SM = 10 x 8 = 80 cutting units in 2 cuttings
1 Com.:   8 x SM =   8 x 8 = 64 cutting units in 3 cuttings
2 Com.:   6 x SM =   6 x 8 = 48 cutting units in 4 cuttings
Modification for walnut: 1 Common standard, unlimited number of cuttings.

Under standard rules (as for oak), this board would grade as excellent No. 2 Common, with 75 units in four cuttings. (Since only four cuttings are permitted for No. 2 Common, the smallest cutting, 9 cutting units, is not included in the total.) But because a modification to the rules allows an unlimited number of cuttings for walnut, the grade of the board is No. 1 Common.

(Poor face shown)

1 cutting, 4˝ wide x 4´ long   1 cutting, 4˝ wide x 4¼´ long   1 cutting, 3˝ wide x 3´ long
split   1 cutting, 4˝ wide x 5½´ long   1 cutting, 4˝ wide by 5´ long   12˝ split

(Boards are not drawn to scale)

simple. It is a matter of calculating the number of cutting units available and comparing the total to the number required for a given grade. A cutting unit is a portion of clear lumber one inch wide and one foot long. Thus the number of cutting units in each clear portion is determined by multiplying its width in inches by its length in feet. When calculating the total yield of clear material, only those cutting units making up the surface of the clear-face cuttings may be counted. There may be additional cutting units in the board, but in areas too small for furniture cuttings, and thus not available for grade computation. Within each grade there is some leeway because the rules describe the poorest pieces—thus there are both borderline and "good" boards. A good No. 2 Common would be just shy of the total cutting units it would need to qualify as a No. 1 Common. The table lists the requirements for determining standard grades.

As can be seen from the table and the two examples, hardwood grading can be detailed and quite exacting. Grading is a 100% inspection procedure, but in a given pile of lumber an experienced grader can accurately judge whether most boards contain the proper percentage of clear area in the allowable size and number of cuttings without using the complete method. However, for a borderline board he will go through all the necessary measurements and calculations, if the lumber value warrants the effort.

Grading and the woodworker

Although grading rules are of particular use to furniture manufacturers, they can also guide the cabinetmaker in selecting lumber. In sum, Firsts and Seconds are relatively clear boards of good widths and lengths. They yield on the average, 80% to 90% clear material, depending on cutting requirements, and the pieces will be good on both sides. Select boards are about 80% clear on one face and of good widths and lengths. They are often used for items that show only one side. No. 1 Common is probably the best all-around grade, considering both yield (about 65%) and price. This grade can include some long (over 4 ft.) cuttings. If most of your cabinet parts are 16 in. to 4 ft. long, consider the economy of No. 2 Common. Often the grade yield of 50% can be exceeded, especially if the parts are glued into assemblies.

A cabinetmaker who wants to use graded lumber should visit a lumber supplier and look over the available stock in the various grades to become familiar with the typical array of defects (and their spacing) that is permitted. Look for grade stamps on softwoods so you will know you are getting what you are paying for. But most important, try to associate the character and size of the cabinet (or parts) with the appearance of the lumber. Then select the grade that will permit you to cut out the parts with the least waste. Not all parts need to be blemish-free; in fact, defects more often than not add character and interest. The lower grades are less expensive, but figure the waste before buying on price alone. □

AUTHOR'S NOTE: Lumber-grading rules can be obtained from the following associations:

National Hardwood Lumber Assn., PO Box 34518, Memphis, Tenn. 38134 (*Rules for Measurement of Hardwood and Cypress Lumber*).

Northeastern Lumber Manufacturers Assn., 4 Fundy Rd., Falmouth, Maine 04105 (*Grading Rules for Northeastern Lumber*).

Western Wood Products Assn., 1500 S.W. Yeon Bldg., Portland, Ore. 97204 (*Grading Rules for Western Lumber*).

Q & A

Formaldehyde in particleboard—*I plan to use particleboard for flooring in my home. Are there any sealants that will stop formaldehyde emissions? If so, will they affect any subsequent finish I put on the floor, such as wax, varnish, or tile?* —Christina Pierce, Hayfork, Calif.

GEORGE MYERS REPLIES: At least two companies make sealants designed to keep the formaldehyde inside the particleboard, although neither is endorsed by the USDA Forest Products Lab. Chemical Products Development Corp. (PO Box 283, Oklahoma City, Okla. 73119) makes a polymer coating in clear and colored mixtures. Mortell Co. (550 North Hobbie Ave., Kankakee, Ill. 60901) sells a clear latex varnish called Hyde-check. Both can be applied with brush or roller, and other finishes can be put over them.

Aging particleboard in a warm, humid place for weeks or months before use will drive off some formaldehyde. An attic or covered shed exposed to sunlight and with a high ventilation rate should work. Stack and sticker the boards or stand them against a wall so air can circulate freely. Ordinary household ammonia, which acts as a formaldehyde scavenger, can further reduce outgassing. Paint it on the boards and let it dry. Be sure to work in a well-ventilated area. If possible, coat the particleboard with a sealant following the aging and ammonia treatments. Formaldehyde levels in the room can be further reduced with good ventilation both inside the room and, if possible, below the floor joists. Finally, you can avoid the problem almost entirely by using plywoods, most of which are glued with phenol-formaldehyde adhesives. This glue emits far less gas than the urea-formaldehyde adhesives used for most particleboards. [For more information on the hazards of formaldehyde, write the Formaldehyde Institute, 1075 Central Park Ave., Scarsdale, N.Y. 10583, or the Center for Occupational Hazards, 5 Beekman St., New York, N.Y. 10038.]

Toxic dusts from plywood and particleboard—*Products like plywood and particleboard are constructed with formaldehyde glues and since I use a lot of them, I wonder about the danger of breathing dust when cutting them. I have built a shroud for my table saw and connected it to a shop vacuum. This setup reduces the dust level, but does it limit exposure to possible toxins?*

—John M. Gaffin, Gualala, Calif.

MICHAEL McCANN REPLIES: Formaldehyde from glues used in woodworking shops is a real health concern for two reasons: it is a suspected carcinogen, and breathing it can sensitize some people so that they experience allergic reactions when exposed subsequently. The chemical is released when materials glued with formaldehyde adhesives are cut or processed in woodshops. In fact, a certain level of "outgassing" releases formaldehyde into the air even when the panels are in storage. Dust masks are of little help because the formaldehyde is in gaseous form. Probably the best way to minimize the hazard is to install a dust collection system that exhausts air and dust outside the shop itself. Although it will raise utility bills by pumping heat out during the winter, this ventilation method will reduce formaldehyde levels. Pending more conclusive data on the cancer-causing effects of formaldehyde, those exposed to it should watch out for such allergic reactions as asthma, skin problems, headaches or other medical symptoms that may have no other clear cause. Once you are sensitized to the chemical, you can get allergic reactions from many sources including carpets, insulation and a range of synthetic fabrics.

As Dries the Air, So Shrinks the Wood

Why woodworkers keep a weather eye on relative humidity

by R. Bruce Hoadley

Most woodworkers realize that wood moves, shrinking and swelling according to its moisture content. Accordingly, we use joints and constructions that allow for a moderate amount of wood movement, and many of us now use moisture meters to ensure that our wood has been dried to a safe level. But a one-time check of moisture content isn't enough. Here in the northeast, you can take delivery of wood kiln-dried to 7% moisture content, but if you then store it in an unheated garage, it will gradually adsorb moisture from the air and increase to a new level of up to 14%, which, if unanticipated, would come as an unpleasant surprise.

The amount of moisture in wood balances and adjusts to the relative humidity of the air around it. Assessing the humidity of the air in shop or storage areas, therefore, is as important as working with wood that has been properly dried in the first place. An extremely dry or damp period may not last long enough to cause much dimensional change in a board, but moisture exchange in the board's surface layer, which takes place immediately, can cause disheartening problems with glues and finishes.

Equilibrium moisture content—One sometimes comes across wood that has been sitting in a well-ventilated, unheated barn for thirty or forty years. It probably reached its lowest moisture content within the first two or three years, and it is not any drier or more stable today than it was then. In wood, *moisture content* (MC) is the ratio (expressed as a percent) of the weight of water in a piece of wood to the weight of the wood if it were completely dry. Green wood may start off with more than 100% moisture content (the sapwood of green sugar pine is actually more than twice as much water as wood, averaging 219% MC), but it will commonly be dried to about 7% to 9% MC for woodworking purposes. Water is held in the wood in two ways: *free water*, held in the cell

---

Weather, temperature and humidity

Weather systems bring air masses having a certain *absolute humidity,* the actual amount of moisture in the air at a given time, expressed in grains per cubic foot (there are 7,000 grains in a pound). Because the maximum amount of water the air can hold depends on the temperature of the air, temperature determines the upper limit of absolute humidity.

As shown at right, at 70°F the air can hold 8 gr./cu. ft., whereas at 41°F the air can hold only 3 gr./cu. ft. We naturally associate cold weather with low absolute humidity and hot weather with high absolute humidity. It isn't absolute humidity, however, that causes the problems for woodworkers but relative humidity. And where relative humidity is concerned, the generalization does not always hold true. A hot summer day can be dry; winters can be cold and damp.

Relative humidity (RH) is the ratio (expressed as a percent) of the amount of water in the air at a given temperature to the amount it could hold at that temperature. Since air at 70°F could hold 8 gr./cu. ft., if it actually held only 4 gr./cu. ft., the RH would be 50%; if it held 2 gr./cu. ft., the RH would be 25%, and so forth.

Dew point is the temperature at which air of a given absolute humidity becomes saturated. As an example, air that contains 4 gr./cu. ft. has a dew point of 49.3°F. That is, when cooled to 49.3°F the air will be saturated and therefore will be at 100% RH. If it gets any colder, moisture will condense out. —*R.B.H.*

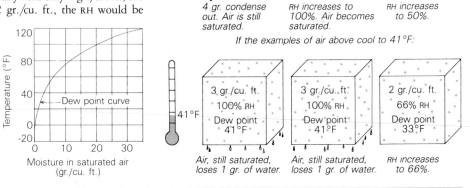

Humidity   *Boxes represent a cubic foot of air.*

If the examples of air above cool to 49°F:

4 gr. condense out. Air is still saturated.   RH increases to 100%. Air becomes saturated.   RH increases to 50%.

If the examples of air above cool to 41°F:

Air, still saturated, loses 1 gr. of water.   Air, still saturated, loses 1 gr. of water.   RH increases to 66%.

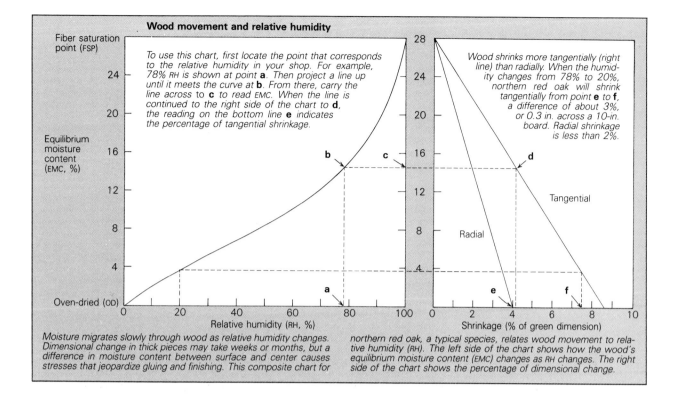

Wood movement and relative humidity

*To use this chart, first locate the point that corresponds to the relative humidity in your shop. For example, 78% RH is shown at point **a**. Then project a line up until it meets the curve at **b**. From there, carry the line across to **c** to read EMC. When the line is continued to the right side of the chart to **d**, the reading on the bottom line **e** indicates the percentage of tangential shrinkage.*

*Wood shrinks more tangentially (right line) than radially. When the humidity changes from 78% to 20%, northern red oak will shrink tangentially from point **e** to **f**, a difference of about 3%, or 0.3 in. across a 10-in. board. Radial shrinkage is less than 2%.*

Fiber saturation point (FSP)

Equilibrium moisture content (EMC, %)

Oven-dried (OD)

Relative humidity (RH, %)

Tangential

Radial

Shrinkage (% of green dimension)

Moisture migrates slowly through wood as relative humidity changes. Dimensional change in thick pieces may take weeks or months, but a difference in moisture content between surface and center causes stresses that jeopardize gluing and finishing. This composite chart for northern red oak, a typical species, relates wood movement to relative humidity (RH). The left side of the chart shows how the wood's equilibrium moisture content (EMC) changes as RH changes. The right side of the chart shows the percentage of dimensional change.

cavities, and *bound water,* held within the cell walls themselves. When wood dries, it loses free water until the moisture content drops to about 30%; from then on it loses bound water. As the cells lose bound water they shrink, creating stresses that can lead to checking and warping.

Even after kiln-drying, wood cells continue to lose and gain moisture until there is an equilibrium between the amount of bound water and the surrounding air's *relative humidity* (RH, explained in the box on the facing page). When this balance with RH is reached, the MC of the wood is called the *equilibrium moisture content* (EMC). Note the left side of the chart above, which is based on red oak, a typical species; other species differ only slightly. Generally the EMC can vary from 0% (when oven-dried, in effect at 0% RH) to a maximum of about 30% (in an atmosphere where the air is saturated with moisture, in effect at 100% RH). A 30% moisture content is all the bound water the cells can hold, the *fiber saturation point* (FSP). The wood will not adsorb more moisture from the air than this, although if rained on or soaked it would absorb some free water again at the surface layers.

Left outdoors (as in a typical drying pile), the wood will arrive at an average equilibrium moisture content depending on the average relative humidity of the area. This is called its *air-dried moisture content,* and once the wood reaches this point it will more or less stay there, varying slightly with environmental fluctuations. Air-dried moisture content can vary widely from region to region—wood reaches a different EMC in southwestern deserts than it does in the northwest's rain forests. EMC can vary depending on local conditions within an area; the windward side of a lake, for instance, is measurably drier than the leeward. As I mentioned earlier, air-dried wood reaches an equilibrium at about 14% EMC in the northeast. This is because the relative humidity here averages about 75%. In your own part of the country, you can determine the EMC for air-dried wood if you know the average RH.

Some people define EMC as *surface moisture content,* an appropriate reminder that the wood cells at the surface attain an immediate equilibrium with the surrounding air. When we put a finish on a wooden object, it slows down moisture exchange, giving some protection from sudden changes in relative humidity. And even raw wood takes time to adjust fully—the rate of moisture migration into wood is quite slow, and one or two days of high humidity are not enough to cause much dimensional change in thick pieces. But even temporary change in a raw-wood surface layer can have critical consequences, and abrupt changes in relative humidity, particularly in the workshop, can cause serious problems: drawers that will never work right, faulty glue joints, finishes that won't shine or, at worst, won't adhere at all. These problems can come as a surprise because human beings are relatively insensitive to changes in relative humidity. While the average person can estimate indoor temperatures within a few degrees, sensitivity to relative humidity is quite another matter. We become acclimated to gradual seasonal changes, and our sense of "normal" adjusts to summer humidity and winter dryness.

I'm frequently reminded of this in my daily work. Our laboratory has an experimental room closely controlled at 72°F and 50% RH. When I enter it in winter it seems oppressively muggy and damp, while in summer it seems cool and dry. We cannot trust our senses, but must rely on instruments such as those shown on page 69 to tell us of conditions that to us may feel only moderately uncomfortable, but to a woodworking project may spell disaster.

Effects of changes in RH—The chart above correlates dimensional change in wood to EMC and RH. My basement, surrounded by bedrock, is also my workshop, and its RH can swing from more than 90% in August (relative humidity rises when hot, muggy air is cooled by the basement) to 5% in midwinter when I have been using the woodstove. Extremes of this magnitude can cause as much as a ½-in. variation in the width of a 10-in., flatsawn red oak board. Wood exchanges moisture with the air fastest on the surface and through the end grain. Abrupt changes in RH mean that the inside of a piece of wood is at an EMC (and size) different from the surface. A sudden dry day can cause microscopic surface checking that will interfere with the quality or adhesion of finishes. Wood has a certain elasticity that allows it to absorb stresses caused by moisture changes, but this elasticity can be lost. A sudden damp day can have somewhat the same effect as a dry one—the surface, restrained from swelling by the center, becomes *compression set* (that is, the wood cells become deformed). When the surface redries, checks result.

EMC can interfere with gluing. Silicone adhesives will not bond properly if the EMC of the wood surface is too high, and plastic resin glues (urea-formaldehyde) will not bond well if the wood is *drier* than about 7% MC. As the left side of the chart on p. 93 shows, one might encounter problems with urea-formaldehyde glues when the shop RH drops below 40%.

While thick pieces of wood may take days, weeks or even months to completely adjust to a new RH, thin veneers can reach equilibrium within an hour or less. Thus they don't surface-check, but they may quickly undergo the maximum overall change in size. I would not work veneer in my basement when its RH is approaching either extreme.

With the RH in my basement so unstable, even moderate-size pieces of wood, drawer parts for instance, can move enough from one weekend to the next to make precision cuts meaningless. Although I manage to store my wood someplace else, upstairs usually, in a closet, under the bed, in the mudroom or wherever, it still leaves me with the problem of what to do with projects that are half-done. I routinely wrap wood sculptures in plastic between work sessions to protect them, because changes in RH can cause extreme stress between the center and the surface of a thick block. Plastic film or bags have the same effect as a coat of finish—while they can't maintain the moisture content of a piece of wood indefinitely, they can isolate the wood against drastic responses to temporary swings by making changes slow and uniform.

Controlling RH—The ideal moisture content for wood is not necessarily the numerical mean between the highest and lowest extremes, but depends on the yearlong seasonal variation. Indoors, the average RH in the northeast averages close to 40%, mostly due to heating in winter, which commonly lowers levels to 20% for weeks at a time. Red oak furniture, therefore, will eventually reach an average EMC indoors of about 7% to 8%. This is the reason woodworkers in the northeast start out with wood dried to this level. Our workshops, then, should be maintained at a humidity level of about 35% to 40% in order to keep our stock at a 7% to 8% EMC. One would do well to think: "My lumber should be at an equilibrium with 40% relative humidity," rather than thinking only about the wood's 7.5% moisture content. This approach has the advantage of automatically accommodating the different EMCs of various wood species and of wood products such as particleboard, fiberboard and hardboard.

Without its being our intent, many of our daily activities affect indoor RH. In our homes and workshops, we routinely modify temperature by heating and cooling the air. If we increase the temperature while the absolute humidity remains unchanged, the relative humidity will be lowered. If we cool the air, such as happens when I ventilate my cool basement with warmer air from outside, the relative humidity will rise. Routine activities such as cooking and washing may release surprising amounts of water. Mopping a kitchen floor and allowing it to dry, for instance, may add several *pounds* of water to the indoor air. So will moving a quantity of green wood into a storage area filled with wood that has been carefully dried. On the other hand, air conditioners and dehumidifiers cool the air below its dew point. The water condenses out and drips away. Muggy summer air can lose so much moisture as it passes through an air conditioner that it will be comfortably dry when it mingles with the warmer air inside the room. The principles involved above are the basic ways we can control humidity. Some of the methods are expensive, and corrective methods are, in the end, based on economics.

One key factor in deliberately controlling humidity is the size of the area—the smaller and better insulated, the more isolated from volumes of outdoor air, the easier (and cheaper) the job. It is probably futile to try to control RH in a drafty area with leaky doors and windows. Where an entire workshop is too large to be brought under control at a reasonable cost, part of it can be sealed with polyethylene sheet, and small heaters or dehumidifiers can be used to lower RH. If RH must be raised, a humidifier such as the vaporizers sold in drugstores for respiratory relief (about $15 and up) will suffice. In a tight shop, even a pan of water placed on a heater outlet may be enough.

The individual woodworker must decide how much variation he can stand. Rough drawshaving of green-wood chair parts can be done at just about any RH. A marquetarian, however, should monitor humidity very carefully, in both workshop and storage area.

One way to keep an eye on RH is to listen to weather reports, and perhaps to arrange a visit with a local meteorologist (television, radio or university) to get information about local high and low periods and the times of year when drastic change is most likely. This, combined with good instruments, will give you a jump on the most dangerous periods.

In winter, with my woodstove drawing in and heating large amounts of already dry winter air, there is a practical limit to the RH that I can maintain in my basement shop. As it gets to a reasonable level, water condenses on cold walls and windows. In summer the outdoor temperature may reach into the 90s, with RH levels above 85% for days at a time. Letting this air into my basement is disastrous. It is frustrating to get ready to spend a weekend on a project, only to discover that low or high humidity makes it unwise to work. For many of us, woodworking is a periodic or a sporadic activity. We can, perhaps, choose our work times to coincide with suitable shop conditions. Someday, when I get to it, I'll partition and insulate part of my basement, at least enough for storage, and I'll use a small heater, dehumidifier and humidifier to get me through the extremes. In the meantime, I'll watch my instruments, exercise restraint, and keep exhorting woodworkers to pay attention to humidity.   □

R. Bruce Hoadley is professor of wood technology at the University of Massachusetts at Amherst, and author of Understanding Wood, *published by The Taunton Press, PO Box 355, Newtown, Conn. 06470.*

Measuring relative humidity

Perhaps the most familiar instrument for measuring relative humidity is the dial-type hygrometer commonly found in home weather stations. This type uses a hygroscopic material, such as animal skin or hair, connected to the pointer on the dial. It has the distinct advantage of providing continuous readings at a glance. But it is subject to inaccuracy for several reasons: the sensing element may react differently to rising humidity than it does to falling, it may lose accuracy after being exposed to extremes, and it can be quickly contaminated by sawdust. These instruments are cheap ($15 and up in 1983) and convenient, but most of them come with inadequate directions. If you use one, keep it clean, mount it where there will be good air circulation around it, and check its calibration regularly.

The instrument most frequently used to calibrate other hygrometers is the sling psychrometer (about $35). It consists of two thermometers mounted side by side. One thermometer bulb is covered with a dampened wick. As water evaporates from the wick, it lowers the temperature of the wet-bulb thermometer. The difference is called the *wet-bulb depression*. On dry days, the water evaporates more rapidly than it does on damp days, so the drier the day, the greater the wet-bulb depression. Wet-bulb depression can be converted (by consulting a chart such as the one be-

low) to relative humidity. To ensure that the air around the wet bulb does not become saturated with evaporating moisture, the instrument is swung in vertical circles (by means of its swiveled handle) until the wet-bulb temperature no longer drops.

A variation of the sling psychrometer is the stationary dual-bulb hygrometer ($10 and up). You can easily make one from a pair of matched thermometers. Wicks can be made from stretchy cotton slipped tightly over one bulb with the free end dangling in a small reservoir. It's best to use distilled water so that mineral deposits don't accumulate in the wick. Keep a good airflow (fan it until the wet-bulb temperature no longer drops), avoid mounting the instrument where conditions such as direct sunlight would affect the dry-bulb reading, and keep the wick clean.—*R.B.H.*

Sources—Here are some suppliers who carry instruments for monitoring RH:
Abbeon Cal. Inc., 123-78A Gray St., Santa Barbara, Calif. 93101 (805) 966-0810
The Ben Meadows Co., PO Box 80549, Atlanta, Ga. 30366 (800) 241-6401
Edmund Scientific Co., 5975 Edscorp Bldg., Barrington, N.J. 08007 (609) 547-3488
Fisher Scientific Co., 711 Forbes Ave., Pittsburgh, Pa. 15219 (412) 562-8300
Fine Tool & Wood Store, 724 West Britton Rd., Oklahoma City, Okla. 73114, Tel: (800) 255-9800
TSI Company, PO Box 151, Flanders, N.J. 07836, Tel: (201) 584-3417
Sporty's Tool Shop, Clermont County Airport, Batavia, Ohio 45103 (513) 732-2411

Part of a dry-kiln control system, this cellulose wafer (left) reacts almost instantly to changing RH levels to yield EMC readings directly, without reference to conversion charts. Available from Lignomat USA (14345 NE Morris Court, Portland, Ore. 97230), the device currently costs $80 without the meter, mostly due to the cost of the kiln-proof holder—the wafers themselves, which are replaced every three weeks, are only about 35¢.

Reading a psychrometer

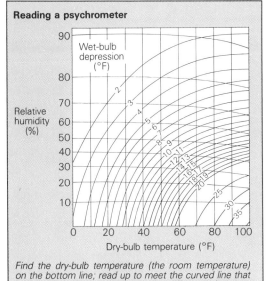

Relative humidity (%) / Dry-bulb temperature (°F)

Wet-bulb depression (°F)

Find the dry-bulb temperature (the room temperature) on the bottom line; read up to meet the curved line that indicates wet-bulb depression (the difference between wet-bulb and dry-bulb readings), and then read the RH, as indicated by the lines numbered at the left.

Instruments to help you avoid the frustrating woodworking problems caused by uncontrolled relative humidity in work and storage areas. Clockwise from upper left: dial hygrometer, dual-bulb hygrometer, sling psychrometer.

Health Hazards in Woodworking

Simple precautions minimize risks

by Stanley N. Wellborn

Industrial woodworkers have long recognized the risks of their trade. But it has been only in the past few years that artists and craftsmen have become concerned about—or even aware of— the many hidden dangers in woodworking.

Of course everyone recognizes those hazards that cause immediate and traumatic injury—blades that cut fingers and limbs, wood chips and fragments that fly into eyes, loose clothing or long hair that catches in whirling machinery, smashed fingers and toes, muscle strains from heavy lifting. But now medical authorities in the United States, Canada and England cite a number of insidious causes of disease that can be directly attributed to woodworking. Their list includes wood dust, sap and oils, mold and fungus, chemical additives, toxic solvents and adhesives, vibration and noise.

A diligent search of medical literature, or a chat with an industrial hygiene specialist, will turn up dozens of horror stories about the health hazards of woodworking. For example, the 43-year-old woodworker who had operated a lathe for more than 25 years and became worried about a persistent sinus irritation and sore throat. His doctor prescribed a standard treatment, yet the condition did not improve. Finally, lab tests revealed cancer of the nasal passages. Or the art student who broke out in a rash, with blisters resembling second-degree burns, shortly after she began to sculpt wood. When she stopped woodworking, her skin healed.

The mere existence of a medical case history doesn't mean every woodworker will succumb to serious disease; the biggest unknown factor is often the size of the risk. In most cases, woodworkers will find they can take adequate precautionary measures for relatively little cost. Some of the common and most basic protective measures are described in the box on page 72. Woodworkers who notice something wrong with their health would be wise to suspect something in the shop; some potential problems are discussed below.

Respiratory ailments

Health authorities warn that woodworkers should be most on guard against inhaling foreign substances.

To most woodworkers, concern about the cancer-causing potential of wood dust overrides all other health worries. Indeed, this concern appears justified, at least on the surface. Woodworkers are 500 times more likely to have certain types of nasal cancer than non-woodworkers. However, the risk of developing cancer solely through exposure to wood dust is quite low.

Stan Wellborn is an associate editor of U.S. News & World Report.

"The statistics on cancer in woodworkers can be made to sound quite alarming," says Dr. Julian A. Waller of the University of Vermont Medical School and an authority on health hazards in the arts. "But the actual risk advances only from 'extremely rare' to 'rare.' Only one woodworker in 1,400 will get this cancer, and at that after an average of 40 years of exposure."

Nevertheless, in various health hazard evaluations conducted by the National Institute of Occupational Health and Safety (NIOSH) in Cincinnati, Ohio, investigators have concluded that wood dust is at least a contributing factor in the development of some other types of cancer. In a report prepared after an evaluation of the Cooper Union School of Art in New York City, the Institute cites studies pointing out that "cancers of the larynx, tonsils, tongue and lung have been reported to have resulted from inhalation of wood dust" among furniture workers in England and Sweden.

In addition, the NIOSH report mentions that many researchers have found that the normal functions of the mucous membranes in the nose, throat and lungs were impaired in workers exposed to wood dust for more than ten years.

Among the most recent and thorough research on this problem is a study done by Dr. Samuel Milham, Jr., of the State Department of Social and Health Services in Olympia, Wash. He reviewed the death records of more than 16,000 members of the United Brotherhood of Carpenters and Joiners of America, and found that the results supported the hypothesis that wood contains carcinogens. The study also found an above-average incidence of leukemia and lymphoma among millwrights, lumber workers and cabinetmakers.

Although risk of cancer from exposure to wood does appear to be low for most woodcrafters, the incidence of other forms of respiratory illness is high. At one time or another, virtually all woodworkers have suffered irritation of the upper respiratory tract after breathing sawdust. The condition is usually transient and produces coughing, wheezing and tightness in the chest. Frequently, however, long-term exposure produces "fogged lungs" on X-rays and a type of occupational asthma that can become virtually permanent.

Redwood dust, for example, is the cause of sequoiosis, an acute illness that resembles pneumonia. It usually appears within a few hours after exposure, and its symptoms are shortness of breath, bronchio-constriction, dry coughing, chills, sweating, fever and general malaise. Repeated episodes of this ailment can cause permanent scarring of lung tissue.

Wood dust from another tree, the Western or Canadian red cedar, causes similar symptoms that can develop into asthma or rhinitis, an inflammation of the nasal passages.

Medical researchers believe the causative agent in red cedar is plicatic acid, which is thought to give the wood its characteristic fragrance. Lumber workers in the Pacific Northwest are frequently affected by cedar dust. One medical case history tells of a 30-year-old worker who could breathe at night only by kneeling on his hands and knees. When he left the woodworking industry, he regained his health.

Another source of respiratory difficulties is the mold and fungus that grow in damp areas of the shop, particularly in piles of sawdust. Mold has also been known to cause serious reactions in skin and fingernails after continuous exposure.

Occupational health experts agree that the obvious and best way to prevent respiratory problems is to cut down the amount of airborne dust in the shop. Although no specific environmental standards for allergenic wood dust have been established by the federal Occupational Safety and Health Administration (OSHA), the American Conference of Governmental Industrial Hygienists has set a provisional (and very low) limit on ''nuisance dust'' of 5 mg per cubic meter of air space. A few minutes of steady hand-sanding normally produce about 15 mg per cubic meter in the immediate work area; a portable or stationary belt sander will generate about 150 mg per cubic meter. Without ventilation, the dust will remain airborne for hours and spread through the shop.

Skin irritations and allergies

A large number of wood species will produce skin irritation or glandular swelling in sensitive individuals who are directly exposed to their dust, oil or sap. Some woods, such as West Indian satinwood and mansonia, are classified as ''primary irritants'' because they are highly toxic and are likely to produce skin eruptions or blisters in most people on first contact. Others, such as cocobolo, are ''sensitizers'' that may cause allergic dermatitis only after repeated exposure.

A number of domestic U. S. woods have been mentioned in medical literature as causing skin irritations, such as hives and rashes, but such skin reactions are actually quite infrequent, occurring in less than 2% of the population. However, the problem becomes much more serious with tropical or exotic woods. A partial list of toxic timbers is given in the box on this page.

Dermatologists who have investigated wood allergies note several common characteristics. Allergic reactions are more pronounced during the summer, or when a person's skin is moist from perspiration, or when the wood dust itself is damp. Reactions are more frequent among persons older than 40. Freshly cut wood is much more likely to be an irritant than older, seasoned wood. Occasionally, a wood species from one geographic area will not affect a woodworker, while the same species grown somewhere else will.

In most cases, it is the heartwood rather than the sapwood that is responsible for skin allergies, and it is the accessory substances, or ''extractives,'' from the heartwood that produce the toxic effects. Extractives are whatever can be leached out of the wood (with water or other solvents) without changing its structure. These powerful chemical components—resins, alkaloids, tannins, acids, salts and gums—vary widely from species to species and even from log to log. In some trees they make up as much as 20% of the wood structure. Most woods contain about 4% to 10% extractives. The effect of extractives can be devastating. One report cited a serious outbreak of dermatitis among workers at an English

Toxic Woods

This list includes woods that are known to cause allergic, toxic, infectious or respiratory reactions. Although researchers point out that not everyone is sensitive to these woods, they warn that woodworkers should be particularly cautious when sanding or milling them. The category ''respiratory ailments'' includes bronchial disorders, asthma, rhinitis and mucosal irritations; ''skin and eye allergies'' includes contact dermatitis, conjunctivitis, itching and rashes.

—S. N. W.

Respiratory ailments
Skin and eye allergies

•		Arbor vitae (*Thuja standishii*)
	•	Ayan (*Distemonanthus benthamianus*)
	•	Blackwood, African (*Dalbergia melanoxylon*)
•	•	Boxwood, Knysna (*Gonioma kamassi*)
	•	Cashew (*Anacardium occidentale*)
•	•	Cedar, Western red (*Thuja plicata*)
	•	Cocobolo (*Dalbergia retusa*)
	•	Cocus (*Brya ebenus*)
•		Dahoma (*Piptadeniastrum africanum*)
•	•	Ebony (*Diospyros*)
•	•	Greenheart (*Ocotea rodiaei*)
•	•	Guarea (*Guarea thompsonii*)
•	•	Ipe [lapacho] (*Tabebuia ipe*)
•		Iroko (*Chlorophora excelsa*)
	•	Katon (*Sandoricum indicum*)
•	•	Mahogany, African (*Khaya ivorensis*)
	•	Mahogany, American (*Swietenia macrophylla*)
•	•	Makore (*Tieghemella heckelii*)
•	•	Mansonia (*Mansonia altissima*)
•	•	Obeche (*Triplochiton scleroxylon*)
•	•	Opepe (*Nauclea trillesii*)
•	•	Peroba rosa (*Aspidosperma peroba*)
•	•	Peroba, white (*Paratecoma peroba*)
	•	Ramin (*Gonystylus bancanus*)
	•	Rosewood, Brazilian (*Dalbergia nigra*)
	•	Rosewood, East Indian (*Dalbergia latifolia*)
	•	Satinwood, Ceylon (*Chloroxylon swietenia*)
	•	Satinwood, West Indian (*Fagara flava*)
•		Sequoia Redwood (*Sequoia sempervirens*)
•		Sneezewood (*Ptaeroxylon obliquum*)
	•	Stavewood (*Dysoxylum muelleri*)
	•	Sucupira (*Bowdichia nitida*)
	•	Teak (*Tectona grandis*)
•	•	Wenge (*Millettia laurentii*)

This information has been taken from:
National Institute of Occupational Safety and Health
International Labor Organization *Encyclopedia of Occupational Safety and Health*
Sculpture in Wood by Jack C. Rich, Da Capo Press, New York, 1977.
''Toxic Woods'' by Brian Woods and C. D. Calnan, *British Journal of Dermatology*, Vol. 95, Supplement 13, 1976 (an excellent source on skin reactions to woods, with case histories and an inclusive list of toxic species).

furniture plant that used mansonia wood. The entire operation had to be shut down for weeks.

Obviously, the occasional case of dermatitis won't discourage woodworkers from continuing to use exotic woods. The best path to follow is one of prevention, including dust control, protective clothing, washing and shower facilities and barrier creams, such as DuPont's Pro-Tek. Persons who suspect they are sensitive to certain woods should have a doctor do a skin-patch test to find the cause of the allergy.

Pesticides and preservatives introduced to wood while it is being timbered, processed and shipped may also cause dermatitis. These include everything from the highly toxic pentachlorophenol to the relatively innocuous polyethylene glycol (PEG) and denatured alcohol. Other chemicals often used in domestic wood processing are potassium dichromate, ethyl triethanol amine, glycol humectant, naphthenic acid, copper hydrate and zinc naphthenate. Standard threshold limit values (TLV's) based on current medical knowledge have been established for many of these chemicals, with the intention of protecting people whose jobs expose them constantly to these substances. But many chemicals banned in this country are routinely used by foreign loggers and shipping companies to prevent insect infestation, mold growth and dry rot in transit.

It is almost impossible for a woodworker to ascertain which additives have been used. Michael McCann, an industrial hygienist and chemist with the Center for Occupational Hazards in New York City, says, "The best procedure to follow is to assume that the wood being used has been processed with dangerous chemicals and take the necessary precautions. It is also important to remember that it is not uncommon for woodworkers to toil 12 or more hours a day for weeks on end when preparing for a show or fair, or just plain getting caught up with a work order. Under these conditions, it becomes doubtful that established TLV's for an eight-hour work day are applicable.''

Dr. Bertram W. Carnow, professor of occupational and environmental medicine at the University of Illinois, points out that the key factor in determining toxic levels for an individual is what he calls ''total body burden''—the sum that each person's metabolism and general health will accommodate. ''Liquid or solid particles such as fumes or vapors in aerosol form, cigarette smoke and other exposures in addition to those from materials used at work all contribute to the burden on the lungs, skin and other organs, and should be minimized,'' says Dr. Carnow.

Many skin irritations are caused by contact with adhesives and solvents that dry the skin and make it more subject to infection. In addition, fumes from such chemicals often are not only toxic if inhaled or swallowed, but also highly flammable.

Epoxies, for example, can cause severe blistering and scaling. Liquid, uncured epoxy resin and hardener will cause adverse reactions in more than 40% of all workers who come in contact with it. Synthetic adhesives, such as urea-formalde-

Preventive Measures

Few occupational health experts would advocate giving up one's craft unless there were overwhelming evidence that a person's health was being seriously impaired, or that an irreversible allergy to materials had developed. In virtually all cases, simple modifications of the working environment and a few changes in work habits will resolve any hazards to health.

Dr. Julian A. Waller believes that ''a reasonably good margin of protection'' can be obtained in most shops for under $100. He and other authorities in the field suggest the following preventive measures for woodworkers:

Adequate ventilation is the basic, and probably most important, requirement of a safe shop. The exhaust system should begin as close as possible to the source of dust or fumes, so they cannot accumulate and will flow rapidly away from the worker's face. The exhaust should be vented to the outside whenever possible, and dust should be collected in a bag or bin. A shop vacuum with a homemade clamp that holds the nozzle near the source of dust and chips is a relatively inexpensive way to remove particles from the air. Fresh air should be allowed to enter the working area freely.

Shop cleanliness is another fundamental. A general cleanup is recommended at the end of each working day. When not in use, jars, cans and bags should be sealed, and spills should be wiped up promptly. For fine sawdust and sanding dust, the best cleanup methods are wet cloths, wet mopping or industrial-type wet vacuuming. Dry sweeping or blowing with an air hose only stirs up the dust.

Personal hygiene also plays an important role. Dirty clothes, long fingernails and unwashed skin and hair can trap dust, solids and dried liquids, and thus exposure continues even when the woodworker leaves the shop. Plastic disposable coveralls, gloves and hats can help reduce these hazards. Work clothes and equipment should be washed separately from other household items.

Protective equipment such as face masks, respirators, eye goggles, ear plugs or muffs, and plastic or rubber gloves are essential for certain operations. Many safety devices, such as respirators and ear protectors, are rated for effectiveness by the federal government or the American National Standards Institute in New York City. A simple filter-type respirator will keep exotic dusts out of your lungs.

Recent workshops on health hazards in the arts have placed heavy responsibility on craftsmen for maintaining awareness about medical matters related to their work. Most doctors are not well informed about occupational hazards associated with the crafts, and many of the cumulative diseases do not become apparent until their damage is fairly extensive. Symptoms of slow-developing occupational diseases are often attributed to another cause or dismissed as psychosomatic.

For these reasons, health authorities suggest four guidelines for woodworkers:

—Know as much as possible about the woods and other materials you use, what diseases they can cause, and what the danger signs are.

—Suspect that a health problem may be related to woodworking if it improves after a layoff of a few days and gets worse when work is resumed.

—Have a physician arrange a pulmonary-function test every two or three years. This test detects lung problems much sooner than X-rays can.

—If a doctor's diagnosis or treatment does not seem satisfactory, consult specialists on particular problems.

—S. N. W.

hyde and phenol-formaldehyde resin, are other irritants with which woodworkers commonly come in contact. Although few woodworkers have occasion to use uncured formaldehyde or phenol resins, they should be aware that "thermal degradation" of these compounds has been reported when heat produced during high-speed machining of wood breaks down glues into separate components, or produces entirely new compounds.

Vibration disease

Another woodworking hazard, well-defined over the years by occupational health specialists, is a disease that develops and spreads slowly through the muscles and circulatory system of the fingers, hands and forearms. Vibration disease is closely related to an affliction known as Raynaud's phenomenon, and is triggered by lengthy use of machinery that vibrates in the 40 to 3,000 cycle-per-second frequency range.

Most woodworkers have experienced a rhythmic tingling in the hands and arms after using such vibrating tools as orbital sanders, chain saws and pneumatic chisels. In most cases, the spasms disappear within an hour. Now, recent medical research among lumbermen in Canada has shown that serious side effects of this reaction may develop, although the process may take from several months to ten years. Smoking and cold weather tend to hasten the onset of the problem. In some cases, tendonitis of the elbow and shoulder may set in. Eventually, numbness and a heightened sensitivity to cold and humidity will occur, and the fingers and palms of the hands will become extremely pale—giving the condition its more common name of "white hand" or "dead fingers." In a few extreme cases, it has been necessary to amputate the fingers.

"We know that vibrations may cause definite lesions to the hands with serious potential consequences," says Dr. Gilles Laroche, a cardiovascular surgeon with the Hotel-Dieu Hospital in Quebec City, in the March 7, 1977, issue of the Canadian periodical *Maclean's*. "Once severe occlusive arterial disease is established, the condition is permanent and little or no improvement will result from cessation of work. In fact, the condition may worsen in a large proportion of patients."

Safety experts advise that cutting down on extensive use of vibrating tools is the best way to prevent this condition, although some authorities have urged tool manufacturers to build shock absorbers into vibrating equipment. Many chain saws now have rubber bumpers between the engine and the handles, and users report them nearly vibration-free. OSHA has not set a vibration standard for tools.

Noise

High levels of noise have long been recognized by industrial safety technicians as unsafe to workers. In a typical wood shop, decibel levels often exceed industry limits and may cause hearing loss.

One study cited by NIOSH found that nearly one shop worker in four had suffered some permanent damage to hearing because of high noise levels from operating machinery. Other studies have found that excessive noise can also contribute to heart problems and gastrointestinal disorders.

Noise levels are measured in decibels (dB) on a logarithmic scale on which every increase of 10 dB means a tenfold increase in noise intensity. Ordinary conversation averages about 60 dB.

OSHA has set a maximum permissible average noise level of 90 dB per eight-hour working day. The permissible noise exposure rises to a maximum of 115 dB, a level that can be tolerated for only 15 minutes or less per day. A circular saw produces between 100 and 109 dB, a medium-sized woodworking shop in full operation averages about 110 dB, and a chain saw may peak at 130 dB. One report cited by NIOSH states that "operators of saws, planers, routers, molding machines, shapers, jointers and sanders are exposed to average overall sound-pressure levels that exceed 95 dB. For several of these operations, the average may be as high as 115 dB."

Protection from noise involves damping machinery with mufflers and sound-absorbing material, keeping machines in good repair and well-oiled, and mounting machines on rubber bases to reduce vibration and rattling. In addition, OSHA-approved ear muffs and ear plugs—rather than improvised cotton or wax devices—are recommended. In general, industrial hygienists recommend ear muffs as the most effective sound reducer.

Fire hazards

Although most woodworkers are extremely cautious when using flammable materials, the danger persists. The National Fire Protection Association reports that the combination of machinery, wood, volatile fumes and finely dispersed dust in woodworking shops results in scores of fires and explosions annually. Small grains of wood dust, when scattered throughout a confined area, can explode with tremendous force if ignited by a spark or match. If flammable solvents are present, the hazard becomes much greater.

Fire prevention authorities agree that the best way to curb the possibility of fire is adequate ventilation. If dust and fumes are vented by a vacuum or "cyclone" air cleaner, and fresh air is continually available, most fire hazards will be sharply reduced.

Campaign begins

Although many potential hazards have now been identified, there is still a great deal that remains unknown. Several state and national art and craft groups have begun a campaign to inform their members about occupational risks, and to seek more government assistance in improving environmental health and safety factors for the craft community. Gail Barazani of Chicago, who is editor of the newsletter "Hazards in the Arts," terms these dangers a "silent enemy" that can seriously harm the health of artists, craftspersons, hobbyists, and their families.

Most of the hazards that woodworkers encounter in their craft are obvious ones that will be recognized and dealt with immediately. The less obvious ones require more diligence and attention, along with a determined effort to learn as much as possible about the materials being used. Dr. Waller, a craftsman himself, sums up by observing that the general rule of thumb for safety should be "common sense and simple precautions. That will eliminate virtually all the hazards anyone is likely to experience." □

[AUTHOR'S NOTE: *Clinical Toxicology of Commercial Products* by Gosslin, Hodge, Gleason and Smith is a standard medical reference text. Another source, with more detailed information, is *Health Hazards Manual for Artists* by Michael McCann, Center for Occupational Hazards, 5 Beekman St., New York, N.Y. 10038.]

Respiratory Hazards
Choosing the right protection

by George Mustoe

When the first woodworker whittled a stick with a sharp rock, millions of years of evolution had already provided safety devices to protect him against the occupational hazards of shaping wood. Living in a landscape sculpted by windstorms and volcanic ash eruptions favored the development of physiological defenses against airborne irritants. Nasal hair filters large particles, while the cilia-lined and mucus-coated respiratory tract keeps all but the smallest dust from reaching the lungs. Unfortunately, nature's defenses are meant to counter occasional dust storms and pollen outbreaks, not the dust and vapors encountered by present-day woodworkers. Though woodworking is relatively clean compared with other manufacturing, woodworkers face two hazards: wood dust produced by sawing and sanding, and toxic vapors emitted by adhesives and finishing agents.

How dangerous is wood dust?—The dust problem has usually been considered to be an unpleasant but unavoidable aspect of the craft. Vacuum filters are often connected to power saws and sanders, but most woodworkers still find themselves breathing more wood than they like, producing the familiar symptoms of sneezing, coughing, runny nose and phlegm. To some degree these are natural reactions, as the body traps and moves dust up and out of the respiratory tract. But the defenses can be overloaded. Just how hazardous is this dust? Inorganic dusts from coal, silica and asbestos have long been known to provoke serious lung damage. Recent research strongly suggests that the relatively larger-sized particles generated by sawing or sanding wood also pose a threat, not to the lungs but to the upper respiratory tract. While some abrasive dust is generated by abrasives themselves, the concentrations are not regarded as hazardous.

A 1968 report in the *British Medical Journal* described an unusually high rate of nasal cancer, *adenocarcinoma*, among furnituremakers in the Oxford area. This disease occurs in only 6 out of 10,000,000 people among the general population each year, compared to 7 out of 10,000 among the furnituremakers, who typically worked with beech, oak and mahogany, often in factories lacking dust-collection systems. The figures suggest that about 2.5% of all woodworkers will develop nasal cancer within 50 years of entering the industry. The disease wasn't found in wood finishers, who typically work in separate shops, suggesting that nasal cancer is linked to dust rather than to chemical exposure. Neither were high cancer rates found among carpenters, who worked mostly outdoors where dust doesn't persist. A 1982 survey of medical records from 12 countries found that 78.5% of nasal adenocarcinoma victims were woodworkers, further indicating the potential hazards associated with dust exposure.

Current data on the relationship between cancer and wood is confusing because woodworkers commonly work with other materials as well. For example, several 1980 reports indicate

If you have a beard, no mask will seal adequately against your face. Instead of shaving, you can wear an air helmet, which blows filtered air over your face. The helmet shown above is 3M's model #W316 ($400 in 1983), available from Direct Safety Co., PO Box 8018, Phoenix, Ariz. 85066.

greater than expected rates of colon, rectal and salivary-gland cancers among woodworkers employed as patternmakers in the U.S. auto industry, but these workers are exposed to plywood, treated lumber, and plastics as well as to solid wood.

Though the relationship between cancer and wood products is just beginning to be explored, particular wood species are definitely known to cause allergenic reactions among many people (see pages 70 through 73). Rosewood, yew, boxwood, cashew, satinwood, teak, ebony and mahogany are among the well noted examples. Western red cedar is particularly notorious because not only is the dust irritating, but the wood contains irritating volatile oils that can evade dust-collection systems. The most detailed descriptions of its effects come from Japan, where occupational asthma was first reported among woodworkers in 1926 after large quantities of cedar were imported from the United States to repair damage done by the Tokyo earthquake. Since 1965, Japanese mill workers and carpenters have again evidenced allergic reactions, as furniture factories have greatly expanded their use of Western red cedar. A 1973 investigation of 1,300 furniture workers revealed that 24.5% suffered some kind of allergic response to red cedar, sometimes developing symptoms within 30 minutes of contact. These symptoms include dermatitis, conjunctivitis, rhinitis and asthma attacks. Sawmill workers are particularly likely to suffer from eye inflammation (conjunctivitis). In Japan, saws are by law equipped with dust collectors, suggesting that irritation comes from exposure to volatile oils. These oils eventually evaporate from the sawn lumber, and respiratory ailments experienced in later processing are more likely dust-induced. In the United States, respiratory irritation has also been linked to inhalation of redwood dust, leading to a form of *pneumonitis* known as "sequoisis." British furniture-makers use the term "mahogany cough" to describe the medical condition *coryza,* an acute inflammation of the nasal membranes accompanied by profuse discharge.

What to do about dust—There are three ways to reduce your exposure to dust. In some situations you can choose another tool that produces less dust; a plane, for example, can substitute for a belt sander. Second, you can trap the dust at its source, using vacuum collection (see the articles on pages 78 to 79 and 80 to 82). Adequate ventilation is the best defense against respiratory dangers, but for those who won't or can't spend the money for a dust-collection and ventilation system, there is a third alternative: you can wear a mask.

Dust masks have been used since Roman times, and simple respirators are described by Pliny the Elder in his *Natural History,* written during the first century AD. Early masks consisted of animal bladders or rags worn over the nose and mouth. During the 1800s, major advances in mask design were aimed primarily at protecting firefighters: masks were developed to filter toxic gases as well as particulates. Chemical warfare during World War I led to further developments. In the United States, this research was led by the Bureau of Mines, which later set performance standards for civilian-use respirators. At present, the National Institute of Occupational Safety and Health (NIOSH) evaluates respirator performance, and specifies acceptability for specific models.

Many woodworkers use "nuisance-dust" masks, which are designed to trap large-diameter, non-toxic particulates. These devices offer fairly good protection for general woodworking, but they are inadequate for dusts released from home insulation, chemically treated lumber or allergenic species. Nuisance-dust masks, though they are light, comfortable and inexpensive, are not manufactured to meet NIOSH standards. The 3M company's popular model #8500 disposable paper mask is available at hardware stores for about 30¢. Another common nuisance-dust mask design, the Norton Bantam model #7200 ($3.50) or the Willson "Dustite" ($3.00), for instance, uses a replaceable filter element (1983 prices).

Given the new-found dangers of wood dust, it is better to use what NIOSH approves as a "toxic-dust" mask, which provides about twice the filtration efficiency of nuisance-dust masks. Disposable types such as those shown below can be purchased locally or from mail-order safety-equipment suppliers. For a permanent facepiece with disposable filter ele-

NIOSH-approved disposable toxic-dust masks include 3M's model #8710 ($1.25), left, and Norton's model 7170 ($3.75), both available from Edcor, Box 768, Kansas City, Mo. 64141.

ments, a toxic-vapor mask (to be discussed shortly) can be fitted with NIOSH-approved toxic-dust filters.

While a mask can offer significant protection, its effectiveness may be reduced by 90% or more if you wear it over a beard. One alternative to shaving is a positive-pressure air-purifying respirator, which fits like a helmet and blows filtered air over your face. These are expensive; 3M's air helmet, model #W316 (facing page), runs about $400. It includes a face shield and a rechargeable battery, and weighs about 3½ lb.

Solvent vapors—While the body's respiratory defense mechanisms can filter moderate amounts of dust, toxic vapors present a more serious threat. Hydrocarbons seldom occur in nature, thus we have developed only a limited ability to trap and detoxify these compounds. Unlike inhaled particles, vapors from paints, glues and solvents are readily absorbed into the bloodstream, often causing toxic reactions in organs other than the lungs. The liver and kidneys are particularly vulnerable.

Volatile compounds are widely used in wood finishes and adhesives, and there is no easy way for a worker to judge their hazards. Odor alone is not reliable. For example, highly-odoriferous acetone ranks relatively low on the toxicity scale, while mild-smelling epoxy gives off very toxic vapors. People all too often assume that the mere presence of products on store shelves indicates their safety, a mistake that is compounded by the tendency to ignore warning labels.

The hazards in using synthetic organic compounds are best known from cases where large numbers of industrial workers developed similar symptoms. The home worker, unprotected by expensive ventilation systems, may be at even higher risk. In 1969, ninety-three Japanese workers were found to be suffering from polyneuropathy resulting from exposure to hexane-based glue, used in home manufacture of sandals. Symptoms included muscle weakness, impairment of sensation, and temporary paralysis in the arms and legs. Reactions continued long after contact with the glue ceased, and four years later eleven of the workers still showed some ill effects.

Understanding the toxic properties of solvents is difficult because of the complex biochemical processes that occur once the solvents enter the body. For example, methylene chloride (a major ingredient in paint remover) metabolizes to form carbon monoxide, and methyl alcohol is converted to formaldehyde. In both cases, the toxic effects are partly due to these intermediate metabolites rather than to the original solvent. Many new products reach the market before their health hazards are well understood. When epoxies were introduced to industry in the late 1940s, numerous incidents occurred. A 1947 study revealed that 47% to 100% of workers at various electrical assembly plants suffered skin ailments from epoxy exposure. Many people become sensitized after repeated contact, but the full range of risks remains unknown. Animal studies suggest that at least some epoxy resins are carcinogenic.

Organic vapors are tissue irritants and central nervous system depressants. Workers are most likely to notice irritation of the eyes, skin and respiratory tract, as well as headache, dizziness, confusion, loss of appetite, nausea, malaise and fatigue. Though these symptoms usually disappear within hours or days, the long-term effects may pose different risks. Kidney and liver damage may result from chronic exposure to many solvents, particularly the chlorinated hydrocarbons (methylene chloride, perchloroethylene, etc.) and the aromatic compounds (toluene, xylene, benzene). A 1981 study by Swedish investi-

Several companies make twin-cartridge organic-vapor respirators, usually available in small, medium and large sizes. American Optical Corp.'s 'Sureguard' model #R5051P (shown being worn at right) is priced at about $17, and has an optional hemispherical fiber pre-filter to trap mists and dust. The Norton 'Protex' model #7531 (held at right) is similar, but uses a flat pre-filter pad. It sells for about $26. The 3M model #8712, worn and held at left, does not have a replaceable filter, but costs only about $8. The mask's wide, soft plastic facepiece is unusually comfortable.

gators revealed that painters with more than 25 years' experience showed a 15% greater than expected death rate from cancer. These deaths included unusually high incidences of cancers of the esophagus, larynx and bile ducts. The study also showed abnormally high rates of fatal diseases of the respiratory tract and upper gastrointestinal tract.

What to do about toxic vapors—Though exposure to vapors can be minimized by providing good ventilation, this remedy is not always feasible for woodworkers. Open doors and windows that vent fumes also invite airborne debris and insects to land on wet surfaces, and in winter one may be loathe to allow heat to escape. Most frustrating is the prospect of stripping floors or painting walls in a room that has inadequate ventilation. The danger level is not known for many compounds, and harmful exposure may not produce immediately noticeable effects. Concentrations of methylene chloride vapor as low as 300 parts per million (PPM) can cause drowsiness and reduced coordination after 3 to 4 hours of exposure. This concentration can easily be reached when paint remover is used with poor ventilation. Other compounds are much more toxic; the wood preservative pentachlorophenol, suspected of causing cancer and chromosome damage, is considered hazardous at vapor levels of only a few PPM. Allowing 2 teaspoonfuls to evaporate in an 8x10 room would exceed the danger level.

Besides working with adequate ventilation, wearing an appropriate mask will provide additional protection against even small concentrations of many of these vapors. The modern

organic vapor respirator is a direct descendant of the World War I gas mask, with several modifications. The glass-windowed, full-face mask is still used when eye-irritating vapors or gases are encountered, but the half-mask style is most common. This consists of a soft rubber facepiece containing one or two vapor-absorbing cartridges. These typically contain about half a cup of activated carbon or charcoal granules, though silica gel and synthetic molecular-sieve resins are sometimes used. The vapor-absorbing property of these compounds comes from the extremely large surface area of their porous particles. Cartridges are available to protect against a variety of toxic substances. They are made by impregnating the cartridge material with reactive compounds: a filter treated with iodine will absorb mercury vapor, while one impregnated with metal oxides will absorb acid fumes. The standard "organic vapor" cartridges have been found to provide protection against all but 18 of the 197 substances tested. These filters absorb the most common vapors emitted by wood finishes and adhesives. One exception is methyl alcohol. For this reason, when alcohol is needed as a solvent for shellac or other materials, it is safest to substitute denatured ethyl alcohol.

Respirator performance is evaluated by NIOSH. Testing is performed using carbon tetrachloride at vapor concentrations of 1,000 PPM. A cartridge is considered spent when the vapor concentration of air passing through it reaches 10 PPM. Under these conditions, cartridge life must be at least 50 minutes. As vapor levels during wood finishing are likely to be much under 1,000 PPM, the actual lifespan of a cartridge is usually 4 to 16 hours.

In addition to the vapor-absorbing cartridge, the organic-vapor respirator usually comes equipped with a fiber-filter disc designed to remove particulates such as paint-spray mist. In particle-free environments, these filters can be removed to make breathing easier. Or the mask can be used with a filter alone, simply as a dust mask. Masks generally contain a low-resistance port for exhaled air to leave the mask. This exhalation valve prevents exhaled air from leaving through the filter, keeping moisture from saturating the absorbing medium. If the exhalation valve leaks, or if the mask does not seal against the face, the mask is ineffective, allowing unfiltered air to enter. Make certain that your mask fits tightly and that the exhaust port functions.

Respirators have some drawbacks. They restrict your field of vision and make talking difficult. Breathing requires more effort than normal, and some people suffer claustrophobia. These problems tend to become less noticeable as you become accustomed to wearing a respirator. The benefits of both dust and organic-vapor masks are most apparent at the end of the day. Gone are the clogged nostrils, gummy throat and rasping cough. Solvents no longer produce headaches, respiratory irritation or that vague hung-over feeling, and you no longer have to rush through the application of a finish just to get away from the smell.

As a woodworker, I try to produce items that will last for many years, and it seems only an extension of that goal to expect my own components to hold up equally well. Though I sometimes feel like a giant anteater as I wander around the shop wearing my bulbous black proboscis, the health benefits seem well worth the minor inconvenience. □

George Mustoe, of Bellingham, Wash., has worked as an analytic chemist. He also makes harps.

What's in a label: common solvents in the woodshop

Aliphatic hydrocarbons: Also known as "paraffins," these petroleum derivatives consist of chains of carbon and hydrogen atoms. Gaseous forms include *methane, butane* and *propane;* molecules containing five or more carbon atoms are liquid at room temperature. *Pentane, hexane, heptane* and *octane* are major constituents of gasoline, kerosene, mineral spirits and VM&P (varnishmakers' and painters') naphtha. Hexane is widely used in rubber-based liquids such as contact cement and rubber cement. Isobutane and propane serve as propellants in some spray cans.

Aliphatic solvents are generally less toxic than other classes of organic liquids, though they are not risk-free. Common symptoms resulting from excessive exposure include skin and respiratory irritation and central nervous system (CNS) depression.

Aromatic hydrocarbons: These compounds are ring-shaped molecules distilled from coal tar. These liquids are powerful solvents, but their use is limited by low flash-points, high volatility and high toxicity. Three compounds are common: *Toluene (toluol)* and *xylene (xylol)* are often added to aliphatic solvents to increase their effectiveness. *Benzene* is not used in most areas, owing to its high toxicity and carcinogenic properties, but it is commonly present in small amounts as a contaminant in commercial-grade solvents. Benzene is commonly confused with benzine, an alternate name for VM&P naphtha, a variety of mineral spirits.

Alcohols: Denatured ethyl alcohol (ethanol) is widely used as a solvent for shellac, and consists of grain alcohol made poisonous to drink by the addition of methyl alcohol or some other toxic liquid. *Methyl alcohol (methanol,* "wood alcohol") is used in lacquer thinner, paint remover, shellac, and aniline-based wood stains. Methyl alcohol can be absorbed through the skin and its vapors are much more toxic than those of denatured alcohol, so the latter product should be employed for general shop use.

Ketones and esters: This group includes a number of compounds which contain oxygen as well as carbon and hydrogen. *Ethyl acetate, butyl acetate* and *amyl acetate* are esters used in nitrocellulose lacquer. Common ketones include *acetone, methyl ethyl ketone* and *methyl isobutyl ketone.* Esters and ketones typically have strong odors and high flammability. They are particularly likely to irritate the skin because of their ability to dissolve natural oils, and they may produce respiratory irritation and symptoms of CNS depression. A ketone derivative, *methyl ethyl ketone peroxide,* is used as a catalyst for polyester resins. This strong oxidizing agent will cause serious damage to the skin and eyes, and demands careful handling.

Glycol ethers: These are another type of oxygenated organic compound used in solvents, most commonly in slow-drying lacquer. Glycol ethers are highly toxic, and can cause liver, kidney and CNS damage. In addition, they may adversely affect reproductive organs, causing birth defects and miscarriages.

Halogenated hydrocarbons: This group of compounds contains fluorine, chlorine, and less commonly iodine and bromine. Gaseous forms such as *freon* have been widely used as spray-can propellants, but these are now restricted because of evidence that their use is destructive to the earth's protective ozone layer. Though some of the fluorocarbons have low toxicity, the chlorinated hydrocarbons rank high on the list of hazardous solvents. Degreasers and dry-cleaning agents such as *dichloroethane, trichloroethane* and *perchloroethylene* are generally weak solvents, being most effective for removing wax, grease and oil. (Mineral spirits is a safer solvent for removing oil and wax residues.) *Carbon tetrachloride* is no longer widely used because of its toxicity, but *methylene chloride* remains a common ingredient of paint remover and spray finishes. These volatile solvents produce hazardous vapors, and liquids can be absorbed through the skin. In addition, air-supplied respirators, not air-purifying organic-vapor (charcoal cartridge) respirators, should be used to protect against methylene chloride, as air-purifying cartridges will not adequately remove this essentially odorless material. Health risks include liver and kidney damage, CNS depression, narcosis and possibly cancer. Unlike most other solvents, halogenated hydrocarbons are not flammable, but when heated they break down to produce phosgene and other poison gases. The solvent vapors commonly have anaesthetic properties, and *chloroform* and *halothane (bromochlorotrifluoroethane)* have been widely used in medicine for this purpose.

Mineral spirits (VM&P naphtha, white spirits): These are distilled from petroleum, and consist mostly of the aliphatic hydrocarbons *hexane, heptane* and *octane.* Composition varies according to the source of the crude oil and manufacturing differences from batch to batch, and chemical analysis reveals the presence of as many as 100 separate compounds in some samples. Mineral spirits are grouped into three categories. Low-boiling-point (140° to 180°F), "odorless" spirits consist mostly of aliphatic compounds with fast evaporation rates and relatively weak solvency. Medium-boiling-point (200° to 300°F), "low odor" spirits are predominantly *heptane* and *octane* fortified with small amounts of *xylene* and *toluene.* High-boiling-point (300° to 400°F), "regular odor" mineral spirits comprise about 75% of all solvents used in the paint industry. They consist of 15% to 25% aromatic hydrocarbons. Mineral spirits are less toxic than most other solvents, but vapors can cause skin and respiratory irritation and CNS depression. Toxicity increases in proportion to the aromatic hydrocarbon content, so odorless spirits are best for general use.

Turpentine: This is produced by steam distillation of pine gum, and consists mostly of carbon-ring compounds called *turpenes.* Pine gum contains about 68% solid rosin, 20% turpentine and 12% water. Turpentine has a strong, characteristic odor, but its physical properties are very similar to mineral spirits, which has largely replaced it as a solvent. Turpentine is more chemically reactive, and will discolor upon long exposure to light or to air. Its vapors can cause respiratory irritation as well as dizziness, headache and other signs of CNS depression. It is a strong skin irritant, and can cause severe allergic reactions after repeated contact.

Lacquer thinner: Lacquers are usually made by dissolving a cellulose derivative in a suitable solvent, though modern formulations may include alkyd resin, natural rosin or other dissolved solids. Lacquer thinner usually consists of about 30% esters and ketones as the active solvent, diluted with aromatic and aliphatic hydrocarbons. The ester, ketone and aromatic content makes these solvents very volatile and relatively toxic, so they should be used only when needed and not as a general substitute for mineral spirits when thinning liquids or cleaning brushes. —*G.M.*

Return-Air Dust Collection

Shavings into barrels, dust into bags, heated air stays in the shop

by Mac Campbell

The woodworker must dispose of three types of shop waste: large chunks such as saw cut-offs, heavy particles such as jointer shavings and floating dust. The collection system I will describe can comfortably handle shavings and dust, as well as small chunks (large chunks go directly into the stove), and it exhausts through filter bags so that heated air can remain in the shop. This system could remove toxic vapors and fumes, but only if it were vented outdoors, whereupon heat would also be exhausted. The system is based on the principle that a given volume of air moves more slowly through a large passage than a small one. If the air carries a stream of particles, they will settle out as the airstream slows down.

My drop-box/blower/bag-box system is diagrammed below. A high-velocity airstream carrying waste from the machines enters the drop box on one side of an interior baffle. Because the box increases the size of the passage, the airstream slows down, and most of the larger particles settle into the collection hopper. At the outlet on the other side of the baffle plate, the airstream picks up speed and goes through the blower into the bag box. Here again it slows down, and returns to the shop only after being filtered of fine particles by the polyester-felt bags. If the system is to be vented to the outside, the bags would be enclosed in a separate box, which would then be vented through an exterior wall.

The size of your drop box is determined by the type of ma-

chines serviced and by space limitations in the shop. My drop box is 3 ft. square and 8 ft. high; the collection hopper consists of four 18-in. diameter barrels 36 in. high, with a baffle board over them to keep particles from falling in between them. Feeding 24-in. laminated panels through the planer as fast as I can fills the barrels in about 20 minutes, but normal shop use requires emptying them only once or twice a week. (In winter they are emptied more or less continuously into the stove.) The drop box should be carefully sealed, using either caulking compound, duct tape or both. The access door should be weatherstripped and latched; the internal vacuum holds it tightly closed when the system is operating.

The bag box must be sealed even more tightly than the drop box because it's under pressure (rather than vacuum), and because fine particles escape back into the shop through the smallest of openings. A barrel or cart system is usually not necessary here; I just open the tightly sealed door and shovel out the dust as required. Though I've been unable to dig up any firm guidelines relating bag area to system capacity, my system, which exhausts one machine at a time, has a total bag area of about 180 sq. ft., and this seems to be about the minimum. These bags need an occasional cleaning, and you can do this two ways. One is to suspend each bag by a rope that runs through a pulley; cleaning is then just a matter of jerking on the rope a few times. A simpler method is to hang the

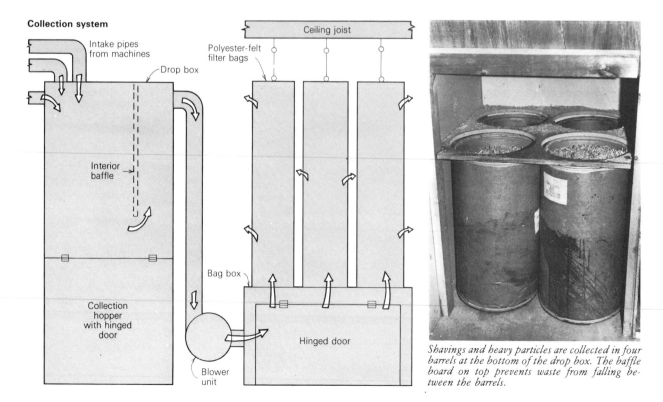

Collection system

Intake pipes from machines

Drop box

Polyester-felt filter bags

Ceiling joist

Interior baffle

Collection hopper with hinged door

Bag box

Blower unit

Hinged door

Shavings and heavy particles are collected in four barrels at the bottom of the drop box. The baffle board on top prevents waste from falling between the barrels.

Photos: Jim DiVeto

Polyester-felt filter bags hang from stringers nailed to ceiling joists. Bag box must be strong and hermetically sealed with caulking and duct tape to keep dust from escaping into shop.

Usual branch sizes and exhaust volumes			
Machine	Size (in.)	Branch pipe (in.)	Cu. ft./min. (CFM)
Jointers	Up to 6	3½	270
	6 to 12	4	350
	12 to 20	4½	440
Planers (single)	Up to 20	5	550
	20 to 26	6	790
	26 to 36	7	1070
Belt sanders	Belt width to 6	4	350
	6 to 9	4½	440
	9 to 14	5	550
Disc sanders	Up to 12	3½	270
Table saws	Up to 16	4	350
Band saws	Blade width to ½	3	200
	½ to 1	3½	270
	1 to 2	4	350

From *Design of Industrial Exhaust Systems* by John L. Alden and John M. Kane (Industrial Press Inc., 200 Madison Ave., New York, N.Y. 10016). This is an excellent source of technical information on all types of dust collection.

bags and beat them with a stick, much like old-fashioned carpet cleaning. Whichever way you go, bear in mind that the dust cake on the inside of the bag is what actually traps the finest particles. The cloth traps coarse particles, which trap finer particles, which trap even finer particles; so excessive bag cleaning will reduce the efficiency of the system. Experimenting will teach you the right balance between ease of air passage and effective filtration.

Mount the blower and motor anywhere between the drop box and bag box. The compact type of blower/motor combination used by Doyle Johnson (described on pages 80 to 82) works well mounted directly on top of the drop box since the

intake is on the bottom. The system is quite flexible, and parts of it can be placed around the shop as space permits. Johnson's suggestions for machine hoods are adequate, though I suggest sticking with the pipe sizes given in the table above. Each intake should be about twice the area of the pipe it supplies in order to provide enough air to carry the chips. Corrugated flex hose, while quite useful for making difficult connections, should be kept to a minimum since it significantly increases resistance. □

Mac Campbell designs and builds cabinets and furniture in Harvey Station, New Brunswick.

EDITOR'S NOTE: For a system in a small shop, the Cincinnati Fan and Ventilator Co. recommends using their model PB-10 blower unit with a 3,450-RPM, 1½-HP motor. It's rated at 490 CFM for 6-in. static pressure, and it costs about $300. Their address is 5345 Creek Rd., Cincinnati, Ohio 45242.

Though it is considerably more expensive, some woodworkers may want to install a centrifugal cyclone separator (shown at right). A cyclone separator employs a cone-shaped collector to create two concentric, helical air currents. Dust particles and shavings are separated from the airstream by centrifugal force and settle into a bin at the bottom of the cone. Cyclone systems can be used with or without filter bags. Cyclone collectors are manufactured in the United States by Torit Division/Donaldson Co., Inc., Drawer 1299, St. Paul, Minn. 55440 (in Canada, 2399 Cawthra Rd., Mississauga, Ont. L5A 2W9), and by Murphy-Rodgers, Inc., 2301 Belgrave Ave., Huntington Park, Calif. 90255.

You can get polyester-felt filter bags for your dust-collection system from Nauset Engineering and Equipment, Inc., PO Box 578, Lincoln, Mass. 01773. This company will sell bags in standard sizes or will

custom-make odd-sized bags to order.

If you don't like fans, ducts and filter bags cluttering your shop, consider APSEE (Air Purification through Stimulated Emission of Electrons). An APSEE machine just whirs quietly high up in one corner of a shop. It makes fine sanding dust—particles ranging from 2 to 30 microns—fall to the ground instead of lingering in the air.

To check this sales pitch, we visited a busy shop whose employees persuaded owner John Petricka to install an APSEE late last year. Petricka has become a believer. He demonstrated by blowing up an impenetrable cloud of flour-fine dust. We fled outside for 15 minutes. When we returned, the air was clean.

Fine dust floats because the friction of sanding gives it a positive charge of static electricity. The particles repel each other. APSEE saturates the shop air with electrons, whose negative charge neutralizes the charge on the dust, whereupon it wafts to the floor. You still have to sweep, but doing so doesn't stir up the dust again. If anything, the extra electrons are healthy to breathe.

An APSEE costs from $2,500 on up, depending on shop volume. Contact Small Wonder, Inc., 3921 Mayette, Santa Rosa, Calif. 95405. (All prices 1980 estimates.)

Cyclone collector

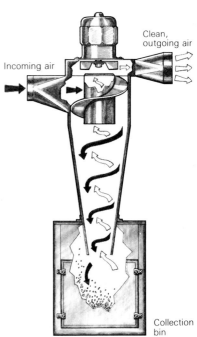

Clean, outgoing air

Incoming air

Collection bin

Dust Collection System
Damper-controlled setup keeps basement shop clean

by Doyle Johnson

Opening the damper slide starts the collector.

One problem confronting all woodworkers is how to combat the dust generated by power tools. My shop is in the basement of my home, and my concern over the mess and health and fire hazards led me to design a dust-collection system for my stationary power tools. I wanted the system to be conveniently located at each tool so no time would be wasted in moving hoses or cords. Therefore I installed permanent piping to the machines with a positive shut-off damper at each, so that the collector would run at full capacity at the operating tool.

In designing and installing a system like this, keep the collector as close as possible to the tools. Use as much pipe and as little hose as you can, to reduce resistance and make the system more efficient. To ensure compatibility, locate sources for all the components before you start construction.

I chose a ½-hp cast aluminum industrial collector (model 50) manufactured by the Cincinnati Fan and Ventilator Co., 5345 Creek Rd., Cincinnati, Ohio 45242. The specifications of this model are 110 volt, 450 cfm, 7-in. static pressure, 9150 fpm velocity using a 3-in. hose, with a noise level of 73 db. The collector retails for $245 (1978). The unit, suitable for outdoor installation, has a totally enclosed fan-cooled motor. It is designed to fit a 20-gal. or 24-gal. waste can, but I

modified a 55-gal. drum with a removable top to accept it. Since the collector is weatherproof, I put it outside to eliminate the chore of carrying the refuse up the stairs, to save space and to get the noise out of the shop. I covered the dust-filter bag with a trash-can liner with the bottom removed to keep it dry. The unit was in service through last winter and survived about 84 in. of snowfall without any problem. I plan to build a small louvered enclosure with doors for it, to muffle the noise and reduce the chance of theft.

I decided on 3-in. schedule 30 (thin-walled) PVC drainage pipe instead of metal vent pipe to reduce the noise and to take advantage of a larger choice of fittings. The smooth sweeping bends of the plastic pipe prevent material from settling out as it passes a drop to another machine. Because of building codes, schedule 30 PVC pipe may not be available in some areas, but it costs about 40% less than the heavier schedule 40 pipe. Schedule 30 pipe costs $6 for 10 feet. Fittings cost a dollar or two each.

PVC pipe can easily be cut on a radial arm saw and can be permanently joined with solvent cement. But I found the joints airtight without cement, and I can remove the pipe if I ever want to rearrange my tools. Duct tape can be used if a joint is suspicious. I secured the pipe to the building with perforated plumber's tape.

After looking through several catalogs, I couldn't find a suitable damper. I could have used standard dampers and wired the system to a wall switch, but instead I designed one of maple and sheet metal, with control contacts to start the collector when any damper is opened. Felt seals make a positive seal on the sheet metal slide. I started with two pieces of maple long enough for all the dampers I needed; the drawing gives the dimensions and steps involved.

Each damper needs two contacts for operating the control relay. They are made of .025-in. brass shim stock. Lay out the contacts on flat stock and drill the holes. Then cut and bend them to shape as shown in the drawing. Smooth the edges and curved end for good electrical contact with the slide. These contacts are suitable only for low-voltage applications.

To assemble the damper, place the slide between a set of damper bodies and bolt together using 3/16-in. by 3-in. screws. Attach the mounting brackets, tighten the bolts and check for smooth operation of the slide. Next place the unit in the vise, insert one of the seals and push it against the slide until it seats evenly. Hold in this position and drill holes to secure the seal with #8 x 1-in. self-tapping screws. Repeat the procedure for the opposite side. The seals should fit into the damper bodies snugly. If the hole is too large, a wrap or two of 1-in. masking tape around the PVC will tighten the fit. Af-

Overhead piping and vertical hoses do not interfere with machines. Dampers are conveniently close to each tool.

Doyle Johnson, of Crown Point, Ind., is electrical supervisor for a steel company and an avid woodworker. His green lumber supply competes with his wife's car for garage space.

Exploded view of damper

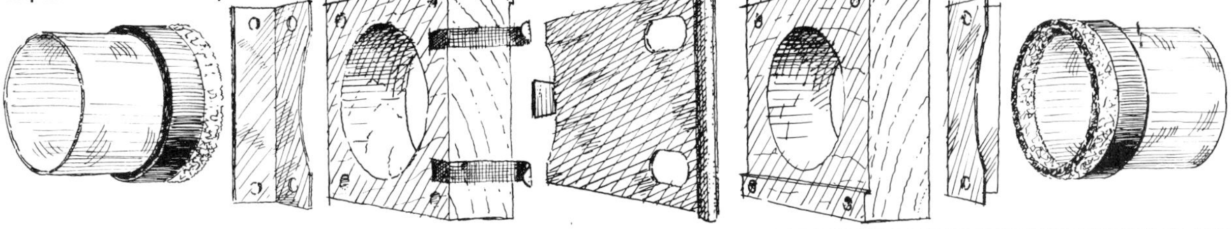

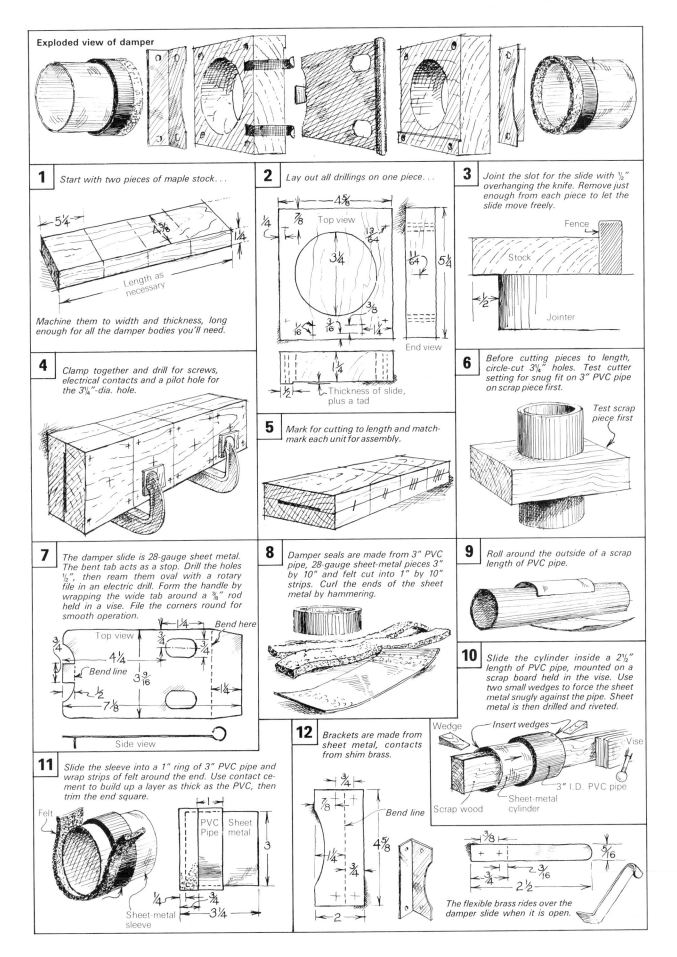

1 *Start with two pieces of maple stock...*

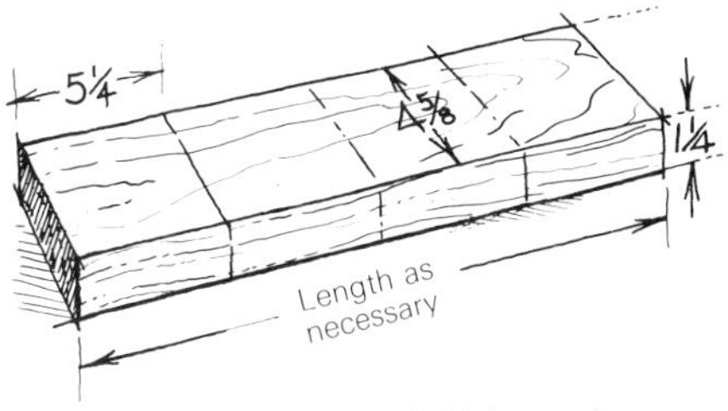

5¼
4⅝
1¼
Length as necessary

Machine them to width and thickness, long enough for all the damper bodies you'll need.

2 *Lay out all drillings on one piece...*

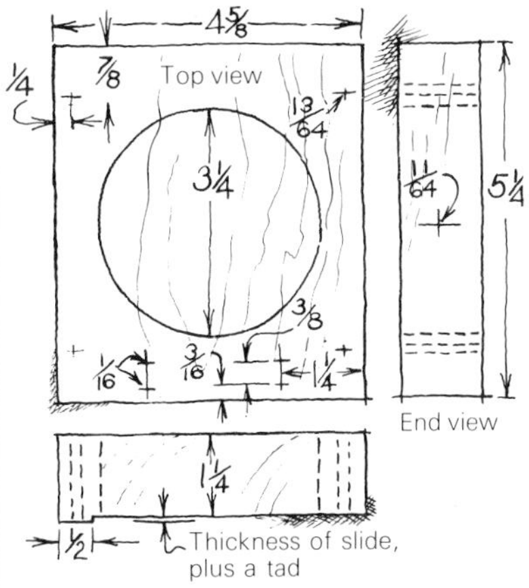

4⅝
¼
⅞
Top view
13/64
3¼
11/64
5¼
⅜
1/16
3/16
1¼
End view
1¼
½
Thickness of slide, plus a tad

3 *Joint the slot for the slide with ½" overhanging the knife. Remove just enough from each piece to let the slide move freely.*

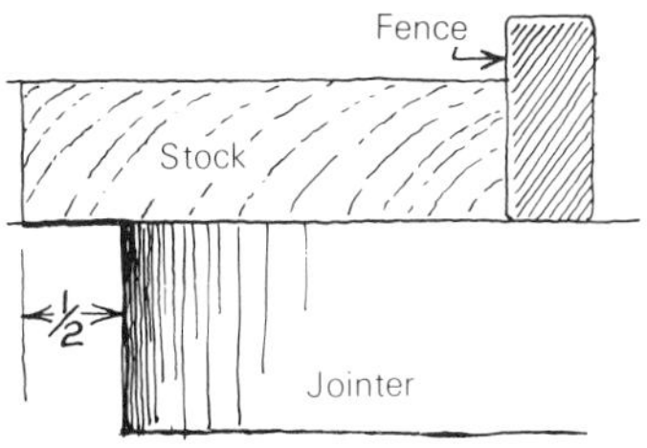

Fence
Stock
½
Jointer

4 *Clamp together and drill for screws, electrical contacts and a pilot hole for the 3¼"-dia. hole.*

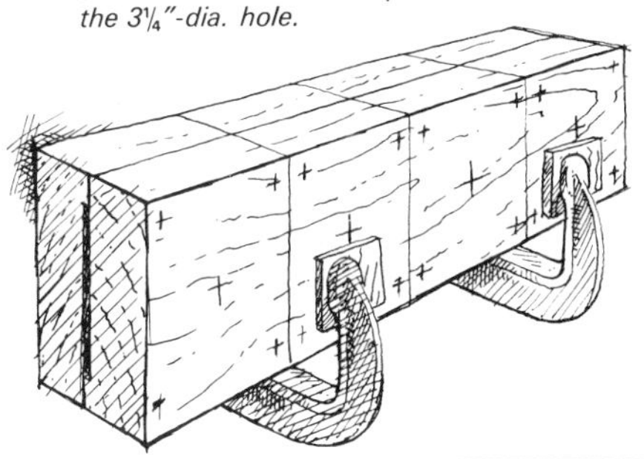

5 *Mark for cutting to length and match-mark each unit for assembly.*

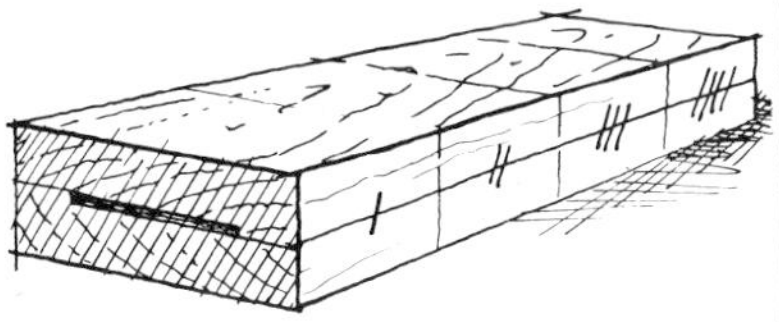

6 *Before cutting pieces to length, circle-cut 3¼" holes. Test cutter setting for snug fit on 3" PVC pipe on scrap piece first.*

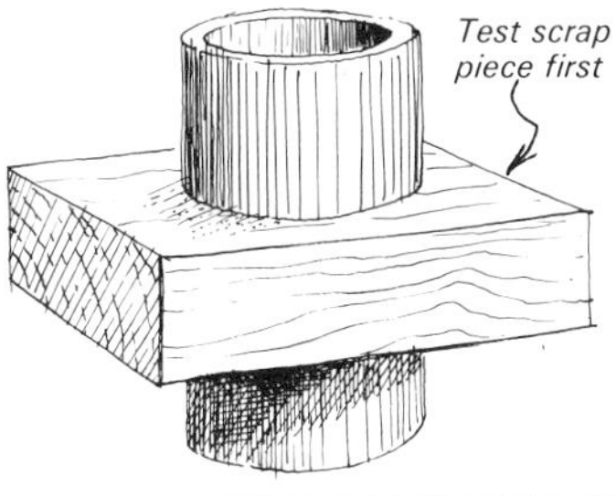

Test scrap piece first

7 *The damper slide is 28-gauge sheet metal. The bent tab acts as a stop. Drill the holes ½", then ream them oval with a rotary file in an electric drill. Form the handle by wrapping the wide tab around a ⅜" rod held in a vise. File the corners round for smooth operation.*

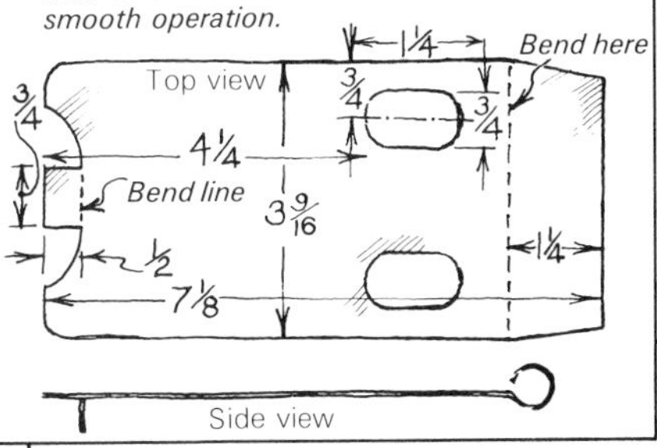

1¼
Bend here
Top view
¾
¾
¾
4¼
Bend line
3 9/16
½
1¼
7⅛
Side view

8 *Damper seals are made from 3" PVC pipe, 28-gauge sheet-metal pieces 3" by 10" and felt cut into 1" by 10" strips. Curl the ends of the sheet metal by hammering.*

9 *Roll around the outside of a scrap length of PVC pipe.*

10 *Slide the cylinder inside a 2½" length of PVC pipe, mounted on a scrap board held in the vise. Use two small wedges to force the sheet metal snugly against the pipe. Sheet metal is then drilled and riveted.*

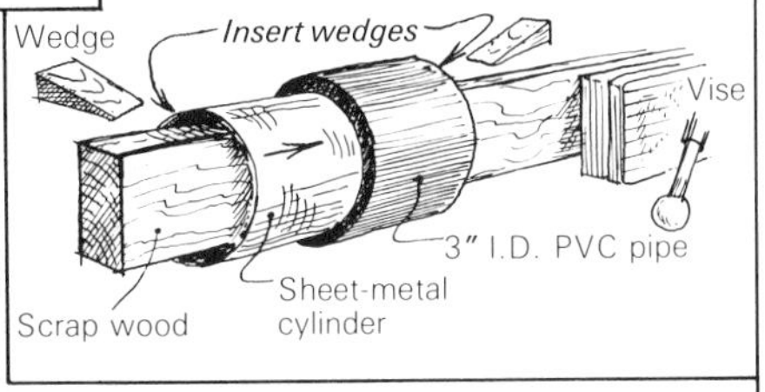

Wedge
Insert wedges
Vise
3" I.D. PVC pipe
Sheet-metal cylinder
Scrap wood

11 *Slide the sleeve into a 1" ring of 3" PVC pipe and wrap strips of felt around the end. Use contact cement to build up a layer as thick as the PVC, then trim the end square.*

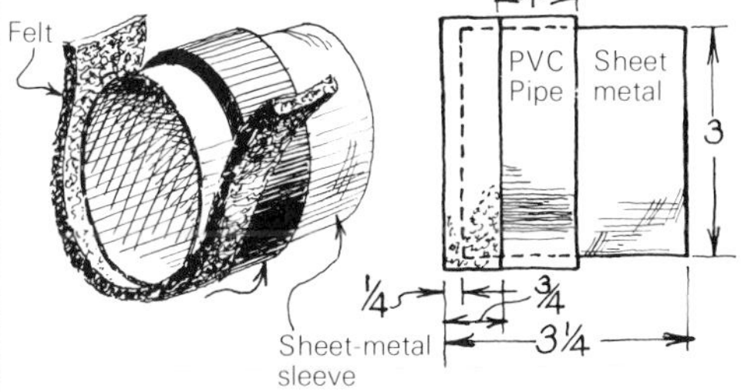

Felt
1
PVC Pipe
Sheet metal
3
¼
¾
3¼
Sheet-metal sleeve

12 *Brackets are made from sheet metal, contacts from shim brass.*

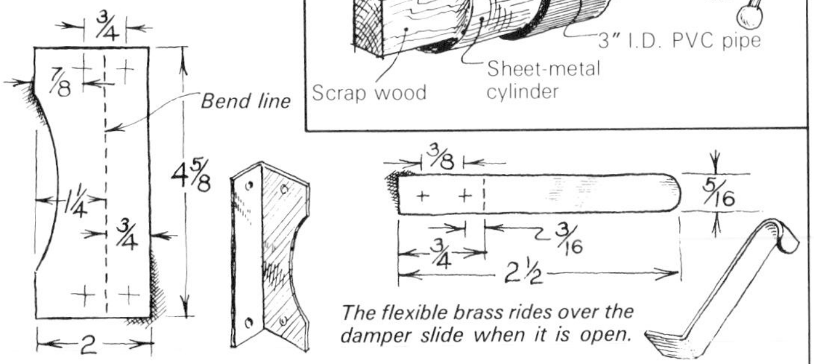

¾
⅞
Bend line
4⅝
1¼
¾
2
⅜
5/16
3/16
¾
2½

The flexible brass rides over the damper slide when it is open.

Collector mounted outdoors on 55-gal. drum, left, is connected to machinery inside shop in various ways. Center, semicircular catcher of ¼-in. Masonite and ½-in. plywood funnels debris from radial arm saw into the pipe about 1 in. above catcher bottom. Blade-guard pick-up could also be built. Saw, used mainly for crosscutting, is tight against wall; more space would permit deeper catcher with bottom pick-up. Right, suction hose attached to short pipe is clamped to drill-press column. Damper links hose to overhead pipes.

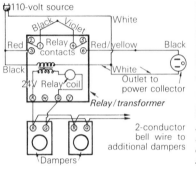

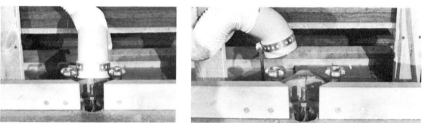

Shaper setup, above, has 45° PVC elbow with sheet-metal sleeve inside. A ⅜-in. threaded rod, bent L-shaped and clamped to elbow with plumber's tape, secures hose to table. Sheet metal closes off area behind cutter. Hose unit swings away to change cutters. Wiring for dust-collection system is diagrammed at left.

Band-saw take-off, far left, is in bottom of sealed-off lower blade guard. Hose is long enough to rest guard on floor while changing blades. Left, table-saw take-off is through a hole in drawer where blade throws sawdust. Hose detaches for vacuuming shop floor. On belt and disc sander, right, system connects to dust pick-ups for shop vacuum.

ter assembly, a small bead of silicone sealer or gutter sealant between seal and body will prevent leakage. This allows the damper to be taken apart if the seals ever need replacement.

The contacts are now attached with #6 x ½-in. sheet-metal screws. Adjust the wipe on the contacts by bending the curved tip up or down to meet the slide. Close the slide and move from side to side; if the contact touches the metal, adjust or trim the contact slightly. Lubricate the slide where the contacts ride by rubbing with a soft lead pencil or graphite-based lubricant to reduce friction and ensure good contact.

For controlling the power to the collector, I selected a 24-volt switching relay/transformer, the kind that controls furnace blowers for air conditioning. The 24-volt circuit is safe to connect to the damper contacts with ordinary doorbell wire. I bought a Sears Model #541.9211D, rated at ¾ hp, 110 volts, for about $15. Its relay controls power to a weatherproof receptacle at the collector. I have enough capacity on the shop lighting circuit to operate the collector system and have it connected so it works only when the lights are on.

I anchored the dampers in easy reach from each machine and ran 3-in. hose to the machine itself. Since hose similar to

the 5-ft. length furnished with the collector cost almost $2/ft., I used 3-in. clothes-dryer vent hose at $.60/ft., which has proved satisfactory. To link the hose to a pipe, one of the sleeves like those on the dampers works fine. To go into a hub on a fitting, just put a short piece of pipe over the sleeve. The metal sleeve protrudes 1½ in. on each side of the damper, which allows connection of 3-in. pipe or hose. To secure the hose I used a double wrap of #14 AWG wire twisted tightly.

In adapting my machines for dust collection, I found that each presented its own problems. The objective is to get maximum air flow around the cutter and into the collector, and I devised solutions (shown above) with that in mind. □

EDITOR'S NOTE: Although the simplified schematic diagram on this page does not show it, electrical circuits of the type described here require a third wire for grounding. In addition, the National Electric Code specifies that outdoor electrical outlets must be protected by a ground fault interruptor, to guard against hazardous shock. For their own safety, readers devising dust collection systems should be sure to consult a licensed electrician.

Woodworking Injuries
A hand surgeon looks at how accidents happen

by Dr. E. Jeff Justis

Woodworkers relish the feel of a tenon sliding into its mortise, and the smooth texture of a newly finished piece of furniture. Our fingertips are so sensitive that we can feel blemishes and flaws in our woodwork that are too slight to be perceived by the eye. Where would we be without these sophisticated sensors? Human evolution is, in part, the result of our early manipulation of our environment with our hands, and this is perhaps at the root of the creative impulses that make woodworking so satisfying.

It's no wonder, then, that people who have severely injured a hand or lost a limb often have emotional difficulty adjusting to their impairment. In fact, sometimes psychiatric care must supplement physical therapy. As a woodworker and a hand surgeon who has seen too many injuries, I am vividly aware of the risk in using power tools. I've also come to realize that virtually all injuries are preventable.

I have treated many patients with hand injuries inflicted by woodworking tools. Surprisingly, about one-third of all accident victims seen in hospital emergency rooms have an injury to the arm or hand. A 1964 study in England found that woodworking tools are responsible for most industrial injuries. Even so, research has not been done on the question of which tools are the most dangerous; hospitals don't generally obtain such information, and medical personnel don't always know the differences among various tools. A medical report may attribute an injury to a handsaw when in fact the injured patient was using a portable circular saw. I've never been injured by my tablesaw or my portable circular saw, but my own experience as a surgeon clearly suggests that circular saws account for the majority of serious hand injuries among woodworkers. I routinely discuss the mechanism of injury with patients, and I have concluded that there are three major causes of serious injuries from a power tool: inattention through repetition, an unanticipated happening, and inexperience or overconfidence. Many accidents involve some combination of the three, not to mention bad judgment brought on by the woodworker's fatigue.

Inattention through repetition—A woodworker performing a number of repetitive cuts, such as a series of crosscuts to length, may become dangerously inattentive. The whine of the machine and the repetitious physical movement can lull the worker in an almost hypnotic way. A tragic example comes to mind: A cabinetmaker with 20 years of experience in a local shop was making repetitive cuts with a radial-arm saw, using his left hand to feed the stock and his right to pull the saw through. In an instant, his right hand moved too fast for his left, and the saw passed over his hand, severing all four fingers of his left hand just above the knuckles but sparing his thumb. Although his ability was permanently im-

paired, the man was able to resume woodworking by, as he put it, "doing the best I can under the circumstances, but I never realized how important my left hand was until this happened." Another patient, who severed his thumb just beyond the base joint in a similar accident, told me afterward that he had never been aware of how much he used his left thumb, especially when trying to hold work against the miter gauge of a tablesaw or the fence of a radial-arm saw.

Interestingly, a 1975 study of 1,071 hand-injury patients showed that although 90% of them were right-handed, their injuries were nearly evenly divided between right and left hands. In virtually every case, the fingers bore the brunt of the injury. Inattention through repetition seems most likely to occur in the production shop, but all woodworkers must avoid being complacent when working with machines. It pays to pause deliberately after every couple of repeat operations to refocus on the task and to carry on with full awareness—a habit that can be acquired.

An unanticipated happening—Power cutting tools operate at high speeds. When something goes afoul, it occurs quickly and surprisingly. Kickbacks caused by binding are a common unanticipated event that can quickly draw fingers into a blade. Putting the fingers too near the blade can result in unpleasant surprises. One patient of mine recently reached with his left hand beyond the sawblade to catch a waste strip. The strip began to slide backward, and as he attempted to catch it, he caught his thumb on the sawblade. Fortunately, the blade was set just above the level of the board and his thumb wasn't severed. But a tendon and two nerves were cut, and although he has regained motion, sensation in his thumb will never be the same. Many of us forget that the regenerative capacity of the human body is limited. Any cut into the sub-dermal layer, no matter how well healed and painless, leaves a scar that is not normal tissue. Thus, a hand that suffers a major injury cannot be fully restored. Even a small cut, on the wrist for example, can result in a nerve injury that is the functional equivalent of an amputation.

Many times an unanticipated event will occur through inexperience, poor planning or a lack of understanding of how tools and machines work. For example, it should be obvious that trying to shape a small piece without a guard or a jig can end in disaster. Jointers can mangle fingers when the operator attempts to machine a small piece. Similarly, failure to anticipate the "breaking through" of the bandsaw blade can result in an injured finger. As a youngster, I recall slicing through the pulp of my left thumb with a scroll saw when the blade passed quickly through a soft spot in the puzzle I was making. My attention was so focused on guiding the saw accurately that I failed to anticipate its moving through the wood so fast. The same can happen with hand tools, particularly sharp edge-cutting tools such as chisels and planes. A cut

---

E. Jeff Justis is a hand surgeon in Memphis, Tenn.

The Small Workshop **83**

A quick way to lose fingers is by passing small pieces over the jointer, above left. Don't machine stock shorter than 12 in., use a push stick and leave the cutterhead guard in place. Some tablesaw operators hold their thumbs near the blade during a rip, as in the photo above. An unanticipated kickback can pull the thumb into the spinning blade. The drill press, left, seems like a benign tool. But when haste wins out over safety, it can do considerable damage in short order. Always clamp the stock being drilled. Bandsawing small pieces is risky enough, but in the photo at right the operator will be in for a painful surprise when the blade breaks through the stock and into his finger.

from a sharp chisel is less traumatic than a severed finger, but both are painful. Yet with attention and care, both injuries can be avoided.

Inexperience or overconfidence—Some general accident studies show that the greatest incidence of injury occurs at two extremes of experience: the rank novice and the highly expert. I've seen many young patients who had summer jobs requiring the use of radial-arm saws, jointers or tablesaws. Within days of beginning work, they sustained serious hand injuries. One young man was using a tablesaw under pressure from his supervisor to keep his speed up while ripping boards. When a board jammed between fence and blade, it pulled his hand into the blade. His index finger was so mangled that it had to be amputated. Fortunately, with reconstructive surgery, he regained acceptable use of his middle finger and hand. Not surprisingly, however, his enthusiasm for woodworking and tools was forever diminished. In his case, the combination of inexperience, repetitive motion and an unanticipated event had tragic results.

At the other end of the scale, a high school shop teacher with 20 years of experience had grown so accustomed to using his tablesaw that he thought nothing of making routine passes with his thumb just millimeters away from the blade. A sudden grabbing of the wood pulled his right thumb into the blade, instantly severing the tip of that digit. Experience, though a good teacher, can lead us to believe we know more than we do, and the subsequent risks we are willing to take can cost us dearly. Even seemingly harmless tools such as the drill press can do grievous damage if they are misused or treated with less respect than they deserve.

The experiences I've described here, no matter how grisly, can teach us important lessons about safety. You can't avoid repetitive operations when using machinery—particularly in production shops. But you can be alert to the hypnotic effect of this type of activity and you can teach yourself to be constantly vigilant. Keep fresh by breaking up a long routine of cutting or machining with another, less redundant operation. And never work around machines when you are tired or under the influence of alcohol or drugs that might make you drowsy.

By definition, the unanticipated happening can't be predicted. Using common sense and a bit of ingenuity, however, will ensure that your hands are out of the way when such events do occur. Build jigs and fixtures to keep the wood under control and your hands well away from cutters and blades. Don't alter or ignore the machinery's own built-in safety devices. And keep the workshop liberally supplied with push sticks—it's far better to have them or a project chewed up than to lose one of your fingers. Push sticks can be made by the dozens and projects can be started over, but damage to the hands may be irreparable, and lost function is an impairment to be carried forever. □

Keeping Ten Fingers
Injury survey pinpoints hazards in the shop

by Paul Bertorelli

In 1982, *Fine Woodworking* magazine asked our readers to tell us about the injuries they had suffered while woodworking. We collected 1,002 survey forms describing all manner of bloody run-ins with power and hand tools, from gruesome, multiple-finger amputations to the cuts and nicks that seem to scar even the most safety-minded. We punched all this data into a microcomputer. What emerged is a clearer picture of which tools pose the highest injury risk and why.

By far and away, the **tablesaw** is involved in more serious hand injuries than any other woodworking tool or machine. It was responsible for 42% of all the injuries reported, followed by the jointer at 18%, the radial-arm saw at 7% and the bandsaw at 6%. Although several other power tools—the shaper, chainsaw and circular saw, for instance—seem more hazardous, all figured in fewer accidents than even the hand chisel, which accounted for 4% of the total.

As several readers correctly noted, the tablesaw may not be inherently the most dangerous machine, but rather the one that's owned and used by more woodworkers more of the time. When I checked with a power-tool trade association, I learned that tablesaws do indeed outnumber radial-arm saws by about five to one, a ratio that nearly matches the injury statistics. But other research by manufacturers and the government also tends to single out the tablesaw. A 1980 study by the National Electronic Injury Surveillance System, for instance, found that tablesaws were involved in more than seven times as many injuries as were radial-arm saws. While our survey indicated that the tablesaw accidents overwhelmingly occurred while ripping, the radial-arm saw can be vicious whether ripping or cross-cutting. The radial-arm saw was also responsible for the goriest multiple amputations.

Our survey confirmed what experienced woodworkers might suspect, that attempting to rip a short, narrow or thin piece of wood on the tablesaw invites an accident. With too little surface to guide against the fence, the stock is liable to twist and bind, resulting in a kickback which pulls the hand that is holding the wood (the left, more often) into the blade. Ripping knotty, warped or checked lumber also increases the chance of a violent kickback, as does plunge- or groove-ripping: lowering the work onto the blade to start a blind cut.

> *"...there was a lot of sawdust on the floor, my eyes saw it, but my mind didn't, until my foot slipped and I lost my balance, and I put my hand on the table to break my fall—but unfortunately my hand landed on the sawblade. I gained an incredible amount of respect for the machine that day..."*
> —Mike Andrews, Martinez, Calif.

> *"...I was trying to finish, I was tired, the machine vibrations had dulled my senses, and I must have just slipped or dragged my finger. I was not using the guard, which I usually do. This time I felt I needed to be able to hold the shutter tight to the fence, and didn't take the time to construct a jig. In my nightmares the last few weeks, I've made jig after jig, and cut off numerous fingers and hands. From another person who thought she was careful, and who never thought it would happen—I was wrong..."*
> —Linda Faulkner, San Angelo, Tex.

Accessories such as **molding, dado and planer attachments** for both the tablesaw and the radial-arm saw were mentioned again and again as being involved in serious injuries, particularly when milling short or narrow stock, say, less than 12 in. long or 3 in. wide. The resultant kickbacks are impossible to control and often forceful enough to injure even without blade contact. Bevan Lavoy of Hornby Island, B.C., told of one such experience: "I was making window trim on my Unisaw with a three-knife molding head...the piece came back, jarring my left hand in such a way that it broke my little finger twice, nearly severing it. I'm sure it happened in less than a millisecond." Lavoy said that he's developed new respect for his tablesaw since the accident, and added, "I abhor molding cutters of any kind...to me, they seem itching to pare my fingernails."

Time and time again, readers confessed to having taken the guards off their tablesaws at the time of their accident. Some said that they now use tablesaw guards, but others continued to maintain that existing guards impair visibility and cause more problems than they solve. Hardly anybody, however, reported a serious tablesaw accident that occurred with a blade cover, kickback pawls and splitter all in place.

From my work with the survey questionnaires I draw several tablesaw lessons. First and most obvious, make guards and push sticks a habit, and train yourself to never put either hand in line with the saw's blade, no matter how safe it seems. Second, plan your work so that you don't need to rip little pieces into littler ones, but can rip them off of big, easy-to-manage chunks of wood. Third, do not attempt to tablesaw-rip warped, checked or knotty pieces. Take them to the bandsaw instead. In fact, one of my colleagues now does all ripping on the bandsaw, although I still prefer the tablesaw. Finally, think twice about those molding heads. Circular saws are designed and equipped for ripping and cross-cutting, not for doing double duty as a shaper or a planer.

Jointer accidents were fewer in number and generally less severe than those associated with the tablesaw, but they occurred for the same reason: trying to mill stock that was too small. Removing the cutterhead guard so that the small, thin stock won't jam under it is a favorite trick that makes this operation all the more hazardous. For some reason, the jointer seems more benign than it actually is, lulling otherwise safety-conscious craftsmen into lapses in judgment that they regret. "I tried to joint a piece shorter than the 12-in. minimum," wrote Bruce Lancaster of Friendship, Md., describing the paring of ⅜ in. from his ring finger. "I was aware of this safety rule, but I tried to shortcut what would otherwise be a tiresome manual operation."

The lesson here is to joint your stock *before* you cut it into little pieces, not afterward. Use a hand plane for short pieces. It may be slower, but it's more pleasant and certainly safer. None of our readers reported being bitten by a hand plane.

As basic stationary power tools go, the **bandsaw** seems like a safe tool, and our survey suggests that it is. It was involved in the fewest, least serious injuries. Two-thirds of the reported bandsaw wounds were bad cuts, often requiring surgery, but this tool was involved in only one amputation. Most of the bandsaw cuts were the direct result of having the pushing hand or thumb in line with the blade when resistance suddenly disappeared due to a check or soft spot in the wood. On the other hand, the **shaper,** with its exposed cutterhead, is one of the scariest tools. That, combined with the fact that fewer woodworkers have one, may explain why it was involved in only 2.3% of the injuries we surveyed, less even than the portable circular saw at 3.7% and the router at 3%.

> "...I was ripping a pine board in which there was a loose knot. All went well until the blade passed through the knot, then the up side of the blade picked up the remaining part of the knot, sending it whisking past my ear..."
> —*Joel B. Johnson, Hendersonville, N.C.*

Chainsaws, surface planers, sanders and drill presses were each associated with fewer than 2% of the injuries reported in this survey.

Before the data from the questionnaires was keyed into the computer, I sorted the survey forms into six categories of injury, with amputations as the most serious, and cuts and tears as the least. I've had no medical training, so my sorting was subjective. But I found that fully a quarter of the injuries reported were described as **permanently impairing**, involving the amputation of one or more fingers, or having done enough bone, nerve and/or tendon damage to never heal right. One-third of the injuries entailed the loss of one or more fingertips, and another third consisted of bad cuts and tears. Likely as not, many of the injuries in this second group were more serious than the descriptions indicated. About 75% of the injuries reported required a visit to a doctor or an emergency room.

Minced by a machine, a finger can take months to heal, and when it does, disfigurement, stiffness, and pain, particularly in cold weather, may persist for years. Amputations or injuries needing tendon or nerve repair almost always require a hospital stay for at least a day or two, sometimes longer, during which the services of hand, orthopedic or plastic sur-

Ripping, grooving and molding safely

by Michael Sandor Podmaniczky

An oldtimer in the model shop where I worked had us take all the guards off the saws. "I want to see the blade that gets me," he used to joke. While I wouldn't go so far as to agree with him, arguments about the effectiveness of guards are pointless if dadoing or ripping of small stock prevents their use.

Modelmakers have many techniques for safely cutting small pieces. For ripping, I prefer the setup shown below (figure 1). Junk the saw's metal throat insert, then make a new one out of Plexiglas or wood. If you raise the blade up through a fresh insert, the resulting slot will hug the blade, leaving no room for small pieces to hang up. For splitters, small scraps of Plexiglas or wood can be glued into the throat slot. For fastening jigs and hold-downs, wide,

double-sided tape is a good alternative to clamps.

Tablesaw cross-cutting isn't as hazardous as ripping, but the fixture shown in figure 2 makes it safer. The stock doesn't touch the table as it slides, so there's almost no chance of a bind and kickback. Stop blocks can be set for re-

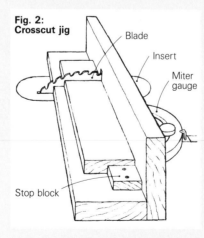

Fig. 2: Crosscut jig
Blade
Insert
Miter gauge
Stop block

petitive cuts to the same length.

Dado and molding heads hog lots of material, and so are prone to nasty kickbacks. The fixture shown in figure 3 will hold the work down. Stop-grooving is most safely done on a router table, as shown in figure 4. Remember two things when performing any kind of rip:

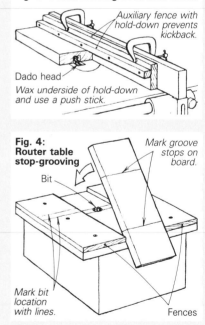

Fig. 3: Dado, molding-head hold-down
Auxiliary fence with hold-down prevents kickback.
Dado head
Wax underside of hold-down and use a push stick.

Fig. 4: Router table stop-grooving
Mark groove stops on board.
Bit
Mark bit location with lines.
Fences

always stand to one side, out of the kickback path, and *never, ever* feed with the blade rotation to correct a miscut. Better to scrap the piece and start over. □

Michael Podmaniczky builds boats in Camden, Maine.

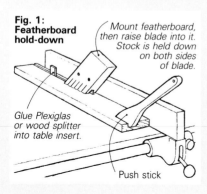

Fig. 1: Featherboard hold-down
Mount featherboard, then raise blade into it. Stock is held down on both sides of blade.
Glue Plexiglas or wood splitter into table insert.
Push stick

Drawings: Lee Hov

geons will be needed. The cost of treatment can be staggering. Ted Walls of Uniontown, Ohio, an amateur woodworker, spent $3800 mending three fingertips lost to a shaper. Though he spent no time in the hospital, Walls' injury kept him from woodworking for two months.

The long-term medical and psychological consequences of losing fingers may be even worse than the initial damage. Reattachment surgery is an onerous, painful procedure whose outcome is always in doubt. The psychic trauma can last longer and cut more deeply than the physical. Andrew McGillivray, a cabinetmaker working in Germany, related a vividly dark tale:

"I *was* a musician; both woodworking and music have been equally important to my enjoyment of life. A year and a half ago, I found two fingers lying on the floor at my feet, as well as having my thumb and other fingers badly cut by a tablesaw." McGillivray's fingers were reattached and his wounds bandaged, but his doctor was reluctant to advise counseling. "His attitude was 'You're broken up by two fingers? I'll show you people with no hands.' With that, he sent me home, where I virtually went crazy for two months. Music was intolerable, I couldn't work...I eventually lost my house and my wife."

McGillivray went on to say, "Now I have strength in my hand and I am working again. I am remarried and have put my life back in order. My point is this: the talk about 'limited flexibility' and 'occupational hazards' skims over the emotional side. No amount of therapy will make it more comfortable for me to put on a glove or make me feel less uncomfortable when I make love to my wife. The effects were more far-reaching than I could have imagined."

I had always thought that **fatigue** after a long day in the shop would lead to most accidents, but our survey suggests that a **heavy lunch** is a more likely cause. The largest number of accidents, 34%, happened right after noon but before 3 PM. Equal numbers of injuries occurred between 6 AM and noon, from 3 PM to 7 PM and from 7 PM to midnight. Experience doesn't seem to be much help either. Seasoned hands with 20 years in the shop were as likely to maim themselves as novices, and amateurs (65% of the sample) were hurt as often and as badly as professionals and teachers. Beginners with less than a year of experience had slightly fewer and less serious accidents than other groups, perhaps because they own fewer power tools and are more afraid of the ones they do have.

As a **left-hander,** I've at times felt frustrated in a world equipped with tools and equipment designed for right-

"Since the time of my accident, I have talked with many people about working injuries, not necessarily exclusive to woodworking. One thing that stood out with many people was that they had 'a feeling' about what they were about to do that had a sense of danger. In other words, they knew that what they were about to do was less safe than it could have been, but they went ahead anyway. After losing both my thumb and forefinger to the tablesaw, I have a rule about those feelings—I act on them immediately."
—Ron Callari, Rochester, N.Y.

"My glasses were loose on my head, and during an operation on the tablesaw they fell off. By reflex I reached for them. By reflex I also reacted to my own reflex, otherwise I believe I might have lost my whole hand, or thereabouts."
—Faz Fazahas, New York, N.Y.

"While I was replacing freshly sharpened knives in my 6-in. jointer, the wrench spread and slipped off the gib screw...my hand hit the edge of the knife, causing a delightfully clean laceration....I have since changed my procedure for changing knives. I put a heavy leather cover on the blade while in the process and I wear gloves. Interestingly enough, I had a premonition that the accident was going to happen just a split second before it did, and couldn't respond quickly enough. I wonder if your research will show any more of this."
—Bill Hoffman, Coventry, Conn.

handers. Many machines are arranged so that the left hand holds the work against the fence, usually near the cutter, while the right does the driving. Our survey suggests that while left-handers don't suffer a disproportionate number of accidents, they are more liable to injure their favored hand. Only 40% of the right-handers reported injury to their favored hand, versus 47% of the lefties. The difference suggests that right-handed fences, controls and handles keep the lefties off balance.

The data collected and analyzed, the question remains: how can you best protect yourself from a woodworking injury? Our survey asked for safety advice, and readers obliged with dozens of suggestions. Some woodworkers swore by guards and splitters, some swore at them. A few sent drawings of their favorite push sticks or hold-down jigs, others thought tool manufacturers ought to bear the onus of designing safer machines. Helpful as they are, none of these ideas breaks any new ground.

The truth is, there's no universal, foolproof gizmo that you can bolt on to every tool in the shop, thereafter ceasing to worry about your fingers. Our survey does indicate, however, that the risk of serious injury can be diminished by *not* ripping, dadoing or molding on the tablesaw, or any circular saw for that matter. Consider using the bandsaw for ripping. With the right blade, it will do it just as fast and it's much safer. For grooving and molding, a router is less risky. Schedule your workday so you can do demanding, hazardous machine operations in the morning, when you're most alert, and not after a full lunch. Don't be a cowboy about guards, hold-downs and push sticks. Use them.

The real safety solution is **attitude.** This point was driven home for me recently when I visited a tool factory where an enormous banner that declared "Safety is a good habit" hung from the rafters. I had seen such banners before and had always considered them a cheap sop for safety hardware. The carnage described in the survey questionnaires made me realize that no amount of money invested in safety equipment will offset a lack of alertness and common sense. The trick is to develop the habit of *always* stopping to get a push stick or a hold-down fixture, or of waiting until the next day when you're fresher. Constant, habitual vigilance is far preferable to a painful, disabling lesson. Time and time again, readers told of being hurt after hurriedly attempting machine operations that they knew to be hazardous. Some even said that they had had premonitions of injury. The point is obvious: if something *feels* dangerous, it probably is. □

Paul Bertorelli is editor of Fine Woodworking *magazine.*

Index

**Fine Woodworking
Editorial Staff, 1975-1984:**

Paul Bertorelli
Mary Blaylock
Dick Burrows
Jim Cummins
Katie de Koster
Ruth Dobsevage
Tage Frid
Roger Holmes
John Kelsey
Linda Kirk
John Lively
Rick Mastelli
Ann E. Michael
Nina Perry
Jim Richey
Paul Roman
David Sloan
Nancy Stabile
Laura Tringali
Linda D. Whipkey

**Fine Woodworking
Art Staff, 1975-1984**

Roger Barnes
Deborah Fillion
Lee Hov Hochgraf
Betsy Levine
Lisa Long
E. Marino III
Karen Pease
Roland Wolf

**Fine Woodworking
Production Staff, 1975-1984**

Claudia Applegate
Barbara Bahr
Pat Byers
Deborah Cooper
Michelle Fryman
Mary Galpin
Barbara Hannah
Annette Hilty
Nancy Knapp
Johnette Luxeder
Gary Mancini
Laura Martin
Mary Eileen McCarthy
JoAnn Muir
Cynthia Lee Nyitray
Kathryn Olsen
Barbara Snyder

If you enjoyed this book, you're going to love our magazine.

A year's subscription to *Fine Woodworking* brings you the kind of practical, hands-on information you found in this book and much more. In issue after issue, you'll find projects that teach new skills, demonstrations of tools and techniques, new design ideas, old-world traditions, shop tests, coverage of current woodworking events, and breathtaking examples of the woodworker's art for inspiration.

To subscribe, just fill out one of the attached subscription cards, or call us toll-free at 1-800-888-8286. As always, **we guarantee your satisfaction.**

Subscribe Today!

6 issues for just $25

TAUNTON
BOOKS & VIDEOS
...by fellow enthusiasts

The Taunton Press
63 S. Main Street, Box 5506, Newtown, CT 06470-5506

FWAE

Fine WoodWorking®

Use this card to subscribe or to request additional information about Taunton Press magazines, books and videos.

1 year (6 issues) for just $25—over 15% off the newsstand price
Outside the U.S. $30/year (U.S. funds, please)

Name _____

Address _____ .

City _____ State _____ Zip _____

☐ My payment is enclosed. ☐ Please bill me.
☐ Please send me information about other Taunton Press magazines and books.
☐ Please send me information about *Fine Woodworking* videotapes.

FWAE

Fine WoodWorking®

Use this card to subscribe or to request additional information about Taunton Press magazines, books and videos.

1 year (6 issues) for just $25—over 15% off the newsstand price
Outside the U.S. $30/year (U.S. funds, please)

Name _____

Address _____

City _____ State _____ Zip _____

☐ My payment is enclosed. ☐ Please bill me.
☐ Please send me information about other Taunton Press magazines and books.
☐ Please send me information about *Fine Woodworking* videotapes.

FWAE

Fine WoodWorking®

Use this card to subscribe or to request additional information about Taunton Press magazines, books and videos.

1 year (6 issues) for just $25—over 15% off the newsstand price
Outside the U.S. $30/year (U.S. funds, please)

Name _____

Address _____

City _____ State _____ Zip _____

☐ My payment is enclosed. ☐ Please bill me.
☐ Please send me information about other Taunton Press magazines and books.
☐ Please send me information about *Fine Woodworking* videotapes.

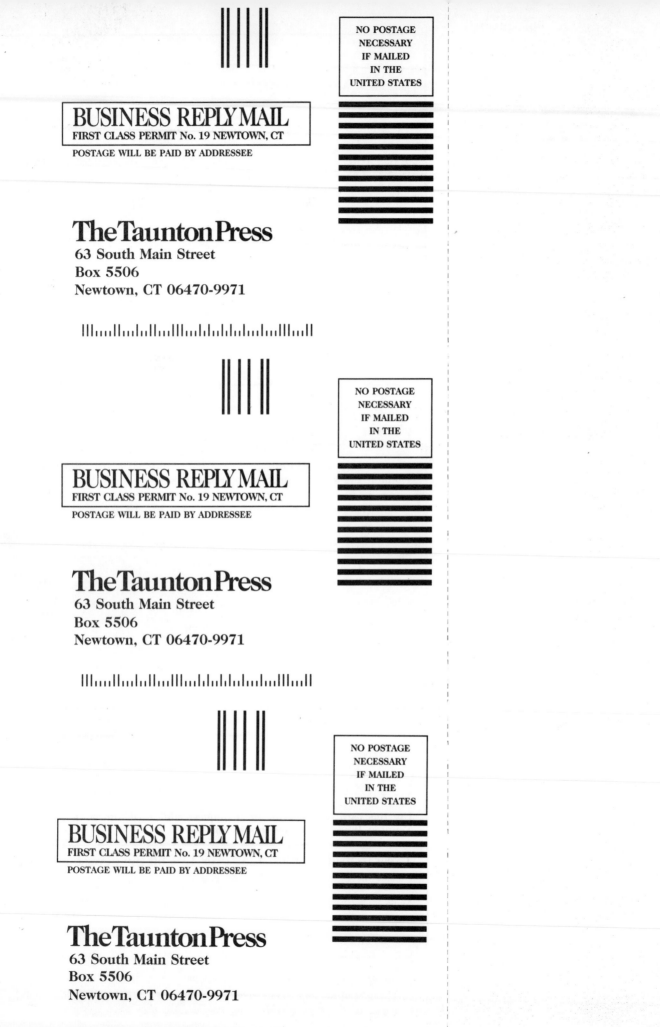

NO POSTAGE
NECESSARY
IF MAILED
IN THE
UNITED STATES

BUSINESS REPLY MAIL
FIRST CLASS PERMIT No. 19 NEWTOWN, CT

POSTAGE WILL BE PAID BY ADDRESSEE

The Taunton Press
63 South Main Street
Box 5506
Newtown, CT 06470-9971

NO POSTAGE
NECESSARY
IF MAILED
IN THE
UNITED STATES

BUSINESS REPLY MAIL
FIRST CLASS PERMIT No. 19 NEWTOWN, CT

POSTAGE WILL BE PAID BY ADDRESSEE

The Taunton Press
63 South Main Street
Box 5506
Newtown, CT 06470-9971

NO POSTAGE
NECESSARY
IF MAILED
IN THE
UNITED STATES

BUSINESS REPLY MAIL
FIRST CLASS PERMIT No. 19 NEWTOWN, CT

POSTAGE WILL BE PAID BY ADDRESSEE

The Taunton Press
63 South Main Street
Box 5506
Newtown, CT 06470-9971